THE ROOTS OF CRISIS IN SOUTHERN AFRICA

Ann Seidman

Oxfam America

Impact Audit No. 4

Africa World Press
of the Africa Research & Publications Project

P.O. Box 1892
Trenton, New Jersey 08608

AFRICA WORLD PRESS
P.O. Box 1892
Trenton, NJ 08607

Copyright © Oxfam America, Inc.

Typeset by Typehouse of Pennington

Cover design by Ife Nii-Owoo

Library of Congress Catalog Card Number: 85-72995

ISBN: 0-86543-025-X cloth
       0-86543-026-8 paper

COVER PHOTO: Rand Daily Mail (Johannesburg) August 20, 1984

A United Democratic Front (UDF) rally that filled
the City Hall in Johannesburg.

NOTE

In July this year, the southern African crisis reached a new peak and burst onto American TV screens. In South Africa, the minority state could no longer rule the black townships. The government imposed a state of emergency. Troops set up roadblocks to cordon off the townships. American audiences watched in horror as South African police, using whips, teargas, armored vehicles, and guns, attacked black men, women, and children. By September, the police had detained over 16,000 blacks. Fourteen people had died in police custody. The officially estimated numbers of dead—mostly shot down by the police or soliders—reached nearly 700. Turning their funerals into mass political rallies, tens of thousands of mourners, wearing the colors of the banned African National Congress, raised their fists and chanted liberation slogans. Meanwhile, the violence spilled over into the white areas.

In August, convinced that the instability of minority rule threatened their money, U.S. banks refused to extend further short-term credit to finance South African foreign trade. The value of South African currency plunged to a record low. Imposing foreign-exchange controls to block growing capital flight, the South African government halted further payments of principal on foreign loans. The head of the South African Reserve Bank flew to Europe and the United States to negotiate secretly with bankers for aid.

Only the United States and Britain abstained as the United Nations Security Council voted overwhelmingly for voluntary member state sanctions to hasten the end of apartheid. Eleven Europen nations voted to ban oil sales to and miliatary and cultural liks with South Africa. The French, Canadians, and Australians banned new investments there.

Americans throughout the nation urged effective U.S. measures. Democratic and Republican Congressmen agreed on a compromise sanctions bill. Seeking to avert its passage, President Reagan ordered limited measures including a ban on nuclear technology; computers to South African agencies which enforce apartheid; loans to the South African government; U.S. export assistance to U.S. firms which have not signed the Sullivan Principles; and possibly the sale of krugerrands. He termed the measures a shift to "active constructive engagement." He sent Ambassador Herman W. Nickel back to South Africa with a letter for President P.W. Botha.

Observers noted that these measures would probably have little impact. For example, in contrast to the unilateral imposition of total sanctions everywhere, as in the case of Nicaragua, President Reagan merely requested permission of the General Agreement on Trade and Tariff administration—likely to take several months—to prohibit sales of South African Kurgerrands in the United States.

Reflecting the increasingly militant mobilization of black South Africans for change, and their growing dismay over President Reagan's policy, Nobel Peace Prize winner Bishop Desmond Tutu, asserted the President was "bending over backwards to save the South African government from the consequences of their own actions." (Boston Globe, Sept. 10, 1985)

In the face of increasingly militant South African blacks' demands and growing international protest, President Botha offered only partial and illusory reforms: He promised "dual citizenship" to blacks, but offered no guarantees that they could vote in national South African elections. His Committee for Constitutional Affairs urged abolition of the pass laws, under which up to 300,000 blacks are annually arrested, but he refused to meet leading blacks to discuss such a reform.

Acting without their government's support, leading South African businessmen, including Gavin Relly, head of the Anglo American Group, the country's biggest mining finance house, met in neighboring Zambia with Oliver Tambo, exiled leader of the African National Congress. Several months earlier that move would have been unthinkable. Apparently, South African businessmen feared for the future of their profitable business enterprises as—in the face of openly violent state-sponsored repression—the black population mounted increasingly effective demonstrations and demands for liberation.

As this book shows, for years the U.S. administration has based "constructive engagement" on a misrepresentation of U.S. interests and the underlying roots of the crisis in southern Africa. The United States needs, not compromise measures to stave off more effective citizen protests at home, but an entirely new southern African policy to support liberation, peace, and self-reliant development throughout the region.

September 16, 1985

ACKNOWLEDGEMENTS

This book has been written as a collective effort involving the contributions of many people: reports of project holders and Oxfam America projects officers working in southern Africa, and research and discussions by staff members, interns, and work-study students in the Boston office. While accepting final responsibility for the contents, I would like to express sincere thanks to those who have contributed information and insights in the preparation of this Impact Audit. In a very real sense, it is the product of a national and even international cooperative effort.

In Oxfam America itself, many individuals contributed to the ideas and research. Shari Zimble and Portia Adams, interns, helped to gather essential data as well as participating in discussions of content. Others who helped gather background information include Nancy Kail, Fernando Olguin, Andrew Swiderski, Anne Robson, and members of the New England Applied Development Research Network, especially Eve Sandberg, Carol Mapoma, and participants from Clark University's International Development and Social Change Program. Deborah Toler, Larry Simon, Pearl Robinson, Edmund Keller, Bud Day, Khethiwe Mhlanga, and many others reviewed drafts and made useful suggestions. Tim Johnson, Lee Farris, Colleen Westbrook, and Ben Soares all helped to prepare the manuscript for publication.

We at Oxfam America would also like to express our appreciation to the following organizations and individuals:

The American Committee on Africa, especially Jennifer Davis, Richard Knight, and Stephanie Urdang;

The Washington Office on Africa, especially Randy Nunnelee;

The Sanctions Working Group on Destabilization in Southern Africa, especially Sean Gervasi;

and the staff of the Solidarity News Service (Gaborone, Botswana).

Ann Seidman
Boston, July, 1985

PREFACE

As this book goes to press, daily headlines report the devastating poverty and hunger in Africa. With heartfelt generosity, millions of Americans have donated funds to alleviate the suffering and starvation. Oxfam America has tried to help channel private U.S. donations to those areas of Africa—Ethiopia, the Sahel, southern Africa—where they can make the greatest contribution to bettering the lives of the people. As part of its underlying philosophy, moreover, Oxfam America aims to ensure that its aid does more than provide temporary relief. In southern Africa, as throughout the African continent, it seeks to assist women and men, working toward long-term self-reliance at the grassroots level, to build sound foundations for improving their lives and working conditions.

Even though southern Africa is roughly the size of the continental United States, with about 90 million inhabitants, not many Americans fully comprehend the nature of the political and economic crisis gripping the region. Because Oxfam America has been working with grassroots projects for some years in several southern African countries, however, its staff members have come to understand the realities of the lives of the people there. Particuarly troubling is the impact of violence on people's lives. In South Africa, a white minority continues its brutal repression of the black majority. Elsewhere in southern Africa, peasants who want to get on with the business of food production see their efforts stymied and thwarted by war. They suffer anxiety, fear, poverty, and even death. Wars are conceived and run by people outside their area, even outside their country.

Drawing on Oxfam America's field experience, this Impact Audit attempts to explain the nature and causes of the crisis confronting the people of southern Africa; the causes as well as the effects of South Africa's domination of the region and its denial of basic human rights to the black majority; and, in that context, the consequences of the U.S. Constructive Engagement Policy. This is not to imply that the African governments of the region have made no mistakes. Rather it is to focus attention on the way the crisis, South African domination, and U.S. policy interact to affect problems which all the governments and peoples of the region confront. The books shows that analysis of the interests of U.S. citizens should lead to an alternative policy of support for the efforts of the majority of southern Africans to achieve self-reliant development.

John Hammock
Executive Director
Oxfam America

FOREWORD

For over four decades the American public has been aware of South Africa's repugnant political system known as apartheid. This awareness has been loaded with ambiguities, however, for the issues are often described as complex. Is it not just one country's internal sociopolitical arrangement that has its own historical roots? Who are we to interfere? Was it not the whites who discovered the country and built it up from scratch? Why should they now be forced to turn it over to the Africans, who will give it over to the communists?

These are but a few of the questions that one encounters among people whose only information about South Africa comes from the South African Information Offices in New York, Washington, Denver, Atlanta, or for that matter, Pretoria. In recent years, the material from these sources has portrayed South Africa as pursuing ostensibly laudable policies:

South Africa is changing for the better, and the U.S. government and business influence are in the vanguard of the forces that are responsible for peaceful change. Moreover, the changes in South Africa are of benefit not only to Africans in that country but to the entire region, for South Africa is a source of modern technology and stability in southern Africa.

The evidence offered to support these claims points to the elimination of some aspects of "petty" apartheid (the desegregation of rest rooms, park benches, and so forth). Sometimes it is even claimed that Africans in South Africa have a standard of life and opportunity superior to Africans anywhere else on that continent. It is even suggested that the regime in South Africa is made up of peace-loving, well-meaning, good Christian people who are constantly threatened by terrorists and communists lodged in hostile neighboring states.

From this perspective it is easy to understand why so many feel that the issues concerning South Africa are either so simple that they will disappear or that they are much too complex for ordinary mortals to comprehend. And yet these issues will not go away. In fact, they become ever more urgent, and hauntingly so!

A South African bishop receives the Nobel Peace Prize, the second time it is presented to an African—another South African. The "Free South Africa" campaign, organized by TransAfrica, intensifies as prominent public figures from all walks of life are arrested and sent to jail for demonstrating at the South African Embassy in Washington, D.C., and at consulates across the country in protest against apartheid. At the same time an ever-increasing number of legislative bodies, from city councils to state legislatures, are enacting measures designed to withdraw public funds from companies and banks doing business with South Africa. Some churches and universities have already led the way, and it appears that similar action might be forthcoming from the U.S. Congress.

Why, one might ask, is all this attention being focused on South Africa when the government there is trying to accommodate African expectations? Would withdrawal of U.S. investments not hurt Africans? And will others with far less compassion for Africans not step in and take over?

These are among the questions that this book answers. It does so with clarity and authority. The book focuses on the impact of the apartheid regime on the situation of poverty and underdevelopment in southern Africa. It takes up the most complex issues, such as:

—the relationship between the low wages paid to South African workers and the high profits of transnational corporations;
—the disenfranchisement of Africans in their own land and their forced removal to "homelands";
—the role of U.S. transnational corporations in strengthening the South African military-industrial complex;
—the role of the U.S. government in retarding the legitimate efforts of the independent nations in southern Africa to develop societies that are democratic, participatory, and self-reliant.

The key issue which one is never allowed to lose sight of is that of human development. This is Oxfam America's concern in southern Africa. The book describes the internal forces within South Africa and the external forces, particularly in the United States, that are arrayed against human development in southern Africa.

It is a study dealing with a region whose total population, excluding South Africa, is more than 60 million; a region rich in arable land, mineral resources, and cultural and social history; a region whose gross domestic product stands today at around $22 billion, with the potential over the next 20 years to total 10 times that figure.

The regional focus is of immense value from another perspective. The book offers the most comprehensive evaluation of the current U.S. administration's "constructive engagement" policy toward southern Africa that has appeared to date. As such, it is a timely document. The larger issues such as divestment, economic and social justice, political and human rights, the linkage between African underdevelopment and U.S. policies toward southern Africa; the linkage between U.S. geopolitical interests and the struggle for liberation and peace in southern Africa; the wider socioeconomic and political impact of global recession, drought, famine—not just in southern Africa but throughout the continent—are moving to the forefront of the political debate concerning foreign policy formulation in the next four years. Senators and congressmen, legislative assistants and lobbyists, academics and church leaders, corporate executives and ordinary citizens, will find here a most readable and well-researched resource.

One cannot overstress how critical it is that this Impact Audit is being published at this time, when events within South Africa are revealing so clearly the bogus character of President Reagan's "constructive engagement" policy. That policy must be reversed. This book offers both the reasons why and some alternatives that would place the United States on the side of liberation, justice, and human development in southern Africa.

Burgess Carr

The Reverend Burgess Carr, associate professor at Yale Divinity School, was formerly general secretary of the All Africa Conference of Churches. He is a member of the board of Oxfam America.

Table of Contents

List of Tables and Boxes

CHAPTER ONE

Introduction: The Crisis in Southern Africa

HUNGER, POVERTY, AND FEAR

Drought in Zimbabwe

As you drive into the Chibi communal area, dust swirls under lowering grey skies. Black tree trunks stand twisted against grey-brown sand. Clusters of thatched huts huddle at the base of black boulders piled haphazardly, as if by a giant in some prehistoric past.

Chibi is one of several communal areas in Zimbabwe, part of a crescent-shaped region stretching from the eastern border with Mozambique down to the southwestern border with Botswana. In the decades before independence, the colonial authorities had forced the African population to live in these areas, which they euphemistically termed "Tribal Trust Lands." They encompass the least fertile, driest soils in the country. At independence, more than 800,000 peasant families lived crowded into communal areas like Chibi, estimated by the previous government at three times as many people as the land could support.[1]

By contrast, the colonial state reserved the more fertile half of the nation's agricultural lands for fewer than 7,000 white commercial farmers. High on the plateau, these farms were well-watered, with easy access to the rail and road network that spread out from the major cities. The average white farmer owned more than 6,000 acres, but cultivated only half that much. During the civil war that finally led to independence, thousands of Zimbabwean men and women joined the liberation struggle in hope of getting more of this land for the black peasants.

In 1980, the first year of Zimbabwe's independence, heavy rains watered the entire nation. The peasants, who returned to settle mainly in the communal areas, rebuilt their homes damaged by years of war. They reaped record crops; then the drought hit. In three years, only a few drops of rain fell in the crowded communal lands. The first year the peasants planted seeds, only to watch the shoots shrivel and die as the soil grew parched and cracked. Scrawny cattle—the peasants' lifetime savings and their only source of draft power—roamed the increasingly barren lands in search of the last blades of grass. Peasants sold some of their cows to the government or to commerical farmers, who herded them onto more lush farmlands farther north. The rest starved. Goats nibbled away the roots of any green plant that might have survived. Women, children, and the elderly lived off the share of the wages sent home by those employed in the cities, the mines, or commerical farms. Yet even this source of income dwindled as the worldwide recession cut Zimbabwe's export prices. Growing unemployment in the "modern sector" forced many able-bodied men home to join their families. By the end of the second year of drought, whole families—almost half the peasant population—lived on government drought relief: small rations of maize and black beans. By the beginning of the third year, the government had to cut back on these already meager allotments. The fragile soils of Chibi and most of the other overcrowded communal areas had turned into near-deserts.

Oxfam America helped the women of Chibi organize cooperatives. They fenced in small plots and carried buckets of water on their heads from the last puddle in the sandy riverbed to grow a few vegetables. The women fed their families relish, a sauce of mixed vegetables, making the drought-relief rations palatable and nutritious. They also sold the relish in a nearby city to earn a few dollars to supplement their drought rations. The women achieved a sense of pride: despite the drought, they were able to help their families live a little better.

At another project, Vukuzenzele, approximately 50 miles west of Chibi, about 70 disabled veterans of the liberation struggle have formed a cooperative. Vukuzenzele, which means "wake up and do it yourself," symbolizes these veterans' determination to improve their living conditions in a peaceful Zimbabwe. They pooled their demobilization pay and, together with funds provided by Oxfam America and other private voluntary organizations, bought a tractor, cleared lands, and built an irrigation system drawing on one of the few rivers remaining during the drought. They succeeded in feeding themselves and their families, and even selling a little surplus in the neighboring peasant communities. They built a clinic for their own use, as well as for others in the nearby communal area; set up a school after hours to raise their own educational levels; and constructed a recreation center where they could meet and talk with their neighbors about their mutual difficulties and ways to overcome them.

Despite the hardships wreaked first by the years of civil war, then by the drought, these hard-working men and women in Chibi, Vukuzenzele, and neighboring areas are determined to carve out a better life for themselves.

* * *

When you fly over Chibi across southwest Zimbabwe, you look down on what appears to be a straight line between the almost endless sands on the southern side, and the greener, better-watered lands to the north. Yet straight lines do not grow in nature. Over the last half century, the white commercial farmers constructed barbed-wire fences to separate their lands from those of the peasants. From the air, these areas appear lush and green in contrast to the crowded, overfarmed, sandy lands of the peasants. The commercial farmers typically could afford to leave as much as half their acreage underutilized. Over the years, they had invested heavily to irrigate large acreages. Throughout 1982 and 1983, despite the drought, they shipped valuable tobacco, cotton, tea, and beef to markets abroad.

Destabilizaton in Mozambique

Across Zimbabwe's eastern border, in Mozambique, the impact of the drought was compounded by attacks by South African-financed and armed rebels of the National Resistance Movement (MNR), which, seeking to destabilize the government, created even worse conditions. Together with private voluntary organizations from many countries, Oxfam America has assisted unemployed Mozambican workers to grow food crops in some of the green belts the government established around major cities to help feed the urban population. For example, in Mahota Green Zone, Oxfam America funded the repair of five broken windmill pumps, ending dependence of the 450 co-op members—mostly women—on costly and scarce fuel for diesel pumps. Once they solved their food-supply problems, the women aimed to improve adult education and to provide day-care for infants.

In January 1984, cyclone Domoina ripped through southern Mozambique. Ironically, the rainfall accompanying it did not bring relief; instead, torrential rains and high winds led to the deaths of more than 100 people. Seventy thousand families lost property, 10,000 of them losing their farms and all their belongings. Some 5,000 head of cattle died. The cyclone destroyed roads, bridges, railways, and electricity networks. It damaged water-supply pipelines and storage reservoirs, cutting off water supplies to Mozambique's capital city, Maputo.

The floods came just at harvest time. The green belt cooperative farms around Maputo were largely destroyed just as Oxfam America received a report indicating that many were "beginning to turn the corner in terms of their economic viability and self-sufficiency." The Ministry of Agriculture sent out an appeal for agricultural implements and seeds. Oxfam America's Zimbabwe office arranged the purchase of 12,500 ring hoes, manufactured in Zimbabwe, to enable family farms and cooperatives in southern Mozambique to plant seeds provided by OXFAM (U.K.).[2]

In northern Mozambique, as the drought dragged on, the MNR attacked distribution networks and burned crops. Unable to grow food or receive government drought-relief assistance, tens of thousands of Mozambicans walked hundreds of miles to cross the border to hoped-for safety in Zimbabwe. Many starved during the trek. More died in Zimbabwe. Cholera broke out. The Zimbabwean government, together with the U.N. High Commissioner for Refugees and private voluntary organizations, stretched resources to build refugee camps.

Barbara Kaim, an Oxfam America representative in Zimbabwe, described their plight:

> The MNR have cut all communication and supply links between the northwest and southern parts of Mozambique so that no food, medication or other goods have reached Tete Province for months. This area was also badly destroyed by the Smith

4

regime's [the minority government which ruled Zimbabwe before independence] raids into Mozambique and it has never benefited from any reconstruction because of the conflict in the south. Refugees speak about whole village communities dying of hunger in Tete Province.

It is estimated that, at present, 60-100 Mozambican families are crossing into Zimbabwe each day. It takes them about 1-3 weeks to walk to the border . . . and, before crossing into Zimbabwe, they have to walk through a mile-wide mine-field laid down by the Rhodesian forces during the liberation struggle. . . .

The Mozambicans enter at Mukosa, and then begin their long trek through Rushinga town and Marymount to the commercial farming areas in Mount Darwin and around Bindura. There, many refugees find employment on the commercial farms. Since they are in such a desperate state, the refugees offer their labour in return for shelter and one meal a day, thereby eroding the government minimum wage regulations for farm workers. . . .

[Most of the refugees are] severely undernourished, and I saw children with clear evidence of kwashiorkor, marasmus, pellagra and other nutritional deficiencies. Most of the adults were emaciated and weakened by a lack of food and their long walk through the bush . . . three to five deaths are reported each week in each of the camps. Many more refugees are assumed to have died on the road.[3]

In Tete, in northwestern Mozambique, Oxfam America supplied seeds and tools to the farmers of Magoe in time for them to resume cultivation when the rains returned in late 1984. In addition, Oxfam America aims to assist them to overcome two basic problems that have hampered their development: the infestation of tsetse flies and the lack of adequate water-supply systems. The tsetse fly spreads a disease affecting domestic animals, thus reducing the availability of draft animals—namely oxen—for plowing. This has reduced overall productivity. Lack of irrigation has reduced production during the dry season, when no rains fall in the region. By working with the people of Magoe, Oxfam America hopes to increase production by introducing simple irrigation devices. Then the people of Magoe can process and store their farm surpluses, not only for their own consumption, but for sale throughout the region.

The Troubled Region

In the 1980s, drought hit all the countries of southern Africa. It imposed a heavy burden on governments already facing financial difficulties as the worldwide recession reduced their export earnings. By 1983, in the semi-arid lands of Botswana, 40 percent of the peasant population survived only on famine-relief rations. Tanzania, Mozambique, and Zambia had to import food grains to feed their growing urban populations.

The drought aggravated the basic problem of poverty confronting the majority of the roughly 90 million people living in southern Africa. A third of the countries in the region are among the world's least developed, with 1984 per capita incomes of $500 or less. In the others, the average national per capita income is higher, but unequal income distribution results in similar poverty-level living standards for the majority of their people.

Box 1.1

```
┌─────────────────────────────────────────────────────────────────────────┐
```

The Impact of Drought in Southern Africa

Angola: Interior stricken, problem compounded by guerrilla war; 200,000 face starvation;[a]

Botswana: Drought spread throughout entire nation; almost half the population estimated on drought relief;[b]

Lesotho: 250,000 people acutely affected;

Mozambique: Southern region and Tete Province stricken, problem compounded by guerrilla war; 100,000 reported to have starved, another 100,000 fled to Zimbabwe;

Namibia: Interior affected;[c] agricultural activity all but collapsed during the seven year drought, the worst in living memory;[d]

Tanzania: Countrywide drought, exacerbated by cattle-killing rinderpest and grain borer outbreaks;

Zambia: 300,000 people in south and west near Angola border severely affected;

Zimbabwe: Southern region (especially communial areas) stricken; problem compounded by migrants crossing the border from Mozambique.

Notes

a. More than 200,000 have been displaced by UNITA attacks "halting production on the fertile central plateau and placing the refugees in grim danger of starvation." Report of International Committee of the Red Cross, *African Business* (Britain), April 1985.

b. Jan Raath, "Botswana waits for rain," *Guardian* (Britain), January 4, 1985.

c. South Africa did not publish data on the effect of the drought on the overcrowded, least well-watered areas of Namibia or South Africa itself, where the bantustans are located (see Chapter 3 below); however, in 1985, 89 percent of the children in one bantustan, Ciskei, suffered malnutrition, and the situation in the others—where 55 percent of the deaths are of children under five years old—is "not much better," according to Mrs. Ina Pearlman, executive director of Operation Hunger, feeding 600,000 people in rural areas. *The Star* (South Africa), April 1, 1985.

d. Tony Weaver, "Nambian Review," *South Africa Review 1983* (South Africa: Raven Press, 1984), p. 220.

Sources: Unless otherwise noted, information appeared in *Washington Post*, February 26, 1984, compiled from U.S. Agency for International Development, World Bank, and U.N. Food and Agriculture Organization; and reports from Oxfam America projects officers.

Low per capita incomes only partially reflect the pervasive impact of poverty. Many, if not most, southern African children are malnourished. In some regions, more than half die before they reach five years of age. Widespread preventable diseases such as malaria, bilharzia, and tuberculosis undermine their health and productive capacity, shortening their life expectancy. Lack of teachers and schools denies children the skills needed to use the 20th-century technologies that could revolutionize their lives. Widespread underemployment thwarts their parents' efforts to earn better incomes.

Yet southern Africa possesses some of the most abundant and varied mineral resources in the world. In addition to gold and diamonds, the region exports copper, nickel, tin, manganese, asbestos, and zinc. It possesses a third of the world's known uranium reserves and the largest known deposits of chrome and vanadium. The region produces more than 80 percent of the world's platinum and has extensive reserves of iron ore and coal, as well as significant deposits of oil, bauxite, antimony, fluorspar, titanium, and vermiculite. (Appendix II indicates southern Africa's share of the production of several major minerals.) In addition, southern Africa boasts extensive and varied conditions for growing every type of agricultural produce. It exports cotton, sugar, tobacco, tea, coffee, and vegetable oils. It grows maize, wheat, rice, sorghum, and millet. Given adequate irrigation and improved farm technology, the region could support several times its present population.

Why is there such hunger and poverty in the midst of some of the world's most valuable resources? Why are thousands of refugees fleeing their homes and countries, seeking aid to start their lives anew? Does the increasing U.S. involvement in the region help the inhabitants to reshape their lives, to find peace and improve their living standards? These are some of the questions this Impact Audit seeks to answer.

THE U.S. POLICY OF CONSTRUCTIVE ENGAGEMENT

By the late 1960s, the "winds of change" that swept down through the African continent after World War II had brought independence to almost 400 million people, including more than 60 million in southern Africa. With relatively little conflict, black governments assumed power in the former British colonies of Tanzania, Zambia, Malawi, Botswana, Lesotho, and Swaziland. Following more than a decade of guerilla warfare, Mozambique and Angola achieved self-rule in 1975. In 1980, the people of Zimbabwe elected Robert Mugabe and his party to form the government, ending years of armed struggle to overthrow the rule of a white minority which represented less than 3 percent of the population.

Only in South Africa and Namibia, inhabited by a third of the regional population, did the white minority cling to power and privilege. Despite growing popular resistance at home and mounting international condemnation of its racist policies, the South African minority intensified economic, political, and military measures to control the black majority at home as well as to perpetuate its domination over the neighboring states.

In 1981, outlining the "major challenges and opportunities" as he viewed them in southern Africa, U.S. Assistant Secretary of State for African Affairs Chester A. Crocker declared:

First, southern Africa is a region of unquestioned importance to U.S. and Western economic and strategic interests. Its potential as a focal point of African economic progress warrants a substantial effort on our part to reinforce these prospects and to forestall heightened conflict and polarization. Second, this region has the tragic potential to become a magnet for internationalized conflict and a cockpit of East-West tension. It contains an explosive combination of forces—Soviet-Cuban military involvement, African guerrilla operations across and within borders, and a politically isolated but militarily and economically strong South Africa. It is imperative that we play our proper role in fostering regional security, countering Soviet influence, and bolstering a climate that makes peaceful change possible.[4]

Dr. Crocker did not specify the nature of the U.S. and Western "economic and strategic interests." Nevertheless, it is true that the United States and Western countries obtain a significant share of several important minerals from southern Africa.[5]

Table 1.1 shows the degree of U.S. reliance on the import of five key minerals from South Africa in 1983. These five minerals are essential to Western industry and defense.[6] (Appendix II includes further data showing the U.S. share of South Africa's exports of these and several other important minerals, compared to those of the major European and Japanese importers.) Other southern African states also mine substantial amounts of copper (Zambia, Namibia, Zimbabwe, and Botswana), diamonds (Botswana and Namibia), and uranium (Namibia), as well as smaller amounts of other minerals.

Southern African countries, and particularly South Africa, are not simply the beneficiaries of an uneven geographical distribution of resources. Over the years, foreign firms, especially British and American companies, have made a disproportionate share of their African investments in developing the mineral wealth of the region. But this is not because deposits of these minerals are lacking elsewhere in Africa or the world.[7] Rather, it is because the companies have chosen to invest their capital to develop the deposits and process the minerals under the conditions prevailing in South Africa.

By the 1980s, total U.S. financial involvement in South Africa, alone, reached almost $15 billion. U.S. manufacturing companies had located almost three-fourths of their investments on the entire continent there.[8] Although direct United States investments in South Africa still lagged behind those of Britain, the United States had become South Africa's leading trading partner. In 1980, it bought about 13.7 percent of South Africa's exports, including uranium; and sold South Africa about 14.35 percent of that country's imports.[9]

Table 1.1
U.S. Dependence on South African Supplies of Five Key Minerals, 1983[a]

Mineral/Alloy	Total Worldwide Imports as % of U.S. Consumption	Imports from South Africa % of U.S. Imports	% of U.S. Consumption
Chromium:			
ore and concentrates	100.0	75.8	44.3
ferro alloys	71.1	49.1	34.8
Manganese:			
ore	65.7	7.1[b]	4.6[b]
ferro alloys	76.2	25.5	19.4
Vanadium pentoxide[c]	40.0	10.4	4.1
Platinum Group Metals	114.0[d]	37.8	43.5[d]
Uranium[e]	16.9	46.2	7.8

Notes

a. For South Africa's major exports to the U.S. and other major buyers of its most important exports, see Appendix I.
b. In 1982, the United States imported 52.1 percent of all manganese exported from South Africa, and South Africa provided 14 percent of all U.S. consumption.
c. The United States was a net exporter of vanadium ferro alloys.
d. Imports exceeded consumption, but net import reliance was 90 percent since the United States exported some platinum group metals and some was put into industry and government stockpiles.
e. Uranium delivered to the Department of Energy for enrichment. Since uranium must be enriched for U.S reactors by the Department of Energy, this represents a useful indicator of imports and consumption.

Source: U.S. Department of the Interior, *Minerals Yearbook*, Vol. I, *Metals and Minerals* (Washington, D.C.: Government Printer, 1984), *Minerals Yearbook*, Vol. III, and *Area Reports: International, 1983* (Washington, D.C.: Government Printer, 1985). For enriched uranium, see *Survey of United States Uranium Marketing Activity, 1983* (Washington, D.C.: Energy Information Administration, 1985).

Crocker did not detail how Soviet-Cuban military involvement, African guerrilla operations, and a politically isolated but militarily and economically strong South Africa combined to create the "tragic potential" for "internationalized conflict and a cockpit of East-West tension." Nevertheless, countering Soviet influence has been a primary theme of the Reagan administration's foreign policy throughout the world. The governments of five southern African states have declared their intention of implementing a transition to socialism, and some leaders subscribed to variants of Marxist ideology. There were an estimated 20,000 to 30,000 Cuban troops in Angola, and liberation movements in Namibia and South Africa used weapons provided by Eastern European countries. Crocker has attributed strategic importance to the region because of its geographic location "astride the sealanes which carry the oil of the Persian Gulf to Western nations."[10]

These economic and East-West geopolitical concerns have continued to underpin the Reagan administration's policy in southern Africa. That policy had led to growing U.S. government aid to the region which, by the mid-1980's, reached about 25 percent of total bilateral U.S. assistance to all sub-Saharan countries. (See Table 1.2.)

Upon coming into office in 1981, President Reagan ordered the National Security Council to conduct a review of U.S. policy toward southern Africa which ultimately laid the foundations for his Constructive Engagement Policy. The interdepartmental committee that conducted the review included senior representatives of the departments of State and Defense, and the CIA.[11] The National Security Council's policy analysis and the president's subsequent directives remain classified. But the broad outlines of what has since become known as the Constructive Engagement Policy have been set forth by Crocker, its chief architect.

In 1980, Crocker had formulated two basic premises. First, change in South Africa—the focal point of the region—had to be controlled and guided toward appropriate goals compatible with the protection of Western interests. Crocker held that the U.S. government should work with a group of "modernizers" within the ruling minority in South Africa to implement appropriate reforms. Eventually, as the black population attained more say in local government and in trade unions, it could begin to negotiate with the minority for a share of power at the national level. The resulting compromises would lead to gradual modification of, and ultimately accommodation to, the demands of the majority.

Second, Crocker urged a stabilization of the region to give the South African government time to implement desirable, if limited, change. As he explained:

> The American stance must be firmly supportive of a regional climate conducive to compromise and accommodation in the face of concerted efforts to discredit evolutionary change and to exploit the inevitable ambiguity and periodic "incidents" that will accompany political liberalization.[13]

AN OVERVIEW

This Impact Audit analyzes the consequences of the Constructive Engagement Policy for the southern African environment in which Oxfam America and other private voluntary organizations seek to help grassroots projects undertake self-reliant development. Self-reliant development is here defined as that which enhances people's control over their own wealth and productive resources, and increases their capacity to meet their own basic needs. The goal of such development is not autarky or isolation, but reduced dependence on foreign interests that prevent people from fulfilling their productive and cultural potential.

Table 1.2
U.S. Grants and Loans to Southern African Governments
(U.S. Fiscal years - Millions of dollars)

Country	Economic Assistance[a]							Military Assistance[b] 1979-1985	Loans[c] 1979-1983	Total Aid 1946-1985	Total[d] Aid Per Capita in 1983 (dollars)
	1979	1980	1981	1982	1983	1984	1985				
Botswana	17.9	19.3	17.6	15.9	13.3	13.3	11.4	23.0	—	211.7	20.60
Lesotho	13.7	18.9	24.9	16.6	21.0	17.4	16.6	1.4	—	142.5	15.00
Malawi	4.1	5.9	9.5	8.7	8.1	7.6	9.7	1.7	—	109.8	1.28
Mozambique	16.8	18.9	8.7	0.6	9.7	16.1	30.0	1.2	n.a.	n.a.	0.75
Swaziland	7.6	9.0	11.5	10.0	8.0	5.7	7.6	0.1	—	73.1	13.33
Tanzania	24.0	25.2	37.2	19.6	n.a.	5.0	3.9	—	1.7	355.3	4.65[f]
Zambia	33.4	46.4	30.6	27.1	27.9	36.4	25.0	—	—	156.7	4.65
Zimbabwe	—	22.9	27.8	75.0	64.0	46.7	39.6	0.8	39.4	323.4	13.80
Region-wide											
Southern Africa[e]	n.a.	n.a.	n.a.	n.a.	8.4	17.6	20.9	n.a.	n.a.	n.a.	n.a.
Total South- ern Africa[g]	17.5	166.5	167.8	173.5	160.4	153.8	164.7	28.2	41.1	1,372.5	8.71

Notes

n.a. Not available. Figures for 1985 are estimates.

a.   Includes Development Assistance, Economic Support Funds, and Food for Peace; excludes Military Assistance and Other Assistance.

b.   Includes Foreign Military Sales, Military Assistance Plan, and International Military Education and Training.

c.   Includes Export-Import Bank loans and other loans. Figures for 1984 and 1985 not available.

d.   Calculated using 1983 aid figures from columns 1 through 3 and population estimates from *1983 World Population Data Sheet* (Washington, D.C.: Population Reference Bureau, 1983.)

e.   Includes projects funded on a region-wide basis, aid to SADCC, and projects specific to South Africa.

f.   Per capita aid figure for Tanzania is for 1984.

g.   This total excludes data not available as indicated in table (n.a.).

Sources: *Agency for International Development (AID) Congressional Presentation, Annex 1, Africa,* Fiscal years '85 and '86. (Washington, D.C.: AID, 1984 and 1985.) Table used for each country; "U.S. Overseas Loans and Grants—Obligations and Loan Authorizations," and for the region, "Resource Flows"; and, for 1984-85 data, U.S. State Department, "U.S. Assistance to Africa," AF/EPS: 2/06/85:1466G:gg.

In order to assess the impact of the Constructive Engagement Policy in southern Africa, it is necessary to comprehend fully the historical complexities of the region. These shape the framework within which U.S. economic and strategic interests have expanded, as well as what Crocker views as the region's "tragic potential to become . . . a cockpit of East-West tension." To help explain this background, the book first explores the roots of poverty in southern Africa: the colonial legacy and South Africa's apartheid system. In that context, it outlines the nature and reasons for the growth of U.S. economic interests. It then analyzes the sources of growing conflicts in the region as southern Africans seek to achieve full political and economic liberation in the face of intensified South Africa repression.

Mozambique refugees after their long trek into Zimbabwe (Oxfam America staff photo by Barbara Kaim)

Ezakheni, a "resettlement" village in KwaZulu bantustan in Natal, South Africa (United Nations photo/151707)

CHAPTER TWO

Institutionalized Poverty in Southern Africa

THE COLONIAL HERITAGE

Decades of colonial rule have left their mark on southern Africa. Over the years, the colonial governments erected institutional structures which impoverished the people and still today render the independent states critically dependent on South Africa.

Even the boundaries of the southern African nations bear witness to the colonial legacy. In their 19-century scramble for Africa, the colonial powers initially carved out countries without regard to economic, ethnic, or geographic realities. Colonial expansion and African efforts to retain some semblance of self-rule divided the vast region into separate mini-economies: the extensive semi-deserts of Botswana and Namibia and the mountainous outcroppings of Lesotho and Swaziland, occupied by a half million to little more than a million inhabitants each; landlocked Zambia, Zimbabwe, and Malawi, each with populations of somewhat more than 5 million, situated on more fertile land and including valuable agricultural and mineral resources; and the much larger, oddly shaped coastal states of Mozambique and Angola, each with populations smaller than New York City. Even Tanzania, with a population of 20 million and a low per capita income, remains economically small. (See Table 2.1.)

The independent countries are not small in land area. Combined, they spread over a territory almost as big as the continental United States and considerably larger than Europe. Overpopulation is not a problem. None of them, even Malawi, the most densely populated, has as many inhabitants per square kilometer as a typical European nation. Nor do they lack resources. Southern Africa, as a region, is rich. It boasts some of the most valuable mineral resources in the world. Its fertile agricultural soils and varied climates allow it to grow and export practically every variety of food and agricultural raw material.

The basic problem confronting all these countries is the poverty of the majority of the population, reflected in part by the relatively low per capita incomes.

This pervasive poverty in the independent countries of southern Africa has been caused largely by inherited colonial institutions which denied the majority of the African population control over the rich resources of the region.

To provide a background for understanding these causes, this chapter summarizes:

★ The way the typical colonial state turned over the best lands in southern Africa to a handful of white settlers and companies to produce export crops and

Table 2.1
Population, Gross Domestic Product, and Per Capita Income
of Southern African States, 1983

Country	Population (millions)	GDP ($ millions)	GDP Per Capita ($ U.S.)
Angola	8.0	2,894[b]	419[b]
Botswana	0.9[a]	956[c]	1,124[c]
Lesotho	1.4	300	214
Malawi	6.5	1,320	203
Mozambique	12.9	2,480[b]	243[b]
Swaziland	0.6[a]	313[d]	614[d]
Tanzania	19.8	4,530	228
Zambia	6.0	3,830	638
Zimbabwe	7.5	5,900	786
Total Independent Southern African States	63.6	22,523	354[e]
South African	30.4	74,330	2,444

Notes
a. The population data are 1982 estimates. Per capita figure is calculated in cases using population and GDP data as noted. *1983 World Population Data Sheet.* (Washington, D.C.: Population Reference Bureau, 1983).
b. 1979 data from United Nations' estimates, converted to U.S. dollars.
c. *International Financial Statistics Yearbook, 1982* (Washington, D.C.: International Monetary Fund, 1983).
d. 1977 data, *International Financial Statistics Yearbook, 1981*, op. cit.
e. This represents a rough estimate because data used above are drawn from different years.
Sources: Unless otherwise stated in notes, the data are calculated from World Bank, *Annual Report, 1984* (Washington, D.C.: International Bank for Reconstruction and Development, 1984).

minerals, forcing African peasant families to provide low-cost labor; and the marginal changes made by the post-independence governments in the distorted allocation of resources.

★ The legacy of social disruption, illiteracy, malnourishment, and shortened life expectancy inherited by the peoples of the region.

★ The impact of the worldwide recession of the late 1970s and early 1980s that—regardless of the widely diverse policies adopted by their respective governments—engulfed the newly independent southern African states.

Land Distribution

Chibi in Zimbabwe typifies the pattern of poverty in the midst of great natural wealth in southern Africa. Colonial governments throughout the region encouraged giant foreign-owned mining and farming corporations as well as white settlers to appropriate the most fertile and best-watered agricultural lands and mineral resources. The transportation network radiating out from South Africa provided these lands with easy access to South African markets and inputs. This landholding pattern has left many African peasants, like the families of Chibi, subsisting on poor land with inadequate water supplies and limited access to transportation. Table 2.2 illustrates how colonial landholding patterns favored the establishment of European-owned farms at the expense of African peasants.

Table 2.2
Landholdings of Settler/Estate Farms as Percentage of Total Farm Area
in Southern Africa Outside South Africa (1974)

Country	Number of Corporate and Settler Farms	% of Farmland
Angola	8,000	n.a.
Botswana	n.a.	15%[a]
Malawi	4,500[b]	50%
Mozambique	6,500	50%[c]
Namibia	6,000-7,000[d]	98%
Swaziland	790	46%
Zambia	700	20 miles both sides of railroad[e]
Zimbabwe[f]	6,682[g]	47%

Notes

n.a. Not available.

a. Botswana's arable land constitutes only 7 percent of total national territory owing to lack of water supplies.

b. Includes 500 corporate farms, 4,000 settler farms.

c. As percentage of total land area of Mozambique.

d. About 10 percent are estimated to be company farms.

e. Railroad runs from Copper Belt to Zimbabwean border.

f. Formerly Rhodesia.

g. Includes 487 corporate farms, 6,195 settler farms.

Sources: *Development Needs and Opportunities for Cooperation in Southern Africa* (Washington, D.C.: U.S. Agency for International Development, 1979). Number of Zimbabwe corporate farms from *Income Tax Report,* Harare, 1980-81. Namibian estimate is from N.K. Duggal, ed., *Manpower Estimates and Development*, based on work of R.H. Green (Lusaka, Zambia: U.N. Institute for Namibia).

In the late 19th century, colonial administrations began to pass laws which enforced these skewed landholding patterns by reserving special areas for the African population. These laws turned over the most fertile soils with the best climatic conditions for food production to a few large European settler- or corporate-owned farms and mines. The colonial administrations then passed laws to resettle the African peasants on overcrowded, infertile reserves. The colonial states exercised police power to coerce the masses of peasants onto these lands.

Colonial Settlers

Over the years, the colonial governments made every effort to assist the settler farmers to produce valuable commercial crops, both to feed the hundreds of thousands of mine workers employed by the foreign mine companies and to provide raw materials and luxury goods for the colonial "motherlands." Meanwhile, the conditions of the African peasants steadily deteriorated.

Take Zimbabwe: When at the end of the 19th century, Cecil Rhodes' "pioneers" marched from South Africa into what is now Zimbabwe, peasants there had for centuries been producing enough food to support themselves as well as whole kingdoms based on gold and ivory trade.[1] African peasants grew the crops that fed the initial European settlements until the colonial government decided to bring in European farmers and give them the best land in the colony.[2] By the time of independence in 1980, almost a century later, fewer than 7,000 European farmers each owned, on average, more than 100 times the land available to the average African peasant. They held more land than they could cultivate adequately, leaving large areas underutilized. Nevertheless, employing more than 330,000 African laborers and using relatively modern machinery and equipment, these large farms produced more than 70 percent of the nation's food requirements and 90 percent of its agricultural exports.[3]

By contrast, on the infertile lands reserved for Africans—the so-called Tribal Trust Lands—about 800,000 families (almost 80 percent of the rural African population) struggled to subsist. By the time of independence in 1980, these areas held an estimated three times more people than economically feasible. In some areas, as many as 40 percent of the men between the ages of 16 and 30 were landless. Struggling to feed their families, the peasants grew crops on land suitable only for grazing; they cultivated 17 times as much land for crops in the Tribal Trust Lands as was ecologically desirable. The remaining uncropped lands were heavily overgrazed. In Zimbabwe, African peasants rely on cattle for draft power and manure to fertilize their crops. Without land to graze their cattle, more and more families were unable to support livestock. Reduced livestock resulted in lower food production. Between 1962 and 1977, the number of families without cattle rose from a third to more than half.

In the face of population growth, these factors led to a sharp decline in the peasants' production of maize, the staple crop. Output per person dropped almost a third, from 352 pounds in 1962 to 231 pounds in 1977. More and more food had to be imported to the Tribal Trust Lands, and their population became increasingly dependent upon the settler-owned commercial farms for basic food requirements.

This inequitable division of land was a key issue spurring the Zimbabwean peasants to support the 15-year guerrilla war. In 1980, that war ended with the election of Robert Mugabe and the Zimbabwe African National Union-Patriotic Front (ZANU-PF) to form the first independent government representing the black Zimbabwean majority.

Not only did the colonial powers take the best lands for the foreign settlers and mining companies, they also invested heavily in an infrastructure which primarily served the European-owned commercial farms and mines. The colonial administrations built roads, railroads, and harbors primarily to facilitate the production and export of crops and minerals produced by settler farms and foreign-owned mine. Railroads invariably run through the heartland of commercial-settler farm areas. In Zambia, the colonial government allocated to settler farmers the 20 miles of land on both sides of the railroad servicing the giant mines on the Copper Belt.[4] In Zimbabwe, no settler-owned commercial farm is more than 50 miles from the nearest railroad, ensuring owners the availability of low-cost and often subsidized bulk transport to the coast for their export crops.

By contrast, places like Chibi in Zimbabwe, Western Province in Zambia, Tete Province in Mozambique, or Kigoma in Tanzania, are relatively inaccessible. Two-lane tarmac highways typically dwindle to single lanes of rutted dirt. Roads leading into many rural villages are little more than grass or dirt tracks, negotiable only by jeep or on foot. In the rainy season, the dirt often turns into impassable mud. Unbridged streams swell into raging torrents. For weeks, even months, villages may be cut off from the rest of the nation. Even if the peasants could overcome the handicap of infertile soils and harsh climate, these added transport problems make it difficult, if not impossible, for them to compete with the more favored, larger settler estates.

Colonial administrations also built electricity-generating facilities only to serve the urban high-income populations, foreign-owned mines, and settler farms.[5] Even today, most peasants must use candles or kerosene lamps, if they can afford them. They have no access to electricity to operate machine tools and small-scale industries, or to ease the burdens of heavy household and agricultural labor.

Arguing that African peasants constituted a poor risk, colonial banks refused to provide them with credit to purchase equipment and materials to expand their output.[6] They preferred to finance foreign-owned mines and big estates. When colonial administrators established state banks, like the Agricultural Finance Corporations found in many British colonies, they imposed terms limiting loans to big commercial farms. Moreover, under pressure from the commercial farmers seeking to prevent African competition, the colonial states created marketing boards geared to handle only settler-produced crops. They either refused to collect the produce of African peasants, or paid them discriminatory low prices.[7]

Creating a Labor Reserve

British colonial administrators adopted measures which pushed more and more men and some women out of the reserves in search of paid employment. They introduced hut and poll taxes to require Africans to take low-paying jobs on foreign-owned mines or settler farms. Sir Harry Johnstone, an architect of British colonial policy in southern Africa, explained:

> All that needs to be done is for the Administration to . . . introduce the Native labourer to the European capitalist. A gentle insistence that the Native should contribute his fair share to the revenue of his country is all that is necessary on our part to ensure his taking a share in life's labour which no human being should avoid.[8]

The lack of adequate land and the discrimination by credit and marketing institutions prevented Africans from earning cash by producing and selling their crops. They had little choice but to take jobs at low wages on settler-owned farms or mines to pay these taxes. In the Portuguese colonies of Mozambique and Angola, the colonial state forced the Africans to work for the settlers. To pay their taxes, Africans were required by legislation to work as contract laborers at least six months a year, either for private employers or the state.[9]

As the decades passed, population growth led to increased overcrowding and landlessness in the areas reserved for Africans.[10] More and more, Africans migrated to search for wage employment, not just to pay their taxes, but to support their families. In addition, they desired manufactured goods that could be acquired only with cash.

Dualistic Development

As Table 2.3 shows, by the time the southern African states attained independence, their economies were geared toward production of crude materials for uncertain world markets. Their continued economic well-being depended on their ability to export enough of their crops and minerals for sufficiently high prices to the industrialized nations.

In short, colonial rule prevented development of local production capabilities, such as food cultivation and small-scale industries in rural areas. Over the decades, the emphasis on mining and commerical farming for export purposes caused an economic imbalance.

Modern skyscrapers etched the skylines of urban centers. Giant foreign-owned mines and sweeping estates extended into the countryside, connected by roads and rail networks reaching down to South Africa. In contrast, the vast majority of people lived in poverty in urban shanties; in brick cubicles shunted off to the side of mine or estate properties; or in thatched-roof huts in neglected hinterlands.

Table 2.3
The Main Exports of the Independent Southern African States

Country (year)	Main Exports as Percent of Total Exports
Angola (1979)	crude oil (68%); coffee (14%); diamonds (11%)
Botswana (1982)	diamonds (56%); copper/nickel (13%); beef (18%)
Lesotho (1979)	diamonds (56%); mohair (11%); wool (9%)
Malawi (1981)	tobacco (41%); sugar (27%); tea (13%)
Mozambique (1981)	cashews (16%); shrimp (15%); sugar (12%); tea (9%); cotton (7%)
Swaziland (1981)	sugar (38%); wood pulp (14%); fertilizer (11%)
Tanzania (1981)	coffee (34%); cotton (16%); cloves (10%); diamonds (6%)
Zambia (1981)	copper (85%); cobalt (10%)
Zimbabwe (1981)	tobacco (28%); gold (9%); iron products (15%); sugar (7%); nickel (5%)

Sources: United Nations, *Direction of Trade Statistics Yearbook, 1983*, except for Botswana, Lesotho, and Swaziland, for which data appear in the Economist Intelligence Unit, *Quarterly Economic Review, Annual Supplement, 1983.*

The disparity between the rural and the "modern" sector resulted in a growing number of men and women fleeing to urban slums, hoping to escape rural poverty. But the settler-ruled businesses could not provide enough jobs. The increasing mechanization of the commercial farm sector and mines reduced the relative numbers they employed. Seeking to enlarge markets for Europe-based industries, colonial administrations encouraged the import of low-cost manufactured goods, which—to the extent they penetrated the rural areas—tended to undermine small-scale rural industries. This further aggravated problems of rural un- and underemployment.[11] Today, the southern African economies must still import machinery and equipment for the mines and commercial farms. With an increased emphasis on export-crop production, some southern African countries even must import staple foods. Decades of neglect and limited access to good farming lands have undermined the peasants' capacity to expand their output enough to feed themselves and growing urban populations.[12]

Only in Zimbabwe, and to a lesser extent in Mozambique and Angola, did the settler population pressure the colonial state to support local industries. Typically located in existing urban centers, these factories depended heavily on the import of capital-intensive machinery, parts, and materials primarily to produce luxury and semi-luxury items for high-income groups. Thus, they did little to alter the lopsided pattern of growth with its focus on urban centers. They provided little employment and only marginally altered the countries' external dependence.[13] As Table 2.4 illustrates, manufacturing remains relatively underdeveloped in most independent southern African states.

Table 2.4
Output of Domestic Manufacturing Industries as a Percent of Gross Domestic Product and Exports, and Manufacturing Employment as a Percent of Total Labor Force in Southern African States

Country (date of data)	Manufactured Output % of GDP	Manufacturing Number Employed	Manufacturing % of Economically Active Population[a]
Angola (1973)	18-20	81,900	7.3
Botswana (1977)	n.a.	4,150	1.2
Lesotho (1978)	2.2	6,582	1.0
Malawi (1977)	12.0	33,379	1.4
Mozambique (1973)	14.0	99,500	2.6
Namibia (1977)	7.4[b]	13,000	4.3
Swaziland (1971)	16.0[b]	6,500	3.2
Tanzania (1980)	9.0	60,226	0.6
Zambia (1982)	19.0	45,510	2.4
Zimbabwe (1982)	25.0	180,500	5.5

Notes
a. This percentage is greatly influenced by the definition of "economically active population," which varies somewhat for each country.
b. Mostly processing agricultural, fish, or forestry products.
Sources: Statistics from *Development Needs and Opportunities for Cooperation in Southern Africa* (Washington, D.C.: U.S. Agency for International Development, 1979); for Namibia, R.G. Green, "Namibia in Transition: Toward a Political Economy of Liberation?" in T. Shaw, ed., *The Future(s) of Africa* (Boulder, CO: Westview Press, 1980); for Tanzania, Zambia, and Zimbabwe, calculated from *World Bank, Annual Development Report, 1984* (Washington, D.C.: International Bank for Reconstruction and Development, 1984); and *The Bulletin of Labour Statistics, 1985-1* (Geneva: International Labour Office, 1985).

SOCIAL DISRUPTION

This colonial pattern of poverty has shaped all aspects of life in the independent countries of southern Africa. Even after independence, hundreds of thousands of men still migrate in search of work. Their prolonged absences disrupt family life. Moreover, the neglect of education for the majority of Africans has left them ill-prepared to use modern technologies. The lack of basic health facilities results in many Africans continuing to suffer from preventable diseases.

Women's Heavy Burden

The continued migration of men for employment has left more and more women, children, and elderly to farm the barren rural lands. In some parts of the region, women are *de facto* heads of more than half the rural households.[14] This has two-fold consequences for rural family life. First, it means that many fathers see their children only a few times a year. While away they often form other attachments, leaving their families without the additional support they need to survive. Second, the loss of male labor imposes a particularly heavy burden on women. They must care for their children, do the cooking, and grow most of their food.[15] Often they walk miles to gather firewood or draw water. They receive little additional cash from their absent men. Historically, government administrators and businessmen did not consider families when allocating salaries. Assuming that women were "taking care of the families back on the farm," they provided wages only sufficient to cover the men's expenses. Large numbers of southern African wage workers still receive less than the minimum necessary to support their families even at a very low estimated poverty level.[16]

Widespread Illiteracy

Viewing Africans primarily as a source of low-cost labor, colonial administrators introduced discriminatory educational policies that perpetuated widespread illiteracy and lack of technological skills. The few schools that were constructed were mostly in urban centers and predominantly for urban whites. Church missions built primary schools in some rural areas, but these reached only a small fraction of the peasants' children. At independence, only a few thousand students had graduated from secondary schools. When Mozambique and Angola won liberation, barely 5 percent of their African populations could read and write.[17]

As Table 2.5 demonstrates, even in 1983 some southern African countries still suffered high rates of illiteracy. Traditional attitudes and heavy workloads left women in most countries with higher rates of illiteracy than men. (The relatively high rate of female literacy in Lesotho is an exception; primarily because most young boys herd sheep and then migrate to work on mines and farms in South Africa, girls have been the main beneficiaries of education.)

Table 2.5
Literacy Rate, As a Percentage of Adult Population,[a] 1983

Country	Males	Females	Country	Males	Females
Angola	35	19	Swaziland	64	58
Botswana	61	61	Tanzania	78	70
Lesotho	58	81	Zambia	79	58
Malawi	48	25	Zimbabwe	76	61
Mozambique	44	23			

Note
a. Literacy refers to the ability to read and write. It does not necessarily indicate acquisition of skills required to run a modern economy.
Source: *1983 World Population Data Sheet* (Washington, D.C.: Population Reference Bureau, 1983).

There were no universities in most southern African states before independence. Only a handful of Africans had obtained university degrees abroad. Only in Zimbabwe, as the capital of the former Central African Federation (which included Zambia and Malawi from 1953 to 1963), was a university established, in 1956. During 15 years of guerrilla warfare against the minority regime after the Unilaterally Declared Independence[18] from Britain, the Zimbabwean liberation movement systematically sent students abroad for higher education. Even in Zimbabwe, however, the 1981 *Manpower Survey* showed that only

Box 2.1

"A Day In The Life of a Sub-Saharan African Woman"*

Morning. Orange and gold. Philomena takes the baby from her breast and eases her onto a fiber mat between the other children. One of the older ones, Nambwere, stretches, rubs her eyes and looks up to see her mother standing in the doorway. Sunlight, rays illuminating the thatched roof, the mud-and-dung walls, sends gray-gold shadows through their home and few possessions: a narrow bed with a three-inch layer of foam brought by the father three years ago; a dresser stuffed with the family's meager belongings; a snapshot of the father in his overalls, standing outside the mine gate in the faraway city; a wedding picture; a table and two chairs; a stool; brooms and calabashes; a clay water pot and a tin can; a hen and her chicks; a small bundle of dry wood. The chickens run out the door, scratching for food. The woman follows, carrying her hoe.

Nambwere dips the tin can in the water pot, takes a drink and uses the rest of the water to wipe her face. She knows her mother will go to the hospital today because the baby is sick. The baby vomits her mother's milk, her stomach distended like a balloon, her skin hot with fever. For days, Philomena has tried the suggestions made by her husband's mother and the neighbors, but nothing seems to help. The nearest hospital is seven miles away, the nearest tarmac road is four miles away, and the few public buses cost too much. She will walk. But for now, Philomena and Nambwere go out to gather greens, firewood, and water in preparation for the day's food.

After picking a few greens, Philomena picks up an old plastic container to walk to the "stream." The stream, which trickles out of a broken-off water pipe, sometimes gets clogged with garbage or a dead animal. But she considers herself lucky because the stream is only one-third mile away from her home. When she arrives, a line has already formed, and a few women are bathing. Philomena joins the line and fills her plastic container. Noticing that a corner of her container has worn through she expertly plugs it with a knot of grass and carefully lifts it onto her head. Only a few drops of water trickle softly down her side as she walks home. She makes two trips.

6,316 professionals, skilled, and semi-skilled workers (a little more than 1 percent of the adult population) had university degrees.[19]

The Neglect of Health

Along with education, colonial administrators neglected to institute basic preventive health measures and to provide facilities to maintain minimum health standards for the majority of Africans. Modern hospitals were built only in the major urban centers, mainly to serve the wealthy minority. A few understaffed and underfunded clinics—some run by governments, some by

---

Soon, Nambwere returns carrying a bundle of branches on her head. Now it is time to make breakfast, which will also be lunch and dinner. Philomena prepares a maize-meal porridge, greens, and strong tea with sugar. Nambwere begins to milk their cow. The cow does not produce much milk because it is a poor breed and underfed; but she produces a few Coke bottles of milk which they may sell in the market to buy salt, soap, and a little kerosene.

Philomena puts on the better of her two dresses, washes the baby and straps her on her back. In the basket she will carry on her head, she puts the two bottles of milk she will sell, a small bottle to hold the medicine she hopes to get at the hospital, and some greens to sell in the market. While she is gone, Nambwere will feed the other children, graze the cow, and do the laundry at the stream.

As she walks to town, Philomena thinks about her troubles: When will I hear from my husband? Will I have to beg my neighbors for maize? Will my baby survive this illness? Two of my other children died when they were this sick. Will the doctor be there? How long will the line be at the hospital? At the kerosene station? What will happen to our family? Will Nambwere ever have time to attend school? This year we did not have enough money for her school fees, and she has been such a help to me. I hope the hospital has medicine today.

And what about the farm? If my husband does not return this year, how will we clear the land? Who will do the first plowing? Who will repair the roof? I wanted to plant maize, millet, and maybe some tomatoes this year to sell, but how can I get the seeds? Well, if the rains don't come soon, it won't matter, it will be another hungry season. And what of the baby?

When my husband and I were together there were fewer fears about the day's needs. We shared the responsibility. Somehow, there was enough. Now I don't know, I don't know how to meet the needs.

* This composite portrait was written by Portia Adams, an intern for Oxfam America, who worked for three years in the Peace Corps in rural Africa.

church missions—provided limited facilities for the Africans living in remote rural areas. Many African babies and mothers still die in childbirth from causes long since eliminated in developed countries and among the high-income urban groups who enjoy modern hospital care. Preventable diseases like tuberculosis, rife among families whose men return from migrant labor contracts in the mines, remain major killers. Every year, malaria and bilharzia, the incidence of which can be significantly reduced by preventive measures, and cured if diagnosed and medicine is available, deplete the energies and shorten the lifespans of thousands of southern Africans. Today the life expectancy of the average southern African is still barely two-thirds that of inhabitants of the industrialized world.

Table 2.6
Life Expectancy in Southern Africa in 1983

Country	Average Years of Life Expectancy	Country	Average Years of Life Expectancy
Angola	42	Swaziland	47
Botswana	50	Tanzania	52
Lesotho	52	Zambia	50
Malawi	47	Zimbabwe	53
Mozambique	47		

Source: *1983 World Population Data Sheet* (Washington, D.C.: Population Reference Bureau, 1983).

POST-INDEPENDENCE POLICIES

On coming into office, the new black governments of southern Africa confronted the tasks of revamping their economies to become more self-reliant. To do this, they needed to give their people access to their countries' resources as well as the opportunity to develop the skills necessary to utilize these resources. They needed to make institutional changes to insure national control of the critical sectors of their economies, and direct investable surpluses toward more balanced industrial and agricultural development. This would enable them to reduce their dependence on uncertain world markets, increase productive employment opportunities, and raise revenues to finance improved social-welfare programs so long neglected by their colonial predecessors.

Growing Expenditures

The new governments of the region had no blueprints for the successful transformation of their nations or the regional economy—indeed, none exist.

Different circumstances within each country as well as fundamental divergences in ideology led them to pursue different paths. One cannot argue they made no mistakes; they did. The literature is full of debates concerning their different policies. For example, critics argue that Malawi, adopting a conventional Western development model, steered a course too dependent on South Africa. In Tanzania, authors have argued for and against the *ujamaa* villagization policy—a policy of bringing peasants together in large villages to stimulate cooperative production. Likewise, there are arguments over the Zambian Mulungushi reforms, through which the state acquired 51 percent ownership of the copper mines. The Mozambicans, themselves, have criticized their initial emphasis on state farms, and have begun to try to assist small peasants to increase their productivity.[20] These governments' mistakes adversely affected their citizens' lives. Nevertheless, pursuing different paths and ideologies, all the independent southern African states faced similar problems—problems stemming from basically similar causes. The results of the first few years of their post-independence efforts exhibited remarkably similar features. This book aims to examine the common factors which constrained the new governments' choices, and the way South African and U.S. policies have affected these factors.

As a result of colonial neglect, the new governments had to double and triple government expenditures to bring educational and health facilities in line with the peoples' needs. In addition, southern African governments had to construct new roads and provide electricity to rural areas. At the same time, as tensions mounted throughout the region, they began to budget more for defense.

The Search for Self-Reliance

These growing expenditures imposed heavy financial burdens on the fledgling southern African governments. In agriculture, several governments sought through a variety of schemes to encourage peasants to expand cultivation and sales of both foodstuffs and export crops. This required major reorientation of marketing, credit, and extension-education structures, as well as land reforms. Some, like Tanzania, through its *ujamaa* program, sought to stimulate cooperative production. Others, like Botswana, encouraged private peasant initiatives. Swaziland permitted transnational corporate investment in large-scale plantation agriculture. All the governments, however, joined in the continent-wide competition to attract major foreign investment, particularly in the construction of manufacturing industries.[21]

The governments of southern African countries laid plans to build factories to process their agricultural and mineral raw materials, rather than sell them in crude form at low prices abroad. Increased local manufacture would both enable these countries to raise their export earnings by selling higher-value manufactured goods, and provide their people with the appropriately designed tools, equipment, and consumer goods they need to increase their productivity

Table 2.7

Government Expenditures on Defense, Education, and Health in Selected Southern African States, 1972 and 1980
(in millions of U.S. dollars and as a percent of total expenditures)

		Defense		Education		Health	
		$m[a]	% Total Exp.	$m[a]	% Total Exp.	$m[a]	% Total Exp.
Angola	1972	(b)	(b)	(b)	(b)	(b)	(b)
	1980	n.a.	n.a.	180	n.a.	63	n.a.
Botswana	1972	0[c]	0	3.8[c]	10	2.5[c]	7
	1980	35.0	10	78.2	22	18.9	5
Lesotho	1972	0[c]	0	3.8[c]	19	1.3[c]	6
	1980	n.a.	n.a.	18.0	n.a.	n.a.	n.a.
Malawi	1972	2.3	3	12.9	15	4.7	6
	1980	54.4	13	37.5	9	23.0	5
Mozambique	1972	(b)	(b)	(b)	(b)	(b)	(b)
	1980	160	n.a.	30.0	n.a.	n.a.	n.a.
Swaziland	1972	0[c]	0	6.3[c]	22	2.6[c]	9
	1980	13.4	9	38.8	25	10.7	7
Tanzania	1972	36.4	12	53.0	17	22.1	7
	1980	403.1	24	192.4	12	88.5	5
Zambia	1972	n.a.	n.a.	114.7	19	44.7	7
	1980	n.a.	n.a.	160.5	11	85.8	6
Zimbabwe	1978	266.4[d]	19	141.1[d]	10	71.4[d]	5
	1980	366.1	19	328.2	17	120.5	6
South Africa	1972	404.2	n.a.	197.6	n.a.	76.3	n.a.
	1980	4509.8	30	2814.4	18	308.2	2

Notes

a. Converted to U.S. dollars using average exchange rate for relevant years reported in International Monetary Fund, *International Financial Statistics* (Washington, D.C.: monthly).

b. Not available for 1972.

c. Still used South African rand as currency in 1972.

d. 1978 data used since 1972 not available.

Sources: *United Nations Statistical Yearbook 1981*, pp. 238-251; for South Africa, *Survey of Race Relations, 1982*; for Zambia, Central Statistical Office, *Monthly Digest of Statistics*, Vol. XVII, Nos. 10-12, October/December 1982; for Zimbabwe, Central Statistical Office, *Monthly Digest of Statistics*, August 1981, November 1981.

and improve the quality of people's lives. Some southern African governments—like Malawi and Swaziland—left productive investment largely to the private sector. Others, like Tanzania, Zambia, Mozambique, and Angola, argued that African entrepreneurs had neither the capital nor the skills required to make the kinds of investments required in key areas to restructure their national economies. They intervened directly in their national economies to encourage integrated industrial and agricultural growth.

Debt and Austerity in the 1980s

Regardless of the differing policies, these countries' failure to adequately restructure their inherited institutions left them subject to external forces beyond their control. Before they had had time to achieve significant changes, the new black governments—whatever their ideology or the development strategy they introduced—found themselves caught up in economic crises that engulfed the entire region. The terms of trade for the export crops and minerals on which all their economies still depended worsened as monetary crises and recessions spread throughout the world.[22] Their foreign-exchange earnings could no longer pay for the imported machinery, equipment, consumer goods,

Table 2.8
**Foreign Debt and Debt-Service Costs of Independent Southern African Governments,
1978 and 1982[a]**

	Foreign Debt (in U.S.\$ millions)		Debt-Service Cost (in U.S.\$ millions)		Debt-Service as % of Export Earnings	
	1978	*1982*	*1978*	*1982*	*1978*	*1982*
Angola	378.0	2,262.0[b]	n.a.	361	n.a.	20.5[c]
Botswana	120.7	209.0	n.a.	n.a.	1.9	2.0
Lesotho	32.7	138.6	3	26	3.82	58.9
Malawi	n.a.	692.0	n.a.	n.a.	8.6	23.0
Swaziland	105.2	177.7	n.a.	n.a.	1.7	3.6[b]
Tanzania	1,142.0	1,632.0	38	113	6.1	n.a.
Zambia	1,449.0	3,294.0	194	642[d]	21.7	67.0
Zimbabwe	418.0	1,221.0	8	146	0.8	13.9

Notes
a. This refers only to public external debt; the presence of private external debt—for which data are unavailable—significantly increases the debt-service ratio.
b. 1981.
c. Using 1981 export figure, and 1982 debt-service payment.
d. Repayments due in 1983.
Source: Economist Intelligence Unit, *Quarterly Economic Reports* for each country, 1983 (data not available for Mozambique); 1982 debt-service ratio for Zambia and Lesotho calculated from *International Financial Statistics* (Washington, D.C.: International Monetary Fund, December 1984).

and even food on which decades of colonialism had rendered their limited industrial and export-oriented agricultural sectors dependent. Falling domestic incomes and lack of spare parts and materials forced factories to lay off workers, while diminished foreign markets led mines and commercial farms to reduce employment. Conventional wisdom urged new governments to create a "hospitable investment climate" to attract more foreign capital, but in fact, foreign investment declined throughout the region.[23] Tax revenues failed to keep pace with mounting government expenditures. Heavy borrowing, both at home and increasingly abroad, fueled inflation and burdened the new governments with growing debt repayments.

On top of all this, prolonged drought struck the region. Peasant farms, like those in Chibi, mostly located in marginal, less well-watered regions, could not produce enough food for bare subsistence, much less the export crops needed to raise cash incomes. Several countries had to import maize simply to avoid mass starvation.

Turning to the International Monetary Fund (IMF) to help finance growing balance-of-payments deficits, several southern African states found themselves forced to impose austerity conditions.[24] In line with developed-country orthodoxy, IMF advisers typically told them to reduce government intervention—intervention through which they had sought to restructure their economies and build more self-reliant industries and agriculture. In the vain hope of attracting more foreign investments, they kept taxes on businesses relatively low. As an alternative source of desperately needed revenue, many raised sales taxes, which tended to fall most heavily on the lower-income groups.[25] They cut back on government spending for health, education, and social services. They laid off workers. And they devalued their currencies, which further reduced their ability to purchase imported machines and other goods on which their economies still depended.[26] As a result, rising prices reduced the real wages of those lucky enough still to have paying jobs—in some cases, back to pre-independence levels.

SUMMARY

The newly independent governments of southern Africa inherited economies geared by decades of colonialism to the export of a narrow range of crude minerals and crops, produced by settler farms and foreign-owned mines, to an uncertain world market; and to the import of high-priced manufactured goods for the minority who could afford them. Over the past century, colonial administrators had built a socioeconomic infrastructure to service these sectors, while institutionalizing land, taxes, marketing, credit, and labor policies to coerce the majority of Africans into a low-paid labor force for minority-owned mines, farms, and factories.

Upon attaining independence, the new black governments of the region sought to overcome colonial neglect by spending heavily to provide roads, electricity, schools, and health facilities. Some attempted to restructure their economies to reduce their external dependence. They sought to encourage investment in new factories as well as to stimulate increased production of cash crops and expand mining output. In all cases, however, as recession from the developed countries spread throughout the region, their markets and the prices for their exports worsened. They could no longer afford to import machinery, equipment, and spare parts on which the "modern" sectors of their economies depended. Unemployment mounted. Tax revenues fell and government deficits increased. Those countries which sought aid from the IMF found themselves forced to pursue austerity policies that threw the burden of the crisis on the increasingly impoverished majority.

30

The city of Johannesburg, South Africa, the center of the world's largest gold-mining industry, was mostly built by black labor, but blacks must live outside the city either in "townships" or remote bantustans. (United Nations photo/151601)

CHAPTER THREE

Apartheid, Transnational Corporate Investments, and South African Domination of the Region

THE IMPOSITION OF APARTHEID

While African states one after another won independence, a white minority in South Africa—barely more than 15 percent of the population—reinforced the institutionalized impoverishment of the majority by enforcing apartheid: a system designed to geographically separate blacks from whites, except when blacks work as low-paid labor on white-owned farms, mines, and factories.

The New 1983 Constitution

One out of three southern Africans lives in South Africa, the only country in the world where the minority justifies its rule solely on racist grounds. Apartheid denies black Africans—almost three-fourths of the population—the right to vote on national issues. The constitutional "reforms" of 1983-84 made no fundamental change in the structure of apartheid. Rather, they reflected the minority's effort to divide further the population and perpetuate its rule in the face of mounting domestic opposition. At the same time, the minority sought to blunt increasing international criticism by promoting the myth of reform.

Only whites were allowed to vote to approve the changes in the South African Constitution. These permitted Indians and coloureds (the South African government's term for people of mixed race) to elect candidates to two newly created, but still racially segregated, houses of Parliament. The whites still elect 178 members to the original and largest house. The coloureds elect 85 members to the second house, the Indians 45 to the third. These "reforms" do not even pretend to give black Africans the right to participate in any of the three houses of the new Parliament.

Each house considers its "own" matters such as housing, education, health, agriculture, and water supply. All three chambers consider "general" matters like defense and foreign affairs. Unless specifically repealed by all three houses, however, existing South African law continues. While Parliament may introduce minor reforms, whites still have an absolute numerical majority, making repeal of the basic system of apartheid unlikely.[1]

Table 3.1
"Racial" Distribution of the South African Population[a], 1982, and Representation in Tricameral Legislation Under New Constitution

	Number	% of Population	Representation in Legislature
Black	22,728,998[b]	73.0	None
White	4,748,000	15.3	178
Coloured	2,765,000	8.9	85
Indian	870,000	2.8	45
Total	31,111,998	100.0	

Notes

a. The concept of distribution according to "race" is in no way scientific, but represents the South African minority's arbitrary allocation as given by the official South African census and population estimates for Bophuthatswana, Transkei, and Venda (generally considered too low).

b. Includes bantustan populations of Transkei, Bophuthatswana, and Venda—almost 4 million people—declared "independent" by South Africa, but unrecognized by any other government.

Source: *Survey of Race Relations in South Africa, 1983* (Johannesburg: South African Institute of Race Relations, 1984), p. 72, 99, following.

Dr. Chester Crocker, U.S. assistant secretary of state for African affairs, characterized white support for the constitutional reforms as a "milestone" in the modern history of South Africa.[2] The Reagan administration based its Constructive Engagement Policy on the premise that this kind of peaceful change coincided with U.S. interests throughout the region.

As background essential for an assessment of this premise, this chapter examines:

★ The way apartheid shapes the lives of the majority of South African citizens;

★ The nature and consequences of investments by transnational corporations (including those from the United States) in South Africa;

★ The role of foreign investment in strengthening South African domination of the region.

The Consequences of Apartheid

Over the centuries since the Dutch first landed in South Africa, the white-ruled state has institutionalized many devices to deny the black majority the right to vote and coerce them into a low-paid labor force. A series of land acts pushed Africans off the best farming land into the desert-like areas today termed bantustans—or "homelands"—comprising only 13 percent of the national territory.[3] The law permits them to leave these areas legally only if they are

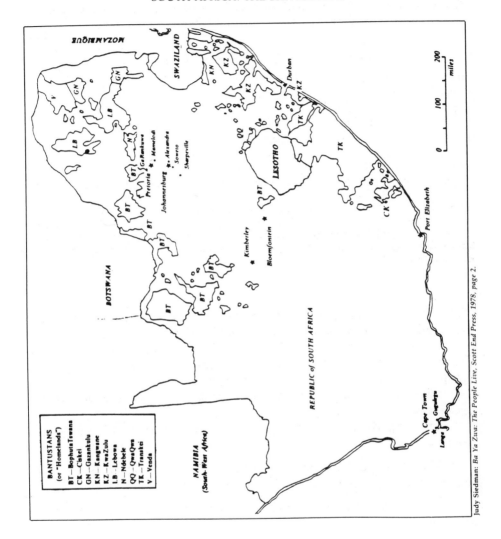

Judy Siedman: *Ba Ya Ziwa: The People Live*, Scott End Press, 1978, page 2.

FIGURE 2

employed by whites and carry "passes" with the required employer and government signatures to prove it. Monopolizing 87 percent of the nation's territory, whites own the farms, mines, and factories that produce the wealth of the nation. As elsewhere in the region, taxes, credit and marketing systems, and the inadequacy of the overcrowded, infertile bantustans force hundreds of thousands of unemployed African men and women to migrate to work at white-owned farms, mines, factories, and kitchens for below-poverty-line wages.

Forced Removals

In 1948, when the Nationalist Party won the white vote in the elections, it proclaimed its aim to enforce apartheid. It accelerated the process of forcing the African majority to live in the bantustans. It forcibly removed 3.5 million black South Africans from what it called "white areas" to those designated for blacks. Men, women, and children, born and brought up in the cities, suddenly found themselves forced to become "citizens" of remote desert lands they had never seen.[4] The government destroyed whole settlements, forcing inhabitants to move to unfamiliar "homelands."

Box 3.1

The Migratory Labor System Viewed from the Bantustans*

The Homeland Magistrates' offices provide the link between work-seekers and the big industrial firms, mines, and businesses who from time to time go to the homelands to contract laborers for a specified employment period. These contracts may or may not be renewable.

For two or three months at the beginning of every year, you may see large numbers of men, who have registered for work, gathered in front of the magistrates' offices, patiently waiting for contracts. Some have traveled distances too long to walk. They have had to pay bus fares and buy food. They have also paid "tribal" taxes in full before their work applications would even be considered. Some have been out of work for two, three, even five years. There is no way they can pay their taxes without obtaining employment. Sometimes the only way a man can break this cycle is to borrow from sympathetic relatives: elderly parents or grandparents willing to sacrifice part of the meager pensions they receive every two months. These relatives know that, as a result of helping to pay these taxes, they will have to live for a week or more on only one meal a day. They can only pray there will be no more serious emergency.

As you see the crowds in front of the magistrates' offices get thinner and thinner, don't deceive yourself into believing that the men are finding jobs. The men desperately throw their passbooks at the labor recruiter in hopes that he will select them; but he only catches those of a lucky few. As the days drag

Despite worldwide protests and claims of reform, the South African government continued this policy. Declaring the remaining "black spots" as "operational areas," police removed whole communities to the nearest bantustans. For example, on February 14, 1984, about 100 police converged on the 70-year-old village of Mogopa near Ventersdorp in the Transvaal. Barricades were set up to prevent anybody—including journalists—from entering the area. Community leaders were rounded up, families and their belongings loaded onto trucks and buses. Resisters were beaten. The trucks drove almost 200 miles to leave the families in a tin-shanty settlement camp, Pachsdraei, in Bophuthatswana.[5]

Today, about 12 million, roughly half of all black South Africans, still work in and live on the outskirts of white areas. This means that about half the black population has been crowded into the bantustans, many of them without even a patch of land on which to grow their own food.

The Myth of Change
Seeking to convince the world that it is actually improving the blacks'

---

on, some men run short of money for food and their return bus fare. More and more simply become discouraged.

This scene is repeated every year in bantustans throughout the country. Tens of thousands of husbands-fathers, with families to care for, suffer embarrassment and shame when they must return to see their wives and children malnourished, clothed in tatters, living in shacks. Yet there is nothing they can do, nowhere else they can turn for work.

Thousands of younger men, little more than boys, have left school because their parents could no longer afford to support them. They are not trained for any job. Most have not even attended high school. They are barely literate. At 16 years of age, they must take the lowest-paying menial jobs—if they can get them—or join the growing ranks of unemployed.

For the women who must remain behind, there is no escape from the grinding round of misery. Those lucky enough to have family plots struggle to till the hard red soils with hand hoes. They have no money to hire tractors or buy fertilizers. In the last four or five years, with little rain, few have produced more than a bag of maize from the exhausted soils. They must search for wild greens which provide their families' only condiments. Yet if they leave their family plots fallow for more than a year, the bantustan authorities will confiscate them and give them to landless families.

*This report was written by a former South African social worker, whose name is being withheld on request to avoid harassment on return to South Africa.

conditions, the South African government has made marginal reforms. New laws were passed permitting local authorities to abolish "petty apartheid," that is, segregation of the races in public facilities in white areas like parks, beaches, and a few hotels. Yet even where such measures are implemented, the facilities are typically located in central urban areas where few blacks live or can afford to go.

In April 1985, Pretoria announced plans to repeal two laws forbidding sex and marriage across racial lines. As one American reporter observed, however:

> For the vast majority of South Africans, who do not have or intend to have relations across racial lines, the significance of the change was largely symbolic. . . .
>
> [T]he network of laws, regulations, customs and Draconian security measures that give force to apartheid remains vast and intrusive. Not even the most optimistic of the system's opponents predicts a fundamental change soon in the apparatus that preserves the power and privilege of 4.5 million whites . . . while denying it to the nonwhite majority.[6]

To promote the myth of change, Pretoria has given blacks "self-government" in the bantustans. It has granted "independence" to four of these: Transkei, Bophuthatswana, Venda, and Ciskei. In actuality, the bantustans remain little more than dumping grounds for women and children, the aged, and the unemployed. Their governing authorities lack the resources to finance adequate social services or carry out policies other than those formulated in Pretoria. No other government in that world recognizes them as sovereign nations; world opinion recognizes their status as just another device to further institutionalize segregation and deprive the African majority of their rights to enjoy the wealth produced from the resources of the entire nation. Yet having granted them "independence," the minority government treats people living in the bantustans as foreigners, requiring them to have not merely the hated passes, but passports to work in South Africa.

The South African government has also established Local Authorities in the urban black townships—located miles from major urban centers—to provide housing for blacks employed in the "white" areas. These Authorities have permission to sell houses to blacks who can afford them. This measure promotes a small black bureaucracy closely controlled by the central government, granting privileges to only a handful of affluent black businessmen.[7]

Donald Woods, former editor of the *Daily Dispatch* in South Africa until he was arrested in 1977 for reporting the details of Steve Biko's death in detention (see below, Chapter 4), wrote an open letter in 1984 to South Africa's Prime Minister P.W. Botha. For the first time, Botha was traveling to Europe to convince European heads of state that the regime's efforts to make reforms were real. Woods reminded him:

> How ironic that you visited Britain and France last week during commemoration of the Normandy D-Day landings which insured the Allied victory in World War II—

during which conflict you and your colleagues in the Afrikaner Nationalist Party fervently hoped that victory would go to the Third Reich.

Considering how bitterly you attacked Jan Christian Smuts' Government for supporting the Allies at that time, and how openly your party admired Hitler, it was in character when you Afrikaner nationalists took power in 1948 to pursue your own Herrenvolk theory of apartheid—and today, under your leadership, the cause of racial purity flourishes more strongly than ever before. Since January, more than 50,000 blacks have been arrested under the Pass Laws, one of your thriving 317 racial statutes that make apartheid first cousin to Hitler's Nuremberg Laws. . . .

Since you became Prime Minister six years ago, things have gotten worse for black South Africans. Forced removals of black communities from white-zoned areas have increased. Penalities under the Pass Laws have been made more severe. Squatters' shelters have been bulldozed and burned, and more blacks than ever before are being stripped of citizenship and consigned to the "homelands." The laws against dissidence have been strengthened, and under your Prime Ministership at least nine dissidents have died in police custody.[8]

"Bantu" Education

Institutionalized apartheid reaches into all aspects of the life of black South Africans. A restricted form of "bantu" education denies black children equal access to schooling, sharply restricting their job options.[9] Primary and secondary schools remain segregated for white, Indian, coloured, and black children. Only in neighborhoods where there are not enough children to establish two separate schools may coloured and Indian children attend school together. Only a tiny handful of black children, whose parents have sufficiently high incomes, may attend selected white schools.

The state spends an average of five times more to educate each white child than it spends for each African child.[10] Many schools designated for black children are overcrowded and in chronic need of repair. The teacher-pupil ratio in white schools is 1:18; in black schools, 1:48. Although the Pretoria government has repeatedly promised educational facilities, a 1980 survey revealed that only a three-fold increase in educational expenditures would provide an acceptable level of education for blacks.[11] That would increase educational expenditures from 4 to 13 percent of the gross national product, a move the government shows no signs of making.

Many black children must leave school to take jobs because their parents' incomes are too low to support them. As a result, only 14 percent of black school-age children actually complete the equivalent of high school. In the late 1970s, an acute shortage of skilled labor led to increased technical and vocational education for blacks. But even then, apartheid severely restricted blacks' technical education; their opportunities remain segregated and limited by bantustanization.

The relatively few blacks who succeed in obtaining the necessary qualifications for university may not attend white universities without government permission. On the other hand, scarce funds severely limit university places and the curriculum in black universities in the bantustans. Furthermore, in 1983 the

Table 3.2
Per Capita Expenditures on Education (Including Capital Expenditure) for 1982-83

	Outside Bantustans[a]
White	$1,689
Indian	$1,063
Coloured	$724
Black[b]	$234

Notes

a. Figures for capital expenditure on education in the bantustans are not readily available. Rand converted to U.S. dollars at exchange rate for 1983 ($0.82 = R1).

b. Estimated current expenditure per capita on black education (excluding capital expenditures) for 1981-82 was $122 inside the bantustans and $177 outside (using 1982 exchange rate $0.93 = R1).

Source: *Survey of Race Relations in South Africa, 1983* (Johannesburg: South African Institute of Race Relations, 1984), p. 426.

authorities introduced age restrictions barring mature black students from continuing their education. In 1984, the authorities permitted fewer than 10 percent of the black high school graduates who took the examinations to enter the universities, as compared to more than half the white students.[12]

Work Opportunities for Blacks

In 1981, blacks constituted almost two-thirds of the paid labor force, but received less than a third of the wage bill. By contrast, white workers making up little more than a fifth of the paid labor force received almost three-fifths of the wage bill.[13] Since the mid-1970s, large firms have promoted a few blacks to supervisory positions, helping to create a small group of black workers who benefit from the *status quo*;[14] the vast majority of blacks still work in menial, low-paying jobs.

Table 3.3
Occupational Structure by Skill (Excluding Agriculture), by Percentage of Workers of Each Population Group Working in Each Category, 1975

	Skilled	Semi-Skilled	Unskilled
White Collar:			
White	36%	62%	2%
Black	10%	22%	68%
Blue Collar:			
White	45%	52%	3%
Black	3%	53%	44%

Source: David Dewar and Vanessa Watson, *Unemployment and the Informal Sector: Some Proposals* (Cape Town: University of Cape Town, Urban Problems Research Unit, Ph.D., 1981).

Table 3.4
Distribution of Wage Bill in South Africa

	% of Work Force	% of Wage Bill
Blacks	62.9	29.4
Whites	21.9	58.7
Coloureds	11.8	8.3
Indians	3.4	3.3

Sources: Distribution of wage bill: Barclays Bank, Johannesburg, March 1983, cited in American Committee on Africa, "South African Fact Sheet" (New York: ACOA, 1984). Distribution of wage labor force: calculated from data in "Labour Statistics Employment and Earnings, March-May, 1983," Statistical News Release, August 25, 1983, published in American Committee on Africa, "South Africa Fact Sheet" (New York: ACOA, 1984). Total in second column less than 100 percent because of rounding.

In 1982, the South African government claimed it had lifted most of the legal restrictions which had for decades reserved more skilled, higher-paying jobs for whites. But the cumulative impact of apartheid remained. Decades of geographical segregation, educational discrimination, and impoverishment had created conditions which automatically excluded all but a few blacks from high-paying, skilled jobs.

As Table 3.5 shows, wages vary per sector, but in every case blacks earn an average of less than a fourth to half the wages received by whites.

The difference in income is even more striking in agriculture. In 1980, black farm workers earned only $28 to $40 a month. They also received some "in kind" payment, but this included only minimal housing and ground corn meal.[15]

Discrimination because of sex, as well as race, further limits the employment opportunities of women. A black woman considers herself lucky to find any kind of paying job. About half of all employed black women work as domestic servants or in related service jobs. Since apartheid legislation prohibits most employed domestics from living with their families, many see their children only a few times a year.[16]

A high proportion of black wage earners receive wages below the minimum subsistence level for an average family. The *1983 Midway Report from the Second Carnegie Study of Poverty in South Africa* revealed that 80 percent of the residents of Soweto—the largest African township in South Africa—live on incomes below the poverty level.[17]

The majority of Africans, now forced to live in the bantustans, can barely survive without remittances from family members who have migrated to work in white areas.[18] The "independent" bantustans, in which about a fourth of South Africa's black population lives, produce barely 3 percent of South Africa's national product. Official South African data do not show any measurable cash income for the 5 million people living in the "dependent" bantustans.[19]

Table 3.5
Employment and Wages (in U.S. $)[a], 1983

	Overall		Mining		Manufacturing	
	Number Employed[b]	Avg. Monthly Wages	Number Employed	Avg. Monthly Wages	Number Employed	Avg. Monthly Wages
Black	1,833,544	$249	621,829	$306	747,806	$439
White	637,723	$1,683	89,272	$1,490	316,100	$1,743
Coloured	342,808	$668	10,423	$610	241,400	$491
Indian	99,324	$998	849	$1,320	86,700	$602

Notes

Figures do not include "independent bantustans."

a. Converted from rands to dollars at 1983 exchange rate ($0.82 = R1).
b. Overall employment figures from Statistical News Release, August 25, 1983, "Labour Statistics Employment and Earnings, March-May 1983" published in American Committee on Africa, "South Africa Fact Sheet," (New York: ACOA, 1984).

Source: Unless otherwise cited, from *Survey of Race Relations in South Africa, 1983* (Johannesburg: South African Institute of Race Relations (1984), pp. 126, 144, 153-54.

Low incomes engender malnutrition and poor health. The Carnegie Study showed that one out of three black, coloured, and Asian children below the age of 14 is underweight and stunted for his or her age.[20] Highly susceptible to disease, the majority of Africans receive grossly inadequate health care. Whereas about 90 percent of all South African doctors are white, only 1 percent are black. One doctor serves 330 whites, compared to one doctor for 91,000 blacks. Many South African black children and adults die every year from preventable and curable diseases. Medical experts report that 25 to 40 percent of the population have tuberculosis in a dormant form. Although there is now a simple cure for this disease, every day six people die from it in South Africa.[21] Even statistics published by the minority establishment show that the black infant mortality rate is seven times higher than that of whites.[22]

THE ROLE OF TRANSNATIONAL CORPORATIONS

During the years the independent southern African states sought in vain to attract foreign investments to develop their economies, two noteworthy events occurred in South Africa: The Nationalists imposed apartheid, and U.S. transnational corporations tripled their investments there.

In the first three decades after World War II, U.S. transnational corporations invested three times as much capital in South Africa as in the entire pre-war era. By 1983, total U.S. financial involvement in South Africa, including direct investment, bank loans, and stockholdings, had reached $14.6 billion[23]—equal to roughly two-thirds of the total gross domestic products of all the neighboring countries combined. Direct investments totaled $2.6 billion, accounting for about 20 percent of all direct foreign investments in South Africa, and surpassed only by those of Great Britain. U.S. financial institutions had outstanding loans to South African borrowers totaling $3.9 billion. U.S. investors were estimated to hold $8.1 billion worth of shares in South African businesses, primarily mines. U.S. manufacturing firms had poured more than three-fourths of the capital they invested in the entire African continent into building factories in South Africa.[24] (See list of U.S. firms with investments in South Africa in Appendix III.)

Apartheid and Foreign Investment

The reasons for this expansion in South Africa, rather than in the independent neighboring countries, reach back into South African history. In the 19th century, under the umbrella of British colonial rule, white-settler-owned capital, accumulated in the diamond mines, combined with British, U.S., and German investments to finance the development of the South African gold industry.[25] Throughout Africa, mining investments remained virtually all foreign-owned, at least until the new African governments obtained independence in the 1960s. In South Africa, the white settlers worked through locally based mining finance houses to collaborate with international financial interests.

This alliance initially excluded the Afrikaners, descendents of the early Dutch settlers, who trekked to the Transvaal in the late 19th century to escape British rule in the Cape. They had enslaved blacks to work their farms and viewed the expansion of English settlers' mining interests as a threat to their claims on African lands and labor. By the end of the 19th century, these conflicts led to the three-year Boer War, which the British finally won.

Following the war, faced with mounting African opposition, the British colonial administration sought to heal the divisions among the whites. Despite bitter differences between them, the English and Afrikaners joined together to control the black majority. In 1910, they created the Union of South Africa as a separate settler-ruled country within the British Commonwealth.

The Union reinforced measures that granted white settlers control over the nation's most productive land areas, exercising state power to coerce the Africans to work for them. The growing labor force in the mines created new markets for white-owned farms. The wealthier Afrikaner farm owners expanded their acreage and squeezed the less successful farmers off their land and into the cities. The resulting "poor white" Afrikaner population, many of them illiterate, could barely compete with the urban blacks who, despite early racist restrictions, had secured better education and skills. To keep the blacks out of the better jobs, therefore, the poor whites used their political influence to agitate for a stricter "Colour Bar."

Throughout most of this period, gold prices remained low. South African mine companies showed profits only because black workers' wages were low. After World War I, the mining companies sought to further reduce labor costs by hiring low-paid Africans to do the skilled jobs historically reserved for higher-paid whites. White miners struck, demanding the exclusion of blacks from all but the most unskilled, lowest-paid work.[26] The Union government used the army to smash the white workers' strike and even hanged some of its leaders. But the mining companies had learned their lesson. In a deliberate effort to win back the support of whites against the black miners, they restored the Colour Bar throughout the mines.

In the mid-1920s, the Afrikaner electorate, seeking to strengthen its position, voted the forerunner of the Nationalist Party into office. The government proceeded to systematize and institutionalize the Colour Bar in all sectors: laws excluded blacks from skilled jobs, reserved certain government posts for whites, and prohibited blacks from supervising whites. Whites received new educational privileges. State and corporate policies aimed specifically to separate and improve conditions of white workers in their living area as well as their work. In return, whites defended the racist system designed to keep black wages low.

Meanwhile the state intervened vigorously to stimulate industrial growth.[27] The Iron and Steel Corporation (ISCOR) and the Electricity Supply Commission (ESCOM) were created as the foundation of domestic industry. An array of inducements was offered to attract domestic and foreign capital into manufacturing. Nevertheless, until after World War II, mining and agriculture continued to form the backbone of the South African economy.

Post-World War II Expansion

At the same time it imposed apartheid after coming to power following World War II, the Nationalist Party introduced new measures to encourage foreign manufacturing investment. These two policies, although seemingly distinct, were intertwined. Attracting new investment was contingent upon guaranteeing profits; profits were realized by keeping black wages low.

In the context of apartheid, U.S. transnational corporations expanded their role in helping the white minority build a powerful military-industrial complex, one enabling the government to perpetuate its undemocratic rule at home and extend its domination throughout the region.

As a consequence of the state's extensive intervention, competitive free market forces advocated by conventional Western theory never existed in South Africa. A handful of locally based mining finance houses, led by the Anglo American Group, with ties to major financial and industrial interests in both Britain and the United States, played a key role in developing South Africa's industrial base.

Box 3.2

The Anglo American Group: A Link to U.S. Transnational Firms

The Anglo American Group, the largest mining finance house in South Africa, typifies the symbiotic relationship that has grown between transnational corporations, banks, the South African state, and domestic capital. Anglo was founded just after World War I by a South African diamond magnate, Ernest Oppenheimer, in cooperation with a U.S. bank, Morgan Guaranty; a U.S. firm, Newmont Mining; and the National Bank of South Africa. The National Bank had originally been founded (in 1890) as a central bank for the Boers' Transvaal Republic, but the British, in effect, confiscated it after the Boer War and transformed it into a private bank. It proceeded to take over several smaller banks, becoming the second largest bank in South Africa, the only major one still in South African hands. In 1918, Oppenheimer obtained a seat on its board, and the relationship between the bank and his mining finance house flourished. In 1918, the National Bank established links to Barclays Bank.

In 1925, the National Bank, the original South African Barclays affiliate,[a] and two other colonial banks merged to form Barclays DCO, one of the earliest transnational banks that operated throughout the British empire in response to the needs of imperial trading and mining corporations. Oppenheimer retained his seat on the board of the new bank, which provided Anglo with invaluable international contacts. Harry Oppenheimer, until recently the chairman of Anglo, inherited his father's place on Barclays International's board. Barclays continues to do a large share of its business in southern Africa.

Using the capital it derived from the low-paid African workers it employed on its South African mines, Anglo collaborated closely with the South African parastatals and transnational corporate interests to develop key sectors of South Africa's basic manufacturing industries. At the same time, it continued to expand, undermining the independence of other mining finance houses while working ever more closely with the ruling Afrikaner interests. It acquired 47 percent of the Johannesburg Consolidated Investment (JCI or "Johnnies"). When the Afrikaner group, Federal Mynbou, took over the General Mining and Finance Corporation (GMFC or GenMin), Anglo also obtained a substantial share. Two Anglo directors sit on GenMin's board.

By the 1980s, Anglo American had grown into an international conglomerate, although its southern African assets still provided its financial foundation. Anglo affiliates penetrated throughout southern Africa in mining, a limited amount of manufacturing, trade, finance, and real estate. An Anglo affiliate managed the huge copper mines that dominated Zambia's economy. Anglo became the largest foreign investor in Zimbabwe, with interests ranging from coal mines to sugar plantations. It opened mines in Botswana, Swaziland, and Namibia, in virtually every case exporting unrefined material to South Africa, Europe, the United States, or Japan. By the early 1980s, the assets of Anglo's group members totaled more than $10 billion.

One Anglo affiliate, De Beers, controls 85 percent of the international production and sale of rough diamonds. It mines diamonds in South Africa, Namibia, Lesotho, and Botswana and buys them from Zaire, Ghana, the Central African Republic, and Sierra Leone. It ships many of its diamonds to Israel and Belgium to be sold, cut, and polished. Together, Israel and Belgium annually export cut diamonds worth more than $1 billion.

In addition to Barclays, Anglo has other major foreign associates. Charter Consolidated, a British transnational affiliated to the Anglo Group, acts as its agent in London. Charter's quoted and unquoted investments total about a billion dollars, mostly in England and South Africa. The Anglo American Group and Charter have made joint investments throughout the world. Together, they obtained 34.75 percent of Hudson Bay Mining and Smelting in Canada. Charter also owned smaller interests in a number of other transnational corporations, including the U.S.-controlled Falconbridge Nickel and several U.S. oil companies.

By the 1970s, Anglo American became closely interlocked with and shared directors with the U.S. firm, Engelhard Minerals and Chemicals (EMC). Engelhard mines and markets ores, metals, and nonmetallic minerals, and refines and trades precious minerals for industry.

The interests of the U.S. mining transnational, American Metal Climax (AMAX), also became increasingly linked with Anglo's in the 1960s and 1970s. In fact, the companies acquired substantial shares in each other. They invested jointly in Zambia's copper mines, developed the Selebi-Pikwe mine in Botswana, and with other companies, controlled the Tsumeb copper mine in Namibia. Both Engelhard and AMAX officials retained close links with the U.S. government.

In the 1980s, Anglo combined its U.S. interests into a new holding company, Minorca, based in Bermuda. It expanded its investments in the United States to become the second largest foreign investor in that country. Walter Wriston, then head of one of the largest U.S. banks, Citicorp, sat on Minorca's board of directors.[28]

Anglo forged a number of additional international connections, as well as building a network of smaller affiliates and subsidiaries throughout Africa, the Americas, Europe, and Australia. It shared directors with top international mining companies, including the British Rio Tinto Zinc. It also established close ties with the West German Dresdner Bank, one of three banks that dominate West German banking.

Note

a. See Footnote 39.

Source: For a well-researched and convenient summary, see Duncan Innes, *Anglo American and the Rise of Modern South Africa* (New York: Monthly Review Press, 1984); see also Anglo American Group, Annual Reports (South Africa); Ann and Neva Seidman, *U.S. Multinational Corporations in Southern Africa* (Westport, CT: Lawrence Hill, 3rd ed., 1979).

State Intervention

Pretoria became an aggressive partner of transnational corporate affiliates[29] and local mining finance houses willing to expand their manufacturing business. Targets were set by sector for increases in annual production. The government provided incentives for transnational corporations to extend their investments from last-stage assembly and processing plants to vertically integrated basic industries.

The Nationalist government broadened the role of the parastatals (partially state-owned corporations) in which it participated through its holding company, the Industrial Corporation of South Africa. Each of the leading parastatal groups had its own complex of affiliates, many of them partially owned by transnational corporations as well as domestic mining finance houses. Box 3.3 shows the close cooperation with mining finance houses and transnational firms, the South African government has operated through this parastatal network to increase investments in manufacturing.

Box 3.3

The Largest South African Parastatals Developed with the Assistance of Transnational Corporations, Including Some from the United States

★ ISCOR, the iron and steel corporation, produces almost three-fourths of the steel consumed in South Africa. It obtains technology and markets from transnational firms. U.S. Steel owns four subsidiaries in South Africa, and has contracted to purchase 3 million tons of ore there for 15 years, beginning in 1978. General Electric's South African affiliate (SAGE) has manufactured electrical controls for ISCOR. In the 1970s, U.S., U.K., West German, and Austrian banks helped finance a $200 million mining, steel-producing, and exporting project controlled by ISCOR.

★ ESCOM, an electricity utility, has constructed a national grid of thermal and hydroelectric power plants, as well as the Koeberg nuclear power plant. These have helped South Africa to reduce its dependence on imported oil to a level lower than that of any other relatively industrialized nation. General Electric's SAGE provided control-relay panels and other technology for ESCOM's projects. Westinghouse, through its French affiliate, helped supply reactors to the Koeberg nuclear plant. Eurocurrency consortia, including U.S. banks, have helped finance ESCOM's growth.

★ SASOL produces oil and petrochemical by-products from coal, which are of particular importance because South Africa, with no known natural oil reserves, faces an international oil boycott. Under strict government secrecy, U.S. firms—Caltex (Standard Oil of California—now Chevron—and Texaco), Mobil, and Exxon—help import, refine and market petroleum throughout South and southern Africa. The French affiliate, Total, owns shares in SASOL. The U.S. firm, Fluor, played a major role in constructing the SASOL oil-from-coal plant, for a time employing the largest number of South Africans of any U.S. firm.

★ IDC, the Industrial Development Corporation, invests in diverse manufacturing industries in cooperation with domestic and foreign private capital. For example, it sponsored the formation of SENTRACHEM (see below), bringing together South Africa and British firms. In the 1970s, it joined with the Swiss Alusaf to invest nearly $100 million to open South Africa's first aluminum company; and joined the Quebec Iron and Titanium Corp., a Canadian subsidiary of the U.S. firm, Kennecott, and South African private firms to build a $200 million project to mine titanium and zirconium.

★ SARR&H, the South African Railroads and Harbours Corporation, owns the most extensive rail network in Africa, and operates and has modernized South Africa's port facilities. General Electric's SAGE and General Motors' South African affiliate have sold it locomotives. In the 1970s, transnational firms collaborated in SARR&H as well as ISCOR to construct the railway and associated infrastructure in opening up the Richards Bay area to spur South African minerals exports.

★ SENTRACHEM, in which the state owns a minority share, relies on its foreign partners for the technology as well as capital to establish a domestic chemicals industry. It was formed in a merger of several South African firms, including affiliates of Anglo American and British Petroleum (BP), sponsored by the South African IDC, which retained a 20 percent share. Foreign oil firms have helped build up South Africa's petrochemicals industry.

★ ARMSCOR, a wholly government-owned parastatal, has contracted with hundreds of private and parastatal firms to produce military parts and equipment. Drawing on the nation's expanding national industrial base, ARMSCOR has achieved an increasingly self-reliant, capital-intensive capacity for production of military hardware.[30]

Source: A. and N. Seidman, *U.S. Multinational Corporations in Southern Africa* (Westport, CT: Lawrence Hill, 1979); Pacific Northwest Research Center, *Unified List of U.S. Companies with Investments or Loans in South Africa or Namibia* (New York: American Committee on Africa, forthcoming 1985); U.N. Committee Against Apartheid, Notes and Documents; and relevant companies' annual reports.

The Key Role of U.S. Firms

U.S. direct investments in South Africa are significant not so much because of their amount, but because they are placed primarily in critical economic sectors that have helped to transform South Africa into an industrialized and increasingly militarized state. Transnationals provide favorable international credit as well as technological and managerial assistance, thus helping South Africa become strategically self-sufficient and better able to defy international sanctions.[31]

U.S. firms have played an increasingly significant role in key basic industries—accounting in 1980 for about 33 percent of the motor vehicles market, 44 percent of the petroleum products market, and 75 percent of the computer market. General Motors and Ford, for example, employ several thousand workers to manufacture cars, trucks, and components, for sale both in the South African market (including some sales to the military and police) and in Europe. Firestone and Goodyear sell tires to South African government agencies, products that can be transferred to the security forces.[32] A General Electric affiliate, SAGE, supplied geothermal turbines to power a nuclear reactor.[33] ITT held shares in a South African firm that produces communications equipment, some of which was sold to the police and South Africa's principal naval base at Simonstown.[34]

Three oil majors—Texaco and Standard Oil of California (together as Caltex), and Mobil—refine and distribute oil products, helping South Africa evade the impact of the OPEC nations' embargo. These petroleum products are used by military and police forces, and help fuel the war of occupation in Namibia.[35]

U.S. computers are used widely in South Africa. IBM South Africa leads the field, with 40 percent or more of South Africa's installed computer base. About 17 percent of IBM's South African revenues come from the central and provincial governments, with more from municipal governments and state-owned corporations. IBM South Africa supplies the Atomic Energy Board; the Industrial Development Corporation; and the government's Council for Scientific and Industrial Research (CSIR), the nerve center of military, nuclear, electronic, and industrial research and development.[36] IBM computers run the Johannesburg Stock Exchange and military communications in Namibia.[37]

Control Data computers and equipment are used by the CSIR, the police, the Atomic Energy Board, ISCOR, and ESCOM. Control Data receives about 50 percent of its revenues from the government sector.[38] Sperry computers are used by the National Petroluem Refiners, the Atomic Energy Board, and a subsidiary of ARMSCOR. Honeywell's customers include SASOL and ISCOR, the latter accounting for 20 percent of Honeywell's business in South Africa.[39]

In the area of finance, U.S. banks like Chase Manhattan and Citicorp, South Africa's top international lender, helped finance the expanding transnational corporate role in the Southern African economy. They have participated in arranging loans from European and U.S. banks to both the public and private sectors. These funds contribute foreign exchange the South African minority needs to purchase the oil, military hardware, and sophisticated machinery it requires to maintain its dominant status.[40]

Corporate Profits and African Poverty

The relationship between corporate profits and African poverty cannot be ignored. After the government's brutal suppression of the 1976 Soweto uprising, the correlation between corporate profits and apartheid became a focus of international criticism. Nevertheless, transnational corporations continued to expand their South African investments.[41] Foreign direct investment grew substantially, especially in manufacturing linked to government-sponsored capital projects, like energy, chemicals, and engineering. These kinds of investments increased South Africa's self-sufficiency in strategic sectors. Direct U.S. investment in South Africa increased 16.8 percent in 1980 and 17 percent in 1981. The U.S. rates of return on this investment reached 29 percent in 1980 and remained at 19 percent even in the recession of 1981. This compares to an average rate of return on foreign investments for U.S. companies in all geographical areas of 18.4 percent and 14.4 percent, respectively. The rate of profit U.S. firms reported on their South African investments subsequently declined, and some began to reduce their investments as renewed recession spread in 1984.[42] Nevertheless, some U.S. firms continued to expand there. For example, Dow Chemical opened an $8.3 million pharmaceutical plant near Johannesburg and asserted that by 1990 it hoped to have invested about $60 million in South Africa.[43]

Two sets of contradictory factors apparently persuaded transnational corporate managers to continue in this triple alliance with South African parastatals and mining finance houses: the relatively high profits they obtained in South Africa, and the fact that their South African investments gave their manufactured output a point of entrance into the extended southern African market.

Foreign firms reap high profits in South Africa primarily because apartheid ensures that black workers' wages remain exceptionally low compared to wages paid to workers in other developed areas. Managers of some firms in relatively labor-intensive manufacturing industries (notably auto and electrical appliances) in the past have explicitly cited low wages to explain their expanding investments in South Africa.[44] Although in the early 1970s South African workers' wages rose as a result of a strike wave in response to inflation, they still remained below the poverty level[45] and well below those of the transnational corporations' home countries.

Although many transnational affiliates operate plants with advanced technologies, employing mainly skilled workers (a high proportion of them white), they still benefit from the institutionalization of poverty for the black labor force for three reasons. First, the cost of infrastructure, provided primarily for white businesses, remains low. This adds to manufacturing firms' profitability. They do not have to provide water, energy, transport links, or skilled labor. Yet by investing primarily in the relatively developed areas of South Africa, foreign firms aggravate the already grossly uneven development between South Africa's urban centers and the rest of South and southern Africa.[46]

Second, the parastatals sell basic inputs to corporations at or below cost. They can do this, in part, because they pay their black employees low wages; in part because they receive state subsidies made possible by the low level of social services provided for the black majority. The state steel company,

Table 3.6

A Comparison of Average Monthly Earnings in South Africa and the United States for the Years 1975 and 1981

	1975	1981
South Africa:		
White	$880	$1,024
Coloured	$224	$337
Indian	$355	$475
Black	$189	$248
United States:	$779	$1,021
Ratio of average U.S. wage to average black African wage	4.12:1	4.11:1

Sources: South African wages: *Survey of Race Relations in South Africa, 1982* (Johannesburg: South African Institute for Race Relations, 1983), p. 64; converted to U.S. dollars at the appropriate International Monetary Fund exchange rate. U.S. wages calculated on the basis of a 40-hour week, four-week month: *Employment and Earnings* (Washington, D.C.: U.S. Department of Labor, Bureau of Labor Statistics), Vol. 29, No. 1, January 1982, p. 198; *U.S. Statistical Abstract, 1978* (Washington, D.C.: U.S. Government Printing Office, 1978), p. 414.

ISCOR, for example, depends on annual subsidies to keep the prices of domestic steel at levels competitive with world prices. And ESCOM charges lower rates for electricity sold to industry and mining firms than to private consumers.

Third, by providing little social security, health care, or education for the black majority, the state holds down effective corporate tax rates to about 25 percent of net corporate income. The fact that 30 percent of the cost of machinery may be deducted from taxable company profits encourages foreign as well as local firms to invest in capital-intensive machinery and equipment. Furthermore, double taxation agreements with Western industrialized nations ensure that once firms have paid taxes on their profits in South Africa, they do not have to pay again in their home countries.[47] Through these agreements, the developed countries effectively subsidize investment in apartheid.

The other set of factors explaining why U.S. and other transnational corporations continue to invest in South Africa relates to their desire to enter the large South African and regional markets. For several reasons, the South African market itself is significant. Although the black majority in South Africa has little money to spend on luxury goods, the 4 million whites constitute an important market for high-priced, manufactured consumer goods. The white minority comprises less than a fifth of the South African population, but its per capita income exceeds those of most industrialized countries of the world. By contrast, the average population of the separate neighboring countries is also about 4 million, but their annual per capita income averages only a few hundred dollars.[48]

Following the independence of Mozambique and Angola and the growth of the liberation movement at home, the Pretoria government spurred parastatals and private firms to invest a significant share of their 1970s profits to mechanize industries and thus reduce the economy's dependence on black labor. While this increased black unemployment and overcrowding in the bantustans, it expanded South Africa's need for sophisticated imported machinery and equipment, purchased from transnational manufacturing corporations.[49]

South Africa's growing military establishment has also become a major component of the country's internal market. The military budget multiplied more than six times in the 1960s, and six times again by 1983 to exceed $3 billion. The state has sought to stimulate local manufacture of military equipment. Secrecy laws conceal the extent of individual transnational corporate involvement in this business. By the end of the 1970s, however, ARMSCOR had contracts with 1,200 firms, of which about a third relied to a significant extent on military sales.[50] General Motors has stated that South Africa's military provides an important market for its trucks.[51] A number of transnational factories in South Africa, which do not market their output directly to the military, produce inputs for other firms that do sell to the military establishment. Others supply licenses used by local South African firms to manufacture military equipment.

The growth of the military establishment, however, has aggravated contradictory tendencies in the South African economy. While substantially expanding the domestic market and strengthening the government's ability to enforce apartheid, this growth has also contributed to rising state expenditures. To avoid discouraging continued investment by imposing higher taxes on corporate profits, the state has raised taxes on lower- and middle-income groups.[52] At the same time, increased government borrowing, combined with heightened spending on military hardware, has stimulated inflation. Rising prices for oil, as well as for heavy machinery and equipment imported to strengthen the state's economic base and its military capacity, further fueled inflation. The cost of living more than doubled in the 1970s and almost doubled again by 1984,[53] reducing the real incomes of the black majority and narrowing the available domestic market.

DOMINATION OF THE NEIGHBORING COUNTRIES

In addition to profiting from South Africa's domestic market and low cost of labor, transnational corporate investors benefit from South Africa's domination of the economies of the neighboring countries. U.S. and other transnational corporations collaborate with the South African government, parastatals, and mining finance houses to gain access in the neighboring countries to additional low-cost labor reserves, markets for surplus manufactured goods, and valuable sources of raw materials.[54]

The Benefits To Transnationals

U.S. and other transnational corporations profit from South Africa's domination of the region in three major respects. First, the surrounding nations have provided a pool of labor which has helped to keep wages low and profits high in South Africa. Initially, as manufacturing firms expanded, they employed more South African blacks. Later, labor recruiting agencies contracted migrant workers from neighboring countries for South Africa's mines and farms so that labor shortages would not boost wages. By the early 1970s, about 80 percent of the workers on South Africa's mines came from neighboring countries. After the independence of Mozambique and Angola and the rise of unemployment in South Africa in the mid-1970s, more South African blacks went to work in the South African mines. Only then did the number of foreign mine workers decline to about half the total South African mine labor force.[55]

Second, because of the limits of the South African market, South African-based manufacturing firms sought to sell their output in neighboring countries. South Africa primarily sells raw and semi-processed materials to the developed nations of Western Europe, North America, and Japan. In exchange, it buys from them the capital and intermediate goods and equipment it requires to build up its manufacturing industries.

By contrast, South Africa sells mainly manufactured goods to its southern African neighbors, including more than half its exports of chemicals and about three-fourths of its machinery, equipment, stone, cement, and glass products. It imports from these countries crude minerals, light consumer goods, and processed and semi-processed agricultural and timber products. As a result, southern Africa is one of the few areas in the world with which South Africa regularly has had a trade surplus.[56] South Africa's trade with its neighbors provides an important source of the income with which it buys machinery and equipment from the industrialized economies. At the same time, the imports of South Africa's manufactured goods in some cases tend to hinder the neighbor's efforts to build their own industries.[57]

Third, transnational corporations collaborate with South African mining finance houses and parastatals to undertake agricultural and forestry ventures and to mine copper, iron, chrome, diamonds, uranium, and other metals and minerals throughout southern Africa. Their projects in the neighboring countries provide the raw materials which they process in their South African factories for both domestic and foreign sales. Foreign banks, with regional headquarters in South Africa, also own the major banks operating in most of the neighboring countries. Thus they increase both their profits and South Africa's foreign-exchange earnings, while draining resources and capital from the neighboring states.

The Exploitation of Namibia

Foreign capital and technology have bolsetered South Africa's refusal, despite international pressures, to liberate Namibia, and have contributed significantly to its ability to employ economic, political, and even military might to maintain its domination of its politically independent neighbors.

South Africa's Illegal Rule

Namibia constitutes the most flagrant example of the way South Africa and the transnational firms based there have dominated and exploited the neighboring countries. South Africa's rule in Namibia dates back to World War I, when, in the name of the Allies, it invaded the German colony, then called South West Africa.[58] After the war, the League of Nations gave South Africa, then still part of the British Empire, a mandate to assume responsibility for the "well-being and social progress" of the Namibian people. Following World War II, when all other mandated territories attained independence, South Africa repeatedly refused U.N. demands, starting in 1966 and supported by a 1971 ruling by the International Court of Justice, that it withdraw.[59] Instead, it extended the apartheid system throughout the country, forcing thousands of Namibians to move from their homes to make way for "white development." It moved the Hereros into the desert, where, their chief protested: "No human being lived here before, it is a country only good for wild beasts." It took over the Namas' hunting grounds to provide more land and labor for white farmers. South African armed forces bombed whole villages in Ovamboland to force the people to move and become migrant workers on the mines, farms, and railroads.[60]

Illegal Transnational Corporate Mining Activities

Diamonds, copper, uranium, lead, tin, and other minerals—these constitute the wealth which South African, American, British, and other transnational corporations, under the umbrella of South African rule, still extract from Namibia. In 1974, the U.N. General Assembly passed Decree No. 1, making the exploitation of natural resources in Namibia illegal without U.N. consent. The Decree declared that any company that continued to operate under the authority of the South African government would be liable for damages to be paid to the future independent government.[61] But transnational corporate mining firms, including some from the United States, continue to mine Namibia's mineral wealth, earning millions of dollars in foreign exchange and paying millions of dollars in taxes to the South African government. (See Box 3.4.) In 1971 alone (before anti-apartheid protests led individual firms to conceal the data), three principal mining operations—the Anglo American Group's Consolidated Diamond Mines, the U.S.-owned Tsumeb, and the South West African Company—generated gross profits of $91 million and net profits after taxes of $59.4 million. Of that, $9.8 million was distributed to residents in the United States, $1.3 million to residents in the United Kingdom, and \$46.3 million to residents (including U.S. and British corporate affiliates) of South Africa.[62] Assuming that those profits remained typical (and if anything, with the opening of the Rossing Uranium Mine, they have probably increased), the mining sector alone may have generated almost \$1 billion in the 1970s. The mining companies paid almost half their profits in tax revenue to the South African government; and the rest to foreign residents, including their transnational parent corporations.

Box 3.4

Some Major Transnational Mining Companies in Namibia

★ The South African Anglo American Group owns the world's largest gem diamond mine, located in Namibia.

★ Until 1983, two U.S. firms, Newmont Mining and American Metal Climax (AMAX), together controlled the Tsumeb copper mine, the largest private employer of migrant contract labor in the country. In 1983, AMAX sold its shares in Tsumeb but Newmont retained its holdings along with its others in South Africa.[a]

★ In the 1970s, the British transnational, Rio Tinto Zinc, invested heavily to open the world's largest uranium mine at Rossing. By the 1980s, it produced a sixth of the world's uranium ore as Rossing speeded extraction, secretly flying planeloads of yellow cake—partially compressed crude uranium—to fill contracts with Britain, France, and Japan.

Note

a. Anne Newman and Cathy Bowers, *Foreign Investment in South Africa and Namibia* (Washington, D.C.: Investor Responsibility Research Center, December 1984).

Source: For details, especially of U.S. corporate involvement, see G. Hovey, *Namibia's Stolen Wealth—North American Investment and South African Occupation* (New York: The Africa Fund, 1982).

Namibian Poverty

Although minerals provide about a third of Namibia's gross domestic product, two-thirds of its exports, and more than half its tax revenues,[63] Namibians themselves never see most of that income.[64] The South African government has helped companies keep cash wages low by enforcing the migrant labor system. As in South Africa, black Namibians—more than 85 percent of the population—must live in bantustans, comprising only about 40 percent of the national land area. As in South Africa, they have little choice but to migrate to work for whites. White-owned farms and domestic service, the lowest-paid categories, employ more than half of all blacks.[65]

Almost three-fourths of all Namibians working in the monetized economy must leave their families to migrate to their jobs. Africans have little say over where they work, or what pay they receive. Their wages are even lower than in South Africa. Men come to the mines and farms sometimes for as long as 30 months, living in barracks, while their families struggle for survival in the desert-like reserves.[66]

Transnational corporations have assisted the South African government in its efforts to retain control over Namibia. First, they mine strategic ores and, through their taxes, help to finance South Africa's army of occupation, which at times has totaled as many as 100,000.[67] Second, the transnationals have set up their own security forces. Rio Tinto Zinc's Rossing, for example, has a private force of 69 to protect its employees and equipment in the event of civil strife.[68] Third, the transnationals have worked directly with the South Africans to reduce the impact of liberation-force attacks. For example, in 1982, the largely U.S.-owned Tsumeb Corporation sent engineers and Rio Tinto Zinc's Rossing mine sent cranes to ensure the quick repair of Windhoek's Van Eck power station after an attack by the South West Africa People's Organization (SWAPO).[69]

In short, instead of obeying U.N. Decree No. 1, which calls for an end to transnational corporate activity in Namibia until independence, the transnationals have collaborated with South Africa's efforts to hinder the liberation forces.

The Independent Neighboring States

In the post-World War II era, South Africa, together with the transnationals based there, spread its economic and political influence into other neighboring countries. This aggravated the contradictory forces that, by the 1970s and 1980s, rendered the region a focal point of international concern.

Transnationals and the "Commanding Heights"

In Africa, the term "commanding heights" refers to the key sectors controlling "modern sector" development: banks and financial institutions, foreign and internal trading companies, and basic industries. As Table 3.7 shows, transnational corporations based in South Africa maintained control over key sectors of all the neighboring economies prior to the independence of Angola and Mozambique.

Separately, the countries of southern Africa cannot afford the development of major industrial projects for many years unless they can entice foreign governments or firms to invest in projects designed to sell output not only in their own, but also in foreign markets. However, transnational manufacturing firms have invested in large integrated manufacturing projects, not in the independent states of southern Africa, but in South Africa. The managers of transnational

Table 3.7
Transnational Corporate Domination of "Commanding Heights" of Economies of South Africa's Neighbors in 1974 (prior to liberation of Portuguese colonies)

					Neighboring Countries				
"Commanding Heights"	*Namibia*	*Botswana*	*Lesotho*	*Swaziland*	*Zimbabwe*	*Malawi*	*Zambia*	*Angola*	*Mozambique*
Banks	Barclays, Standard, French bank	Barclays, Standard	Barclays, Standard	Barclays, Standard	Barclays, Standard, National Grindlays Nedsual	Barclays & Standard own 49% and manage Commercial Bank; government owns 51%	Barclays Standard, National Grindlays, conduct 80-90% of bank business	Barclays, Standard and Anglo-American held shares in Banco Standard-Totta Alliance (a Portuguese bank)	Barclays, Standard and Anglo-American hold shares in Banco Standard-Totta Mozambique (a Portuguese bank)
Basic industries	*uranium* Rio Tinto Zinc			*iron ore* Anglo-American	*asbestos* Turner, Babcock, Newell; *iron & steel* British Steel (32%); *chrome* Union Carbide Rio Tinto Zinc; Phosphates AECI	none		*oil* Gulf Oil Texaco	none
Major Mines	*copper* Anglo-American AMAX, Newmont, Falconbridge; *diamonds* DeBeers	*diamonds* DeBeers; *copper-nickel* Anglo-American AMAMX (government 15% share)					*copper* Anglo-AMAX (in partnership with government, 51%)	*diamonds* DeBeers & Portuguese; *iron ore* Krupp	

	Lonrho	Lonrho	Lonrho	Bat,Tate&Lyle		Anglo-American
Major estates/ Agro-industry	Tate & Lyle Del Monte Nestles	American	Tate & Lyle Anglo- Brook Bond-Leibig	(in partnership with government)		(primarily settler farms)
Foreign and internal wholesale trade	All imports and exports handled by South African and transnational firms with South African Customs Union. handled in close collaboration with South African and transnational firms within South African Customs Union	All imports, exports go through Mozambique	36% of imports from South Africa, unknown % from Rhodesia	CBC (U.K. 49%, Zambia government 51%) ZOK (formerly South African, taken by government 100%	Portuguese interests handled imports; Transnational mining, agribusiness handled most exports	Portuguese interests handled trade, with growing South African and transnational involvement

Source: Government reports and annual reports of companies, cited in Ann Seidman and Neva Seidman Makgetla, *Outposts of Monopoly Capitalism* (Westport, CT: Lawrence Hill, 1980) pp. 240-241.

mining companies, with their regional headquarters in South Africa, make most of the decisions as to whether or not given deposits in the rest of the region will be mined. They have mined some minerals for shipment in crude form to South African factories and for sale overseas. They have simply ignored other deposits when they did not wish to open new mines that might compete with their existing ones elsewhere. They have neglected the potential for building regional industrial capacity outside minority-ruled South Africa.

Enclave Investment

Lacking the capacity to mine and manufacture their own minerals, the independent southern African states remain dependent on imported machinery, equipment, fuel, and even consumer goods—many of them manufactured in South Africa. When, as in the early 1980s, an international recession reduces their foreign-exchange earnings, they cannot even buy the essential spare parts and materials, including the high-cost fuels, on which further development of their limited modern sectors depends.

The case of oil illustrates the problem: Oil is essential, not only as fuel for transport and operation of diesel motors for many kinds of wells and maize mills, but for lubrication of machinery and equipment in large-scale factories. No industrial economy can survive without oil. Angola has reserves considered among the largest in the world. Gulf Oil, a U.S. firm, began drilling for oil in the late 1960s, during the last days of Portuguese rule. By the 1970s, when Angola attained independence, Gulf was pumping millions of barrels from its Cabinda wells each year.

South Africa, on the other hand, has no known oil reserves.[70] Yet the major oil companies built their main refineries, not in Angola or any other independent

Table 3.8
Petroleum Refinery Distillation Capacity in Southern Africa, 1981

	Total Petroleum Refinery Distillation Capacity (in thousands of metric tons)	% of Regional Total
Angola	2,250	7.6
Mozambique	800	2.7
South Africa[a]	23,330	79.2
Tanzania	850	2.9
Zambia	1,220	4.1
Zimbabwe	1,000	3.1

Note

a. Figure includes Namibia data. South Africa sells its output to Botswana, Lesotho, and Swaziland, which have no refining capacity.

Source: *United Nations Statistical Yearbook, 1981* (New York: United Nations, 1983), pp. 810-811. (Total percentage is less than 100 because of rounding.)

oil-producing African state, but in South Africa. Combined, the smaller refineries in the independent southern African countries produce barely a fifth of the output of those built by transnationals in South Africa.[71] Except for Angola, all the independent southern African states remain dependent on importing crude oil at high prices through transnational corporate marketing networks.

Rising oil prices have drained away as much as a fourth of southern African states' foreign-exchange earnings.[72] This has been an important cause of their mounting balance-of-payments deficits and international debt. Shortages and the rising costs of fuels, furthermore, have hindered the expansion of road transport needed by peasants to develop rural areas.

Iron, used for producing steel for machinery and construction, is another mineral essential for both large and small development projects. Several independent African states have extensive known deposits of iron ore. Before independence, the West German firm, Krupp, shipped iron ore from southern Angola to its home steel plants. The South African mining finance house, Anglo American, shipped away a whole mountain of Swazi iron ore to Japanese steel firms.[73] On the other hand, the transnationals have not developed known iron ore deposits in Tanzania, Zambia, and Mozambique.

Only in minority-ruled South Africa and pre-independence Zimbabwe did state corporations, working with transnational corporate affiliates, build industries to produce steel from local ores.[74] Planners in Tanzania and Zambia proposed steel plants to process their countries' iron, but neither government could muster enough funds to constrict them. Tanzania built a small plant to process imported scrap.[75] Yet all South Africa's neighbors continue to import steel machinery and equipment. Some still buy steel from South Africa's ISCOR. In the 1980s, balance-of-payment deficits forced independent southern African states to curtail imports of such items as steel pipes and construction materials. The resulting shortages thwarted such vital rural projects as construction of irrigation systems.

Copper, mostly produced in southern and central Africa, has for decades been a leading African export.[76] Copper is used for electrical cables, which are essential for generating and distributing electric power, and is used in many industrial alloys. After independence, Zambia's government acquired ownership of a majority of the shares of the four vast copper mines which produce more than three-fourths of that nation's exports. The South African Anglo American Group and American Metal Climax (AMAX), nevertheless, still owned the remainder, managing the mines and marketing the output. In Namibia, the U.S.-owned Tsumeb copper mine, as noted above, remained Namibia's largest employer. Botswana's Selebi-Pikwe nickel-copper mine, 85 percent owned by the Anglo American Group and AMAX, began to produce copper in the 1970s. On the other hand, the transnationals for the most part have ignored known copper deposits in northeastern Angola.

Transnational and South African copper firms have long shipped copper in crude ingots from southern African mines to their plants in South Africa,

Table 3.9
Pig Iron and Crude Steel Production and Consumption in Southern Africa, 1980

| | Production (in thousands of metric tons) | | | Consumption | |
	Crude Steel	Pig Iron	Iron Ore	Total (in thousands of metric tons)	Per Capita (kgs)
Angola	0	0	0	81	11
Malawi	0	0	0	2	0
Mozambique	0	0	0	7	1
S. Africa	8,959	7,895	16,471	6,746[b]	211[b]
Swaziland	0	0	3,11[a]	—[b]	—[b]
Tanzania	0	0	0	83	5
Zambia	0	0	0	3.1	5
Zimbabwe	898	1,171	1,038	806	110

Notes

a. 1979.
b. South African data includes the consumption of Namibia, Botswana, Lesotho, and Swaziland; Botswana and Lesotho have no productive capacity, and Swaziland produced only crude iron ore.

Source: *United Nations Statistical Yearbook, 1981* (New York: United Nations, 1983) pp. 591-92, 692, 713-4.

Europe, or the United States for final processing. When the independent southern African countries require copper cable and electrical fixtures, they must import them. The resulting high costs have contributed to the factors hampering efforts to distribute electricity to rural communities.

Southern Africa has abundant possibilities for producing hydroelectric power, a significant alternative to high-cost mineral fuels. Most of the potential sites, however, lie outside the flat plains that comprise much of South Africa's own territory. In the 1950s, the settler-ruled Federation of Rhodesia and Nyasaland built the first phase of the Kariba hydroelectric project on the then-Southern Rhodesian (now Zimbabwean) side of the border. Primarily, it was to provide electricity for the Northern Rhodesian (now Zambian) copper mines, but also for new industries being built in Bulawayo and Salisbury (now Harare). After independence, Zambia built the Kafue hydroelectric project and a second Kariba project in order to reduce its dependence on the minority regime still ruling in Southern Rhodesia. In the 1970s, the South African government collaborated with the Portuguese colonialists and transnational corporate interests to construct the Cabora Bassa Dam in Mozambique and the Kunene project in Angola, both of which it planned to integrate into a regional hydroelectric grid to power its continuing industrial growth.

After independence, these projects provided Zambia, Mozambique, and Angola with surplus power. They illustrate the potential for independent southern African states to join together to construct a regional power grid, which would provide enough power to meet most regional needs until the year 2000.[77] However, instead of participating in the creation of such a grid after independence in 1980, Zimbabwe's new government bowed to Anglo American Group pressures and World Bank advice to build the Hwangwe thermal plant, which uses Anglo American coal. This reduced, rather than strengthened, the possibilities for extended regional cooperation. At the same time, it imposed a major addition to Zimbabwe's rapidly growing foreign debt and more than doubled its electricity rates.[78] Only after an explosion destroyed part of the new Hwangwe thermal plant and after Mozambique had signed the Nkomati Accord (see Chapter 6) did Zimbabwe's government finally agree to buy Cabora Bassa power.

The Drain of Investable Surpluses

Dominating the development of the southern African states' export enclaves, the transnational mining firms also extracted a major share of the investable surpluses generated in those countries. Rather than investing these surpluses to finance national and regional development, however, they typically remitted a major share to their parent companies in South Africa and abroad. In the late 1970s, the direct outflow of profits, interest, and dividends, together with the high salaries of expatriate personnel, consumed about a fourth of Zambia's gross domestic product,[79] and almost 40 percent of Namibia's.[80] Through transfer pricing, the companies drain away an unknown but significant

Table 3.10

Production of Copper Ores, Smelting and Refining in Southern Africa, 1980 (in thousands of metric tons)

	Botswana	South Africa[a]	Zaire	Zambia	Zimbabwe
Copper Ore	15.6	200.7	459.0	713.8	27.0
Smelted	none	185.0	425.7	609.5	26.7
Refined	none	147.9	279.4	607.2	27.0

Note

a. Includes Namibia; Lesotho and Swaziland have no copper production capacity.

Source: *United Nations Statistical Yearbook, 1981* (New York: United Nations, 1983), pp. 594-95, 695.

Table 3.11

Net Installed Capacity of Electric Generating Plants in South Africa, 1982 (in thousands of kilowatts)[a]

	Angola	Malawi	Mozambique	South Africa	Tanzania	Zambia	Zimbabwe
Hydro	400	67	1,520	570	188	1,538	705
Thermal	200	37	280	20,193	70	190	487
Total	600	104	1,800	20,763	258	1,728	1,192
% of Regional Total	2.3	0.4	6.8	78.5	1.0	6.5	4.5

Note

a. No separate data are provided for Namibia, or for Botswana, Lesotho, or Swaziland, which are in the South African Customs Union.

Source: *United Nations Statistical Yearbook, 1981* (New York: United Nations, 1983) pp. 792-6.

additional share of the region's investable surplus.[81]

It is difficult to distinguish what portion of these surpluses go to South African-based enterprises to finance the continued strengthening of the South African economy, and what portion the transnationals remit directly to their overseas head offices. Nevertheless, the consequence for the region's peripheral economies remains the same: loss of capital that might otherwise have helped improve agriculture and build new industries.

Partly as a result of the loss of these surpluses, the independent southern African governments have had to borrow heavily abroad to finance whatever projects they have undertaken, even the infrastructure built to enable transnationals more efficiently to exploit the region's mineral and agricultural resources. By the 1980s, many had borrowed sums totaling a major share of their gross domestic products. (See Chapter 2.)

Unable to build factories to compete with those in South Africa, the independent countries of the region still must import most of their basic equipment and machinery, and some of it comes from South Africa. As members of the South African Customs Union, Botswana, Lesotho, and Swaziland not only cannot build factories capable of competing with those in South Africa, but they must purchase most of their imports directly from that country.[82]

Before independence, white settlers in Southern Rhodesia (now Zimbabwe), Mozambique, and Angola, and after independence, governments in Zambia and Malawi, succeeded in attracting transnational manufacturing firms to invest marginal amounts in last-stage assembly and processing plants to produce goods for local consumption. These factories, however, even when partially financed locally, typically continued to import parts and materials primarily to produce luxury and semi-luxury items for higher-income groups. Located in existing urban centers, they tended to reinforce the geographically lopsided focus of growth around export-oriented enclaves. They purchased relatively capital-intensive factory equipment from transnationals, thus contributing little to increased employment. For example, in the 1970s, locally generated investable surpluses financed two-thirds of the $15.3 million (18 million kwachas) invested in Malawian manufacturing plants. Nevertheless, the new jobs created annually dropped from almost 900 in 1970 to barely 200 in 1976, while the amount invested to create each new job more than doubled, from about K4,000 to K10,234.[83]

Two decades after independence, Zambia remained highly dependent on South Africa for the import of manufactured consumer goods, as well as equipment and machinery. In compliance with the U.N. boycott after minority-ruled Rhodesia's Unilateral Declaration of Independence (UDI), Zambia dramatically reduced trade with Rhodesia. But to do so, Zambia initially expanded purchases of South African goods. Eventually, when it closed the border with Rhodesia, it reduced South African goods to about 10 percent of its imports.[84] In 1978, as South Africa's manufacturing industry stagnated because of the international recession, the International Monetary Fund (IMF) reportedly pressured Zambia to reopen the railroad through Rhodesia, despite the continuation of UDI, and South Africa's share of Zambian imports once again increased.[85]

The 1980s Recession

In the late 1970s and early 1980s, when worldwide recessions sharply reduced their export earnings, the independent southern African states could no longer afford to import the necessary spare parts and materials to keep factories operating at full capacity.[86] The worsening international economic conditions affected not only the independent southern African states, but South Africa itself. Even in the late 1970's, about a fourth of South Africa's productive capacity lay idle. Official South African statistics grossly underrepresented black unemployment, and ignored unemployed black women altogether. By the late 1970s, unofficial estimates indicated that more than 2 million South African blacks were jobless. In 1983, unofficial estimates showed almost 3 million—almost one out of six members of the adult labor force—unemployed.[87]

Workers from the neighboring countries were the first to be displaced as unemployment mounted in South Africa. As South Africans laid off in other sectors of the economy began to take jobs in the mines, the mine companies sent home about a third of the mine labor force, swelling the numbers of unemployed in neighboring countries. The governments, especially Mozambique, Malawi, and Zimbabwe, confronted added problems of reabsorbing tens of thousands of men who, over the years, had lost their skills and interest in agriculture.[88]

SUMMARY

While most southern African states attained political independence in the 1960s and 1970s, South Africa's minority strengthened its rule over the African majority through apartheid. It uprooted and removed growing numbers of the black population onto barely 13 percent of the national land area, forcing them to migrate to work as low-paid labor for white-owned farms, mines, and industries while systematically denying them adequate education, health facilities, and human and political rights.

Yet during these very years, U.S. and other transnational firms, taking advantage of the low-paid labor and tax savings made possible by apartheid, multiplied their profitable investments to build up South Africa's increasingly militarized industrial economy. By the 1980s, U.S. financial involvement in South Africa totaled almost $15 billion.

The growth of foreign investment helped strengthen the South African minority regime's capacity not only to perpetuate apartheid at home, but also to maintain and extend its domination over its neighbors. The profitablility for foreign investors depends not only on the additional low-cost labor, but also on markets and sources of raw materials available throughout the region. After South Africa rejected U.N. demands to liberate Namibia, transnational corporations continued to exploit that country's labor and rich mineral wealth. From their regional industrial base in South Africa, transnational corporate interests also collaborated with South African firms to mine and ship away valuable crude or semi-processed minerals. Transnationals also drained away a major share of these countries' gross domestic products, funds which might otherwise have been invested to build industries and agriculture. As a result, the fledgling independent southern African states found themselves barely able to withstand the impact of the mounting crises of the early 1980s.

SOUTHERN AFRICA

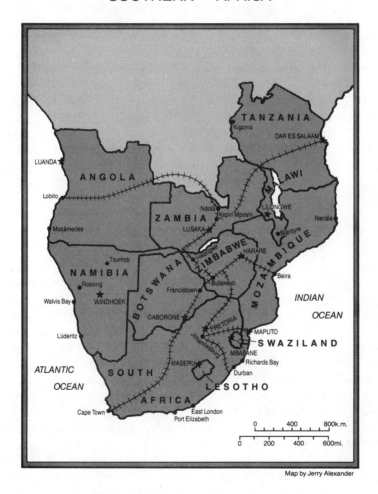

Map by Jerry Alexander

FIGURE 3.1

A woman tending a cooperative garden in Chibi, Zimbabwe (Oxfam America staff photo by Michael Scott)

CHAPTER FOUR

Toward Regional Independence

INTRODUCTION

While the Nationalists imposed apartheid, and with the aid of foreign investors built up South Africa's military-industrial capacity, Africans in country after country, some peacefully, others through bitter struggle, won the right to self-government. By the end of the 1960s, black governments ruled in most southern African states: Tanzania, Zambia, Malawi, Botswana, Lesotho, and Swaziland.

Having failed to achieve independence from the Portuguese through civil demonstrations, the people of Mozambique and Angola fought for more than a decade to win their freedom. In 1974, the Portuguese military toppled the Lisbon dictatorship, in part because the prolonged guerrilla warfare in Africa had destroyed the army's will to fight. The liberation movements—FRELIMO (Front for the Liberation of Mozambique) and the MPLA (Popular Movement for the Liberation of Angola)—began the business of building new, independent governments. The new Mozambican government supported the Zimbabweans' efforts to free their land. Observing U.N. sanctions against the white-minority regime led by Ian Smith, it ended all transport of Rhodesian goods through its ports. The transnational corporations, which owned about 70 percent of the assets in Zimbabwe's developed sector,[1] had until then shipped about three-fourths of their goods through Mozambican ports. Mozambique's action forced them to make major investments to shift their trade to the longer, more expensive routes through South Africa. At the same time, Mozambique lost hundreds of millions of dollars worth of trade. (See Chapter 6 for estimate.)

The Smith regime retaliated. Its plane bombed Zimbabwean refugee camps inside Mozambique, indiscriminately killing men, women, and children. It organized the Mozambique National Resistance Movement (MNR),[2] which sought to disrupt and destabilize Mozambique's economy, killing people in rural areas and destroying essential infrastructure.

By 1980, Zimbabwe's liberation movement had freed much of the country-side. Unable to keep the economy going, the minority regime accepted U.S., British, and South African pressure to meet with the Patriotic Front leaders at Lancaster House in England to formulate a constitution. The resulting document was a compromise.[3] It reflected British and American efforts to limit the possibilities for fundamental change in the new Zimbabwe (see Chapter 6), as well as the Zimbabwean liberation movement's attempts to achieve independence with the fewest possible restrictions.[4] In 1980, the overwhelming

Implication that residue of colonialism has forced dependence of Black African economies on S.A. — due to Western efforts to limit change

election victory of Rogert Mugabe and his party, the Zimbabwe African National Union-Patriotic Front (ZANU-PF), heralded a new era for Zimbabwe.

Political independence, however, did not bring about a solution to the problems of poverty besetting the people of Zimbabwe or elsewhere in southern Africa. The new black governments realized that continued minority rule in South Africa would seriously hamper their efforts to achieve full economic as well as political independence. The Nationalist government, reinforced by foreign investment and technology, still ruled in South Africa and exercised its economic, political, and military might to dominate the people and resources of the region. Here lay the roots of mounting tension in southern Africa. This chapter:

★ Outlines the history of popular resistance which, *by* why the 1960s, had given birth to armed struggle for complete liberation in South Africa and Namibia. These were not isolated phenomena. Despite heightened repression, the South African and Namibian developments grew out of, and played a major role in, the growth and spread of nationalist movements which, by the 1980s, had liberated most of the region.

★ Explains why, upon attainment of independence, the neighboring countries united in the Southern African Development Coordination Conference (SADCC). Its leaders expressed their determination to formulate and implement a strategy designed to reduce their dependence on South Africa and promote coordinated development to provide full employment and higher living standards.

★ Describes how the Pretoria government retaliated. It sought to destabilize its neighbors and thwart their efforts toward self-reliant development, aiming to coerce them, instead, to join its own Constellation of States.

A HISTORY OF SOUTH AFRICAN RESISTANCE

Since the 17th century, southern Africans have resisted European penetration of the region. The colonialists subdued the Africans' armed resistance by turning one people against another and by exercising military force. Only in 1906 did the British defeat the final armed uprising against colonial rule in Natal, South Africa. This signaled the end of the first phase of two-and-a-half centuries of African armed resistance.[5]

The African National Congress (ANC) ~ 1912

Providing early leadership for equality and justice in the region, South Africans created political organizations which cut across tribal divisions that had weakened resistance to colonial conquest. In 1912, two years after the formation of the white-ruled Union of South Africa, the African National

formation of Union of S.A. in 1910

Congress of South Africa (ANC) came into being, dedicated to forging national unity and defending the rights of all Africans in the country. During the next 30 years, the ANC led a series of campaigns against the Pass Laws, the Land Act, and further restrictions on the already severely limited political rights of Africans and others. Emphasizing the unity of all South Africans, regardless of race, the ANC worked closely with the Indian and coloured communities.

The growth of the ANC in South Africa stimulated parallel movements in the neighboring states. Many early nationalist leaders elsewhere established contacts with the ANC. Some even named their first political efforts "ANC" to stress the regional character of their struggle.

In the early 1940s, the formation of the ANC Youth League marked a heightened militancy and a growing organization. In 1949, as the Nationalists further implemented apartheid, the ANC adopted a Program of Action, emphasizing self-determination and the need for blacks to take a leading role in the struggle for liberation. Throughout the 1950s, the ANC led mass actions in the form of protests, demonstrations, and strikes in opposition to the increasingly severe forms of segregation and white domination under apartheid.

On June 26, 1955, the ANC brought together a Congress of the People with nearly 3,000 accredited delegates from all over South Africa. The Congress Alliance symbolized the growing unity of the different sectors of the population. The delegates formulated the Freedom Charter, embodying a program for a nonracial, unitary, democratic state. The South African government held the Charter to be a treasonable document. It charged 156 ANC members with treason. Only after a mass trial that lasted five years were all 156 acquitted.

In 1959, while the ANC's leaders were still on trial, a group of former ANC members organized the Pan Africanist Congress (PAC). They objected to the ANC's cooperation with other organizations in the Congress Alliance around the Freedom Charter. In particular, believing whites might dominate the organization, they objected to any form of cooperation with progressive whites.

In 1960, at a mass meeting in Sharpeville protesting the Pass Laws, the police shot and killed many peaceful demonstrators. Protests, demonstrations, and strikes spread throughout the country. The government declared a state of emergency, arrested approximately 20,000 people, and detained another 2,000 without trial. Within a fortnight, it had banned both the ANC and the PAC, effectively outlawing these organizations; their members could no longer meet together, speak publicly, or be quoted. Rather than comply with the ban, both organizations went underground, changing from being a movement attempting to work within the system to one advocating armed struggle. In 1962, Nelson Mandela, president of the ANC, was convicted of treason and sentenced to a life term in prison.

The government intensified its repression in light of the widespread civil unrest. It passed even harsher laws, extending its use of torture, imprisonment, and detentions without trial. By the late 1960s, it had jailed, banned, or exiled all the known liberation-movement leaders. In response, a new set of organizations emerged. They filled the vacuum created by the government's suppression of the

ANC and PAC. United loosely around a set of ideas described as "Black Consciousness," these organizations helped to educate and organize black people, particularly youth.

The Black Consciousness movement spurred a defiant rejection of apartheid, especially among black workers and youth. The South African Students Organization (SASO) was founded by black students who refused to join the National Union of South African Students (NUSAS). Black workers began to organize trade unions in defiance of anti-strike laws. In 1973, there were strikes throughout the nation. The collapse of Portuguese colonialism and the victories of FRELIMO in Mozambique and the MPLA in Angola stimulated further activity.

The Soweto Uprising

In 1976, student protests against bantu education in Soweto, the sprawling Johannesburg township reserved for Africans, led to a two-year uprising that spread to black townships across the country. The protests grew to encompass the full range of black grievances against the apartheid system, and police killed hundreds of blacks, including students and schoolchildren, over a two-year period. Hundreds of thousands of workers mobilized to protest police killings of demonstrators.

Amid these protests, the Soweto Student Representative Council (SSRC) led a successful campaign against the Soweto Urban Bantu Council. The South African government had instituted the Council as part of its attempt to foster the appearance of increased self-government for the black population. The students challenged this myth. First, they prevented the Council from increasing rents; next, they characterized the Council as a collaborationist institution. Ultimately the Council collapsed.

In 1977, boycotts and unrest among students and teachers grew after Steve Biko, a leader of SASO, died in detention.[6] Within a month of his death, the government had detained scores of people and banned 18 Black Consciousness organizations as well as two newspapers with black readerships.

In the next several years, despite restrictive legislation, black workers organized unions to demand better wages and working conditions. Confronted with mounting opposition to apartheid and growing economic difficulties, the minority government abolished some minor apartheid restrictions, permitting those Africans who could afford transport to use selected public parks, beaches, and other public facilities in white areas. The government permitted blacks to organize unions subject to strict government regulations. It then introduced the 1983 constitutional reforms establishing subordinate parliamentary houses for the Indians and coloureds. The key aspects of apartheid—the exclusion of blacks from political power, the lack of free movement of blacks to "white" areas, and unequal access to education, housing, and social services—remained unchanged. Simultaneously, the state stepped up its efforts to move blacks to the remote bantustans.

Key aspects of Apartheid unchanged despite 1983 const. reforms.

The United Democratic Front (UDF)

In May 1983, representatives of 32 member organizations began to build the multiracial United Democratic Front (UDF). It rapidly became the most powerful alliance of anti-government organizations since the Congress Alliance of the 1950s. Starting with organizing committees in all the major urban centers, the UDF held its inaugural meeting in August. Attended by more than 400 organizations, the meeting stressed popular rejection of Pretoria's 1983 constitutional reforms. It endorsed the statement of Dr. Allan Boesak, president of the World Alliance of Reformed Churches, who declared:

> We are here to say that the government's constitutional proposals are inadequate and that they do not express the will of the vast majority of South Africa's people.
>
> But more than that, we are here to say that we are working for one undivided South Africa which will belong to all of its people, an open democracy from which no single South African will be excluded. We want all our rights, we want them here and we want them now. We have been waiting so long. We have pleaded, cried, petitioned too long now. We have been jailed, exiled, killed for too long. Now is the time.[7]

At the outset, the UDF focused on four tasks: 1) to consolidate its regional structures; 2) to mobilize and express black opinion on the referendum, in which the government permitted only whites to vote on whether to adopt the Constitution; 3) to organize a boycott of the Black Community Council elections, which the government sought to establish to give blacks a pretense of the right to vote under apartheid; and finally, 4) to oppose the Coloured Management Committee elections to demonstrate that the coloured population also opposed the discriminatory institutions proposed by the new Constitution.

The UDF won its first victory when most coloureds and Indians boycotted the 1983 Management Committee elections. Despite the efforts of the pro-government Coloured Labor Party to urge the people to vote, only 8 percent of the coloureds even registered. At the end of 1983, the UDF called for a boycott of the new Act granting blacks a limited franchise to vote for black Local Authorities in the townships. The vast majority of blacks stayed away from the polls. In only a few areas did registered blacks exceed 20 percent of the eligible voters; in major urban areas, barely 10 percent of those registered voted.

During these campaigns, the UDF's membership grew to 600 groups. In every urban and in several rural areas, Youth Congresses were established, particularly committed to organizing working and unemployed youth, scholars, and students. Civic and women's organizations also expanded.

The UDF broadened the anti-apartheid movement. Increased union membership pressured union leaders to take up the political issues of the day, although it remained illegal for black unions to participate in any political action. The 54,000-member Boiler Makers Association came out in opposition to the new Constitution. The Federation of South African Trade Unions (FOSATU) campaigned for a "no" vote from the white electorate. Some unions, like the General and Allied Workers Union (GAWU), the Council of Unions of South

Africa (CUSA), and South African Allied Workers Union (SAAWU), affiliated with the UDF.

The small 1984 turnout among coloured and Indian voters for representatives in the new tricameral legislature reflected the effectiveness of the UDF's campaign against the constitutional reform. Barely 20 percent of the registered Indian voters—15 percent of the eligible adult population—went to the polls. Among the coloured voters fewer than one out of five voted. In the Cape Peninsula, where nearly a third of the coloured population lives, less than 5 percent of those eligible turned out.[8]

In an effort to thwart the UDF campaign, the police whipped protesters at the polling places.[9] The authorities detained many UDF leaders, six of whom sought protection in the British consultate.

Unrest in the black townships grew during the following weeks into a nationwide uprising surpassing that of 1976. Students boycotted schools. Protesters organized strikes against rent hikes. Riots broke out. The police retaliated with tear gas, dogs, and water hoses. They fired on crowds. Hundreds died and hundreds more were wounded. The police detained more than 2,000 blacks, many of whom were attending funerals of those killed.[10]

At the funeral service of four black youths killed when student demonstrators clashed with police, Bishop Desmond Tutu, shortly before he received the 1984 Nobel Peace Prize, expressed the feelings of many:

> We call on the authorities to hear us when we tell them apartheid is evil. . . . We are the victims of a vicious system. Let them hear us when we warn responsibly that we cannot go on like this.
>
> There will be recurring trouble . . . if the real leaders remain in prison and exile, while the government continues to present us with other leaders who we think are collaborators with an evil system.[11]

Intensified Repression

Over the years, while the liberation movement within South Africa mobilized to oppose apartheid and superficial reforms, the South African government strengthened its powerful security apparatus.[12] Gradually the Nationalist government widened the range of prohibited actions. It narrowed people's rights and increased the state's powers to stifle opponents without publishing information about its actions. New laws increasingly vested extensive arbitrary powers in the executive, removing a large part of ministerial and police activity from public or judicial scrutiny.

In 1982, as international criticism of these measures increased, the government adopted an omnibus Internal Security Act to consolidate and replace most of the previous security legislation. This 1982 Act incorporated all the powers contained in the earlier Internal Security Act, the Terrorism Act of 1967, the Unlawful Organizations Act, the Riotous Assemblies Act, and the General

Law Amendment Act. Under the new law, the minister of law and order retained the power to declare certain organizations illegal; to compile lists of officers, members, and active supporters of organizations declared illegal; to ban individuals or place them under house arrest; to ban meetings and gatherings; to ban newspapers and other publications; to detain witnesses for political trials; and to hold people in indefinite preventive detention.

Box 4.1

How the 1982 Internal Security Act in South Africa Increased the State's Arbitrary Repressive Powers

Under the Act:

★ The offense of "terrorism" carries penalities up to and including the death sentence. The Act defines "terrorism" as an act of violence committed with intent to "overthrow and endanger State authority"; to bring about "any constitutional, political, industrial, social or economic aim or change"; to induce "the Government . . . to do or abstain from any act or to adopt or abandon a particular standpoint"; or to "put in fear or demoralize the General Public" or a particular group of inhabitants. Anyone who encourages, aids, or advises another person, or conspires with another to commit a violent act to bring about any of these objects, is also guilty of "terrorism."

★ A conviction for sabotage can result in imprisonment for up to 20 years. Furthermore, anyone who advocates, advises, defends, or encourages the achievement in South Africa of any of the objects of "communism" is liable on conviction for imprisonment for up to 10 years.

★ A new offense, not contained in previous laws, defines "subversion" to include actions aimed at, among other things, "causing or promoting general dislocation or disorder"; prejudicing the production and distribution of essential services or the free movement of traffic; causing "feelings of hostility between different population groups"; and encouraging or aiding other persons to commit any of the acts listed. If the act for which the accused is sentenced results in the use of violence, the state can impose a sentence of up to 25 years' imprisonment. The wide scope of possible interpretation of the Act could, of course, include any strike or boycott.

★ A new offense of "incitement" is defined as any act which encourages or aids others to protest any law or for a change in administration of any law. A person found guilty of "incitement" is liable for a fine of up to R5,000 or up to five years in jail, or both.

Source: International Defense and Aid Fund for Southern Africa, *Apartheid: The Facts,* (London: IDAF in cooperation with the United Nations Centre Against Apartheid, 1983).

Workers for OXFAM (U.K⊸) have directly experienced the impact of South African repression. One OXFAM fieldworker there, Alex Mbatha, had to take refuge in Zimbabwe after he and his wife, Khosi, were detained without charge for six months and tortured by the South African security police. They were released in 1982 as a result of a persistent campaign by OXFAM. Mrs. Mbatha was so badly treated in prison that she suffered a stroke. Alex Mbatha explains:

Today we are outside South Africa—my whole family—as refugees, because of the type of work I was engaged in. The authorities thought that the job I was doing was

Box 4.2

Bantustan "Justice": Government and Repression in Venda

South African declared Venda "independent" in 1979. No other government recognizes it. It inherited South Africa's security laws and inhuman practices toward detainees. In 1981, a bomb exploded in Sibasa, Venda's principal town, killing two policemen. Blaming the explosion on the African National Congress, the police arrested 20 persons, including Tshefhiwa Muofhe, a Black Consciousness supporter and lay preacher of the Lutheran Evangelical Church. Arrested without charge on November 10 while in perfect health, he died in custody two days later. A post mortem examination revealed severe bruising of body, head, and genitals caused by "extensive use of force" accompanied by internal bleeding. Shortly afterwards, the Venda security police arrested four Lutheran church pastors. One was detained for several months without charges and then released. Two were held incommunicado until early 1982. When brought before the magistrate and charged with murdering the Sibasa police, they alleged torture, including electric shocks, and showed injuries on their bodies. The state, after several months, finally withdrew the murder charge. The fourth, the Rev. T.S. Farisani, was detained until the charges against the other two were dropped. At the end of 1982, he visited Europe and North America and gave this account of his treatment:

They made me lie on my back, raise my legs, and they kicked me in my private parts. They banged my head against the wall, pulled off my hair and my beard, karate chops, judo kicks, all the combinations. I lost consciousness many times. There was blood all over and in the evening, when I regained consciousness, they asked me to scrub the blood on the floor and to use the same cloth to wipe the blood off my body. I was swollen. My head was swollen, and I was breathing through the ears because my eardrums were punctured. I had holes in my knees I could put my fingers in. They took me to a more sophisticated torture station at Sibasa and told me that no man comes into this torture room and goes out alive unless he says and does what we want. They then undressed me, covered my head in a canvas bag, poured water on the floor and over my head and connected an electric wire to my earlobes and to subversive—because in that country you do not talk about "development." Development in South Africa is synonymous with agitating, being a troublemaker. If you speak in terms of motivating people for self-help, if you intervene to give them hope, reminding them that there are people outside their country who are at one with them in this struggle, then you are branded as a terrorist. But I knew I had done no wrong—I had neither killed nor maimed anyone. At the depth of torture, I knew I had been right to take on that job—to help those people in the homelands who had lost hope, the sick and the old who had nothing, the helpless, the voiceless and the voteless people. I was paying the price of having identified myself with the sufferings of my people.[13]

---

the back of my head. They poured a glue-like substance down my spinal cord and they set the electric current on. I fell into the water. . . . "

He finally wrote what they wanted. "I could not afford to be brave. I tried but failed. I was defeated." He, too, told the magistrate he had been tortured.

As a result of the electric shocks, Rev. Farisani had a heart attack and was removed to a hospital. A military doctor refused to treat him, saying that he was dying and if he treated him, he would have to answer many questions in court. Rev. Farisani was driven 120 kilometers to another hospital. Some days later, he was taken back to his cell, where he had another heart attack. He then remained in the hospital until his release in June 1982.

During his visit to the Geneva Centre of the Lutheran World Federation on January 31, 1983, Rev. Farisani explained the relationship between the new Constitution and Venda:

People say coloureds and Indians are being brought in Parliament and this is progress. . . .

At the very beginning, I have to say Vendaland and South Africa are to all practical purposes still one country, but for all political propaganda purposes they are two countries . . . . It is on record that over 80 percent of the people [in Venda - ed.] voted against the ruling party and against independence, and the members of the . . . opposition party who won the election were detained. When they were in detention, the governing party had a session to elect a president and in this way he won the vote and became president of Vendaland and the commissioner general. . . . People were appointed into the cabinet; until today they are cabinet ministers. Candidates who performed hopelessly in some instances, getting only 2 percent of the vote, are today members of Parliament through fraud.

So the government we have as of now in Vendaland, per se, has not been elected by the people. To put it in clearer terms, they have been rejected by the people and they must be very grateful to Pretoria that they are still in power.

Source: "Human Rights in the World: South Africa" in *For the Rule of Law - The Review* (International Commission of Jurists: Geneva, July 1983).[15]

Black authorities in the bantustans typically impose repressive measures at least as severe as those of the central government. Some bantustan authorities have issued their own "security" laws modeled closely on national laws. For others, the South African government has issued emergency proclamations embodying similar clauses under the Black Administration Act. The bantustan authorities usually implement the legislation as vigorously, if not more so, than the South African government itself.

In 1984, the Fund for Free Expression issued a 149-page report that details human-rights violations in the four "independent" bantustans. It asserts they have become the main focus of repression. Detention, torture, and general harassment of dissidents, students, lawyers, trade unionists, and clergymen have become a near-pervasive fact of life in the homelands. The territories, while inheriting South Africa's far-reaching security legislation, are removed from media and civil-rights monitoring groups based in the urban centers. In the Ciskei, the chiefs were found to have used their wide powers to torture and kill others in tribal conflicts. The homeland chiefs are invested with control of services, as well as being the dividers of land and the major employers in their areas. As the vice chairman of the Fund for Free Expression, Aryeh Neier, pointed out in his preface to the report:

> Abuses by the white rulers of South Africa are so great that it may seem perverse to discuss abuses by black officials in their homelands. Yet such an approach misses the point. Homelands officials hold their posts and exercise power because the South African government counts on them to further its policy of denationalizing Southern African blacks and to assist in persecuting those who resist white minority rule.[14]

Together with its satellite bantustan authorities, the South African government exercises its powers to harass and destroy the opposition. Police continue to ban and break up meetings of community organizations, and to detain their leaders without trial.

The Pretoria government has sought to suppress the growing trade-union movement among blacks. In 1981, the minister of defense claimed that the ANC promoted labor unrest through "front organizations." The police detained more than 300 trade-union officials and workers. One, Neil Aggett—a white—died in detention in February 1982. Others were tortured or suffered long periods of detention. Nevertheless, trade-union activities and strikes continued. The authorities singled out for harassment the leaders of SAAWU as the most militant section of the labor movement. In a trial in the Ciskei, the union's president, Thozamile Gqweta, gave chilling testimony of the torture he suffered durng his seventh span in detention. To avoid yet another detention spell, Gqweta remained in hiding during SAAWU's fourth annual convention.[16]

The unions demonstrated increasing resourcefulness and sophistication. They made effective use of the Industrial Courts, gaining numerous favorable judgments. Twice, as the unions followed grievance procedures prescribed by law, they came to the brink of legal strikes. Then, in 1984, 90,000 blacks legally struck eight gold mines, all but one owned by the Anglo American Group. In at least three mine compounds, riot police clashed with striking workers. Police shot and killed seven striking miners at the Western Areas mine.[17]

Throughout the country, unions found themselves fighting hostile government action. In late 1984, reinforced by armed troops, police began to make house-to-house searches in black townships in what Minister of Law and Order Louis le Grange announced as an "operation . . . to effectively rid the affected areas of criminal and revolutionary elements. . . ."[18]

By November, hundreds of thousands of people in the townships south of Johannesburg had joined a two-day civil-rights strike called to press demands that included removal of police and army units from the townships, the release of political detainees, and lower rents. Employers reported at least half the 2 million black workers in the industrial areas surrounding Johannesburg supported the strike. Crowds attacked police and black officials of the local administrations, expressing their resentment of Pretoria's efforts to install pliant Local Councils in black townships. The police and army units, setting up roadblocks around the townships, fired shotguns, rubber bullets, and tear gas into the crowds. Hundreds of people were detained, and at least 16 killed.[19]

The Archbishop of Durban and president of the Southern African Catholic Bishops' Conference, Denis Hurley, issued a 38-page report denouncing police conduct as resembling:

> that of an occupying foreign army controlling enemy territory by force without regard for the civilian population and, it appears, without regard for the law.

Archbishop Hurley noted:

> A kind of state of war is developing between the police and the people. They seem to be in a mood which inspires them to say, "The people are our enemy, and we are out to impose our will upon them by any means that we find effective."[20]

International protests against the detentions led to the arrests of leading American citizens in nonviolent demonstrations at the South African Embassy in Washington and at consulates throughout the United States. In response, the South African regime released some of the detainees. However, it reintroduced a disruptive tactic it had used three decades earlier against the African National Congress: it arrested two UDF leaders on charges of treason as they left the British Consulate in Durban, where they had taken refuge for three months to avoid detention. Then, it put them and six others in prison to await a protracted trial. The state charged that the UDF fronted for the banned ANC. Those found guilty would face a death sentence.

At the same time, the state used its security laws to charge and imprison other black activists. The five leaders of the Transvaal general strike, charged with subversion under the Internal Security Act, faced a maximum 25-year penalty. Some 58 political trials were scheduled to begin in July 1985. The imprisonment of the leaders of the opposition for months while awaiting trial, as well as the heavy burden of defense costs, would inevitably disrupt efforts to conduct peaceful protests against apartheid.[21]

Despite this political repression, unrest and resistance continued in 1985, with student boycotts, work stoppages, and rent strikes rendering the black townships almost ungovernable. Most black councillors, criticized as tools of the regime and even physically attacked, their homes burned by aroused township residents, resigned. Pebco, a UDF affiliate, urged people in the manufacturing center of Port Elizabeth to stay away from work for three days in March to protest increases in consumer prices and bus fares. Despite the refusal of the Azanian People's Organization (AZAPO)[22] and major union groups to support the stayaway, almost all of the workers participated. Police reacted by patrolling the townships, urging people to go to work, and firing birdshot at groups of people gathered in the streets. By the end of the "black weekend," police violence had killed 15 people.[23]

Then, on March 21, the 25th anniversary of the Sharpeville massacre, police ordered between 3,000 and 4,000 mourners at Langa, outside Uitenhage, not to board buses and taxis to attend a funeral of one of the victims. The people proceeded, instead, in a peaceful funeral march, accompanied by the police in an armored car. Then a shot, fired without warning, killed a boy riding ahead of the crowd, and a fusillade from the police caught the mourners in a crossfire. At least 19 men, women, and children lay dead. Many more were wounded.[24]

On April 13, 1985, 50,000 blacks filled the soccer stadium of the battle-scarred black township outside Uitenhage to attend funeral services for those killed by police three weeks earlier. The government had banned most black gatherings in eastern Cape Province and other troubled regions of the country. As with other funerals of police victims in South Africa, however, this one turned into a massive political rally. A U.S. reporter described the scene:

> Today's massive gathering was a strange mixture of genuine mourning and an outpouring of political passions. . . . There was much rhythmic dancing, singing and chanting of slogans. . . .
>
> Banners were everywhere, mostly denouncing police violence, the segregationist system called apartheid and the administration of President Pieter W. Botha. Dislike of the Reagan administration and Britain's conservative government also revealed itself. One banner with an original numismatic touch declared: "Botha, Reagan, Thatcher—three sides of the same coin."
>
> The funeral's political dimension was that of the African National Congress, support for which counts as treason. Apart from the ANC flag draped over the row of coffins, there were songs and chants in praise of Congress leaders Nelson Mandela and Oliver Tambo and the underground organization's guerrilla wing, Umkhonto we Sizwe.[25]

At the end of April 1985, the entire workforce of about 40,000 in the Val Reefs gold-mining region went on strike to protest the dismissal of 2,000 workers who refused to do dangerous underground work. One miner was killed when police shot teargas and rubber bullets at the strikers. In retaliation for the mass work stoppage, two mine companies, Anglo American and Anglovaal, fired 14,400 workers, and sent them back to their homes—in the bantustans, Mozambique, and Lesotho—in a massive bus lift. The men, who took refuge in their hostels, had to be dislodged by teargas. Meanwhile, two powerful bomb blasts, which authorities claimed were set off by the African National Congress, ripped through the Anglo American and Anglovaal head offices in Johannesburg.[26]

Armed Resistance

In the mid-1970s, as in the American colonies two centuries earlier, more and more South Africans began to support armed struggle to overthrow minority rule. They attacked selective targets symbolizing authority, especially police, their vehicles and buildings. The lack of apparent pattern in these incidents suggested that most were spontaneous acts inspired by outrage at police violence.[27] After the Soweto uprising in 1976, however, the instances of armed actions, sabotage, and clashes with the armed forces increased rapidly, involving more organized forms of attack and more sophisticated operations by well-trained and well-armed combatants.

Since 1976, in almost all cases where evidence exists, the responsible organization has been Umkhonto we Sizwe, the armed wing of the ANC. In 1979, a new phase began when three ANC combatants, armed with automatic rifles and grenades, attacked a police station. They left leaflets at the scene declaring the attack was in retaliation for the execution of Solomon Mhlangu, an ANC combatant hanged by the authorities a month earlier. After that, several police stations were attacked, and in 1981 and 1982, so were at least two military bases. In 1983, a well-planned bomb attack destroyed a defense headquarters building in Pretoria, killing a number of high military officials as well as many civilians. The South African government's claim that these attacks came from "terrorists" based in the neighboring countries led to military invasions of Lesotho, Angola, and Mozambique.[28]

Umkhonto we Sizwe's success in evading combat action, in spite of massive follow-up operations by security forces, indicates widespread community support. Mass participation in funerals of combatants and the nature of memorial and commemorative services demonstrate more open support. The police have reported discovering caches of arms in urban and rural settings throughout the country. All these signs suggest the guerrillas have established bases inside the country, and do not depend solely on sanctuaries in the neighboring independent states.[29]

South African security forces acknowledge the scale and spread of actions across the country as a serious challenge.[30] This is confirmed by the extent to which the government has been obliged to militarize the society and by its emphasis on building civil defense structures and the commando system. By

1980, the National Security Council—composed of civilians and military officers and chaired by the Prime Minister—had emerged as the most powerful policy-making body in the government.[31]

Speaking at the beginning of 1983, on the 71st anniversary of the ANC's founding, the organization's president, Oliver Tambo, asserted:

> The enemy relies decisively on the use of force to entrench himself in power. We have to meet his murderous onslaught by intensifying the armed struggle. Our task, therefore, is to further strengthen the combat capacity of Umkhonto we Sizwe within South Africa for the immediate purpose of escalating our offensive.[32]

At the end of 1983, Gen. Constant Viljoen, chief of the South African Defense Force, stated in his Christmas message: "In this season of goodwill, I would like to say that the task is done and that peace reigns. Unfortunately, the tempo of the enemy assault is increasing rather than diminishing. . . ."[33]

Almost a year later, on October 9, 1984, an ANC statement declared:

> Deploying the army to assist the police by occupying a residential area is, on the one hand, an indication of the growing loss of control by the regime. . . . On the other hand, it is a clear indication of the strong will and determination of our people to struggle to the bitter end in demand of their national rights and a government elected on the basis of one person, one vote, irrespective of race or colour.[34]

THE NAMIBIAN PEOPLE'S STRUGGLE FOR LIBERATION

Swapo

Organizing into the South West Africa People's Organization (SWAPO) in 1960, the Namibian people also began to demonstrate, to strike, and to send delegations to the United Nations, joining other former League of Nations-mandated territories in calling for independence. After the International Court of Justice ruled in 1971 that South Africa should free Namibia, the United Nations in 1973 declared SWAPO the sole and authentic representative of the Namibian people.[35]

Despite the International Court's decision and U.N. recognition of SWAPO, South Africa continued its illegal rule in Namibia. Given South Africa's intransigence, SWAPO too decided to organize its people for armed struggle. In response, South Africa intensified its efforts to root out and destroy the Namibian liberation forces. It employed the same methods used in South Africa in banning, detaining, and imposing long-term prison sentences on SWAPO leaders. Nevertheless, in 1975, after Angola attained independence from Portugal, the effectiveness of SWAPO activities forced the South African military to send tens of thousands of soldiers to northern Namibia.

The Western "Contact Group"

In 1977, after the election of President Jimmy Carter, the United States joined the United Kingdom, France, West Germany, and Canada to organize a "Contact Group." They sought to engage the African countries, the Organization of African Unity, and SWAPO in discussions leading to implementation of U.N. Security Council Resolution 435. That resolution, adopted in January 1976, set out the principles and conditions to be observed in the transition to Namibian independence.

Expressing skepticism about this new "peace initiative," SWAPO nonetheless agreed to await its outcome. Addressing the U.N. Emergency Conference on Namibia four years later, in March 1981, SWAPO's Permanent Observer to the United Nations, Theo-Ben Gurirab, asserted:

> There are more South African troops and police agents in Namibia now than there were in 1977. There are more South African military bases now in 1981 than were there in 1977. More Namibians have died, including those who died at Kassinga [when South Africans bombed and killed some 600 men, women, and children in a refugee camp for Namibians inside Angola], than in 1977. In the period from 1977 to the present, South Africa has steadily imposed one fait accompli after another in Namibia and today we are being told that there is an elected regime in Namibia led by a so-called Council of Ministers. That is the situation inside Namibia.[36]

From 1977 to 1983, the Contact Group negotiated with South Africa to arrange for U.N.-supervised elections leading to independence. Yet South Africa continually stalled, trying to impose instead an "internal settlement" on the people of Namibia. It provided substantial financial and political support to the Democratic Turnhalle Alliance (DTA), a white-dominated party which included some Namibian blacks. It handed over increasing adminstrative power to the DTA-dominated National Assembly. In 1982, however, Peter Kalangula resigned as the DTA's president and exposed its lack of legitimacy. Kalangula argued that the DTA's structure tied it too closely to South Africa's apartheid system, and would cost it votes in an election contest against SWAPO.[37] Every time the Contact Group managed to bring SWAPO representatives together with South African officials, South Africa had another excuse to postpone the elections. Several times, South Africa invaded Angola, claiming that SWAPO forces attacked targets in Namibia from bases there. The South African government insisted, as proposed by the Reagan administration, that before it would agree to a ceasefire and implement elections, Angola must send home the Cubans who had provided the new Angolan government with technical and military assistance.[38]

At the end of 1983, the French representative withdrew from the Contact Group. He pointed out that the Group had achieved nothing. Its existence had seemed only to provide a pretext for continued stalling of serious efforts to ensure Namibian independence.[39]

While negotiations dragged on, the South African-imposed administration in Namibia began to finance its expenditures, including South Africa's large and growing military presence there, by borrowing funds on the South African and international capital markets. By the time it achieves independence, Namibia is likely to find itself burdened with an official external debt as great, in proportion to its gross national product, as that of other debt-burdened Third World countries.[40]

THE SOUTHERN AFRICAN DEVELOPMENT COORDINATION CONFERENCE

The Potentials

By the 1980s, the governments of the newly independent nations of southern Africa realized that separately they could neither undertake effective development nor reduce their dependence on South Africa.[41] Alone, even the coastal states of Tanzania, Mozambique, and Angola, although much larger in terms of area and population than their neighbors, confronted severely limited growth potentials. By uniting, however, they believed they could transform the region into a powerful, modern industrialized unit. Even excluding South Africa, they possessed the essential resources to build the complex modern industries required to provide productive employment and raise the living standards of the entire regional population.

This is not to suggest that the southern African states possessed a detailed program promising successful regional transformation. They confronted serious difficulties in implementing plans for more equitable allocation and development of their extensive mineral, agricultural, and human resources. In addition, they had to resolve fundamental political and ideological differences, focusing on the minimum threshold of agreement that would enable them to make step-by-step progress. Nevertheless, to the extent that they could constructively address and resolve these difficulties, the potential existed for more effective use of their resources to meet their peoples' needs.

First Steps

As a first step, Tanzania, Mozambique, Angola, Zambia, and Botswana joined together as Front Line States to promote the liberation of Zimbabwe, Namibia, and ultimately, it was hoped, South Africa. In 1979, when Zimbabwe's liberation appeared imminent, they formed the Southern African Development Coordination Conference (SADCC) and, meeting in Arusha, Tanzania, declared as their objectives:

1. The reduction of economic dependence, particularly on the Republic of South Africa;
2. The forging of links to create a genuinely equitable economic integration of the region;

3. The mobilization of resources to carry out national, international, and regional policies;
4. Concerted action to secure international cooperation with a regional strategy for economic liberation.

In pursuit of these objectives, the Front Line States' spokespersons agreed to identify areas where together they could reshape their national development to produce for themselves the goods and services still bought from South Africa, and to weave a fabric of regional cooperation and development. They also agreed to hold annual SADCC meetings as a "mechanism for surveying results, evaluating performance, identifying strengths and weaknesses, and agreeing on future plans . . . [through] sustained cooperation over two decades."[42] The time had come, they declared, to establish a "new economic initiative for southern Africa." They invited the international community to help them within a framework of guidelines:

★ Equitable development must be emphasized within the southern African region, since unbalanced development within or among states is divisive and ultimately weakening.
★ Development must avoid the creation of new and excessively dependent relationships.
★ External aid must be directed to the real needs of the people and countries as identified by their governments.
★ In the interest of reducing external dependencies, regional development strategies should be given special attention.[43]

In 1980, all the other independent states of the region—Malawi, Swaziland, Lesotho, and the newly liberated Zimbabwe—joined SADCC. The SADCC countries viewed improved transport and communications as critical, both to reduce dependence on South Africa and to increase trade within the region. One of their first acts was the creation of the Southern African Regional Transport and Communications Commission, located in Maputo, Mozambique, to coordinate transport and communications among participating states. The new Commission began to investigate the types and locations of transport networks that should be constructed to help spread productive activities.

Although southern Africa is better served by rail than most of the rest of the continent, the colonial regimes had built railroads primarily to ship heavy mineral products from the mines to the coasts for export to foreign markets or to South African factories. The participating states began to plan new railroads to link all the independent states. Mozambique and Zimbabwe sought to improve the railroad service to Maputo and Beira in order to reduce Zimbabwe's transport dependence on South Africa. But railroads are expensive. In the late 1970s, using conventional Western techniques, they cost an estimated $1 million per kilometer. Even the Tazara railway (which extends from Zambia to Dar es Salaam in Tanzania), built by more labor-intensive methods, cost about

$400,000 per kilometer.[44] Roads for truck transport, cheaper to build, require greater maintenance. In the late 1970s, it cost about $43,000 a kilometer to construct a two-lane tarmac road in tropical Africa.[45] Unpaved feeder roads, opening up remote areas, are less expense to build and maintain. The maintenance and repair of trucks used on such roads, however, constitutes a chronic problem; the average life expectancy of these trucks is typically measured in months rather than years.

The SADCC countries also focused on expanding their energy supplies, and they assigned Angola to develop a regional energy plan.[46] Wood and charcoal, the primary sources of energy for the general population, are becoming increasingly scarce. A decade ago in Tanzania, per capita consumption of fuel wood totaled between one-and-a-half and two kilograms per person per day, or about 27 million tons of fuel wood for the entire nation. (Already, women spend one out of every two days scouring the countryside for wood to keep their families warm and provide cooking fuel.) Experts forecast a "critical shortage" of fuel wood in a few generations. Elsewhere in the region, as in mountainous Lesotho, rural familes have already denuded wide areas of trees for firewood, fostering serious soil erosion on the rocky hillsides.[47]

Other potential sources of energy exist in the region. About 11 percent of the world's known coal reserves are located in southern Africa. Southern Africa also abounds in oil, natural gas, and uranium. Most of it still is exported in crude form. Angola has agreed to provide oil to SADCC countries at reduced prices.

Hydroelectric power, once the facilities are installed, is cheaper than either coal or oil. It engenders few of the pollution problems caused by the use of other fuels. The Kariba, Kafue, Cabora Bassa, and Kunene dams, if linked in a regional grid, could probably produce sufficient power for the initial stages of regional industrial and agricultural expansion. Widespread use of this existing power would require substations that could spread the use of electricity to less-developed rural areas. This would expand the market for wire and electrical machinery and equipment, which might be manufactured by factories processing the region's copper.

A third important area of cooperation is that of food reserves, for which Zimbabwe has taken responsibility. This involves identifying productive and storage capacity within the region. Given adequate planning and development of water supplies, the SADCC member states among them have the capacity to grow every variety of food crop. By cooperating, they hope to be able to increase regional trade in food, thereby reducing external dependency.

Long-term Development Possibilities
By combining their national resources, the independent states of southern Africa could take advantage of the economies of scale needed to build basic industries and to reduce their dependence on imported machinery and equipment.[48] But the creation of a more balanced regional economy will require further planning which SADCC has only just begun to undertake. The total

population of the region, excluding South Africa, is more than 60 million. The regional gross domestic product is about $22 billion—providing significant potential markets for new industrial output. At about 25 percent of the regional product, the annual investable surplus generated for investment[49] would total more than $5 billion. Over the next 20 years, this would provide sufficient capital to ensure significant progress in building integrated industrial and agricultural projects.

Viewed over time from a dynamic perspective, the possibilities arising from this first state of regional integration (even given the exclusion of South Africa) would be far greater than if each country developed separately. If the governments could coordinate their investments, both regional markets and surpluses could multiply rapidly. Over a 20-year period, say from 1985 to 2005, assuming an annual growth rate of the regional product of about 6 percent, the annual market could expand to about $50 billion. The investable surplus accumulated over these 20 years could be expected to reach almost $200 billion. Linked to and stimulating the use of the region's labor and other resources, this growth of regional investable surplus would permit financing of an expanding range of new industries and more productive agriculture. Instead of remaining almost entirely dependent on foreign markets and investors, the independent southern African states could then conduct trade on a more equitable basis with the rest of the world.

The SADCC member states invited potential foreign donors, both governmental and nongovernmental, to help finance regional cooperation. Many governments, as well as private voluntary organizations like Oxfam America, have expressed their willingness to support SADCC's development efforts. Yet, despite the determination of the governments of the the independent counties and the declarations of support by the international community in the early 1980s, three factors seemed to threaten these efforts. Chapter 2 discussed two of these factors: international recession and three years of drought. South Africa's clandestine assaults and open invasions became the third danger that threatened the independent southern African states' attempts to undertake self-reliant development.

South African Destabilization Tactics

The Minority Regime's Fears

Until the mid-1970s, the South African minority had felt safely tucked away at the bottom of the continent behind a buffer provided by the Portuguese in Mozambique and Angola and the Smith regime in Rhodesia. Even when, in the 1960s, independence spread throughout southern Africa, South Africa's rulers could feel protected by like-minded governments in neighboring states. But the collapse of the Portuguese empire and the attainment of independence by Angola and Mozambique in 1975 cracked South Africa's protective shield. The last remnants seemed shattered when Robert Mugabe became the first prime minister of independent Zimbabwe.

Several of the new states on South Africa's borders won their independence after armed struggle. Their very existence inspired black South Africans, already displaying rising militancy, with the belief that victory was possible. Angola and Mozambique pledged to build nonracist socialist societies, thus posing a double challenge to South Africa's racist and capitalist socioeconomic structure.

At their March 1982 summit meeting in Maputo, Mozambique, furthermore, the leaders of the Front Line States observed that "under the leadership of the ANC, the people [of South Africa], through strikes and armed action, are vigorously rising against apartheid." Their statement committed them to "intensify their material and diplomatic support for the liberation movements, SWAPO and ANC of South Africa, so that they can intensify the armed struggle for the attainment of the national independence of their peoples."[50]

For a time, South Africa apparently believed it could neutralize neighboring countries, and by using promises of economic and technical assistance, draw them into a "Constellation of States."[51] But the South African government's desire to remain the controlling regional "superpower" made it impossible to draw all its neighbors into the proposed Constellation on a voluntary basis. South Africa therefore carried out a complex combination of economic and political maneuvers, accompanied by military interventions, to destabilize its neighbors.

Military Intervention

South Africa mounted its heaviest military attacks against Angola. Some 6,000 South African troops first invaded Angola in August 1975, with the declared aim of preventing the Angolan national liberation movement, MPLA, from assuming power as the country's first independent government. Then-U.S. Secretary of State Henry Kissinger and the CIA covertly backed the invasion.[52] Nevertheless, it was eventually defeated with the aid of Cuban troops sent in response to the young Angolan government's call for international assistance.

In 1977 and again in 1981, South African troops launched raids into Angola. They established an occupation army in southern Angola. They killed thousands of Angolan citizens, displaced many more, and destroyed roads, villages, factories, food supplies, hospitals, and schools.

At the end of 1983, Pretoria sent in yet another invasion force. This time it was halted by combined Angolan and Cuban forces just north of the area the South Africans had occupied in 1981 in Kunene.[53]

Not only did South Africa invade Angola with its own troops and mercenaries, it also provided extensive support to a paramilitary anti-government group there. With openly acknowledged South African aid, the Union for the Total Independence of Angola (UNITA) engaged in harassment, increasing the pressures exerted on the Luanda government.[54]

U.N. estimates of the costs of the damage wreaked over almost a decade by South Africa's invasions and indirect sabotage of the war-torn Angola countryside total $7 billion.[55] Hundreds of men, women, and children have died, while the lives of tens of thousands more have been disrupted by warfare.

South Africa also carried out direct military attacks in Mozambique and Lesotho. In January 1981, South African commandos invaded Mozambique and killed 13 members of the ANC in the capital city of Maputo. In December 1982, South African commandos crossed into Lesotho and attacked 12 supposed ANC targets, killing 42 people, including 12 Leostho citizens as well as 30 South African refugees. In May 1983, the South African air force bombed an alleged ANC headquarters in Maputo, destroying a jam factory and killing six people, only one of whom had any ANC connections.[56]

Surrogate Sabotage and Terrorism

Pretoria also mounted campaigns of sabotage and terrorism against its neighbors. It sponsored surrogate forces in Mozambique, Lesotho, and Zimbabwe. These frequently attacked and damaged targets like roads, railways, electricity, oil, and water supplies.

South Africa's primary weapon in its undercover war against Mozambique was the Mozambique National Resistance Movement (MNR). No one but South Africa claimed this was a genuinely indigenous movement. After Mozambique achieved independence in 1975, the Rhodesian Central Intelligence Organization created the MNR to provide intelligence and to harass the Zimbabwean liberation movement, which, as it entered the final stages of struggle for independence, drew heavily on Mozambican solidarity. When Zimbabwe became independent, its new government closed the MNR training camps, but the MNR directorate moved to South Africa. From there it operated an irregular force which, according to a U.S. State Department official, received the bulk of its support from South Africa. The South African army financed and armed it, and gave it logistical support in the form of training, command and control equipment, and helicopter transport. Its radio, Voice of Free Africa, made broadcasts from South African soil. The MNR tried to politically destabilize Mozambique by brutally killing schoolteachers, health workers, foreign technicians, and other civilians working with the FRELIMO government.[57]

South Africa also carried out economic destabilization. Mozambique's railways and ports provide five SADCC countries with important alternatives to routing trade through South Africa. MNR sabotage of the Mozambican transit system helped in part to foster continued regional dependency on South African routes. Efforts to block the railway and road to Zimbabwe, to sabotage the port of Beira, and to attack the Beira-Zimbabwe oil pipeline fit into this pattern.[58]

In 1981, after the new Zimbabwean government began to examine critically the extent of South African investment in its economy, the South African government unilaterally terminated a preferential trade agreement that dated back to 1965, only agreeing to restore it after several months of delay. South Africa also abruptly recalled some 80 railway cars and diesel engines on long-term loan to the Zimbabwean railways, sharply reducing Zimbabwe's transport capability.[59]

Some of the attacks in Mozambique clearly were aimed at hurting Zimbabwe. In December 1982, commandos landed at Beira and blew up most of its oil storage facilities. The oil, destined for the newly reopened pipeline to Zimbabwe, amounted to a two-and-a-half month supply and was valued at $12 million. Zimbabwe had only stored enough locally to last two weeks. The sabotage left South Africa with a grip on all Zimbabwe's oil supplies, and it suddenly announced long delays in oil deliveries. The resulting chaos hit Zimbabwe over Christmas. Travel was impossible. Cars were abandoned, factories closed, power cuts became frequent. The situation only eased when the Zimbabwean government reached an agreement to ship its oil through South Africa.[60]

Pretoria also used its close links with elements of Zimbabwe's security and armed forces—forces maintained from the previous regime under the Lancaster House Agreement—to carry out internal sabotage. In 1981, an armory storing some $36 million worth of supplies was blown up. In 1982, 13 planes, a fourth of Zimbabwe's air force, were destroyed at Thornhill Air Force Base. A month later, Zimbabwean forces found and killed three South African Defense Force members at Sengwe, 18 miles inside the Zimbabwe-Mozambican border.[61]

As it had with the MNR in Mozambique and UNITA in Angola, Pretoria supported a group to foster destabilization in Zimbabwe. It established four training camps in South Africa (including at least one in the Bophuthatswana bantustan) to train some 5,000 former Rhodesian troops and dissidents. As land redistribution slowed and drought destroyed crops and cattle, the South Africans stepped up their activities in Zimbabwe. In 1983, Radio Truth, stationed in South Africa, began to beam messages to the region. Jonathan Steele of the British *Guardian* reported "testimony of captured rebels, as well as tests on abandoned arms and ammunition, reveal the existence of a carefully-planned operation by South Africa's military intelligence department." The Zimbabwean government discovered traces of South African involvement in at least 48 incidents of violence in 1983, and more in 1984, including ambushes of government troops, attacks on a bridge and a mine, and the shooting of three white farmers, one of them a senator, together with his daughter and an English visitor. According to Emerson Munangagwa, Zimbabwe's security minister, the South African-armed rebels numbered about 100 men in Zimbabwe at any one time, about a third of the total number of dissidents operating in the country.[62]

In late 1984, South Africa invited reporters to a simulated battle on the plains of Lohatla in its biggest military exercise since World War II. As one reporter pointed out:

> The display of might—sure to be interpreted by black-ruled African neighbors as a
> show of hostile preparedness—seemed to illustrate both the successes and the failures

of South Africa's efforts to circumvent the international arms embargo imposed in 1977.

It also reaffirmed the racially divided nation's military superiority in a region where other armed forces are largely preoccupied with suppressing internal dissent. That dissent is sometimes sponsored by South Africa itself.[63]

SUMMARY

After decades of peaceful petitioning and protest, their leaders jailed or forced underground as the South African government removed Africans to the bantustans and intensified its repressive measures, the liberation movements of South Africa and Namibia embarked on armed struggle. As Pretoria sought to convince international critics that it was introducing a limited constitutional reform at home, South Africans formed the United Democratic Front to express their opposition to the new Constitution and to demand an end to minority rule.

As domestic opposition mounted, South Africa's neighbors also sought to achieve full economic and political liberation. Stalling on U.N. demands for free elections and the complete independence of Namibia, Pretoria poured more and more troops and weapons into its unsuccessful efforts to destroy SWAPO's army.

Meanwhile, the politically independent neighboring states, despite their differing perspectives, created the Southern African Development Coordination Conference, explicitly dedicated to reducing their dependence on South Africa and to transforming the regional economy.

The South African minority government feared the loss of the low-cost labor, rich mineral resources, and markets provided by the neighboring states. When it failed to entice them into its proposed Constellation of States, Pretoria mounted a destabilization campaign to ensure continued dependency. It provided extensive training and material support to the MNR in Mozambique, UNITA in Angola, and dissidents in Zimbabwe. Its military forces invaded and killed civilians in Angola, Mozambique, and Lesotho.

By the 1980s, it was clear that the South African government's determination to perpetuate apartheid and control the region lay at the root of what Dr. Chester Crocker, assistant U.S. secretary of state for African affairs, described as a potential "magnet for international conflict and a cockpit of East-West tension."[64]

Squatters near Cape Town, South Africa, who risk a precarious existence to be near their menfolk (United Nations Photo/161768)

CHAPTER FIVE

Constructive Engagement in South Africa

TO WARD OFF SUBSTANTIAL CHANGE

Over the past two decades, as transnational corporate investments multiplied in South Africa, the U.S. government began to play an increasingly significant role throughout the region. Unfortunately, particularly in recent years, the United States has, in effect, encouraged the South African government to pursue its established policies. This has undermined and weakened the efforts of southern Africans, especially the liberation movements in South Africa and Namibia, to end apartheid and free the region from minority domination.

As noted in Chapter 1, Assistant Secretary of State for African Affairs Chester Crocker maintained that the United States' concern with southern Africa centers around its economic and strategic importance and the danger that it might become a "cockpit of East-West tension." For these reasons, Crocker explained to a 1981 Congressional hearing, "Above all, we seek to dampen the chances for expanded turmoil by encouraging negotiated solutions and an opportunity for peoples of this strategically located region to build their own futures."[1]

He has argued earlier that South Africa's rulers could gradually move in an appropriate direction to facilitate these kinds of negotiations:

[T]he way the white leadership plays its cards will help to shape the question of who sits at the future bargaining tables and under what circumstances. The governing white minority cannot "solve" the domestic political conflict unilaterally. But it could move to defuse a potential crisis, and take steps that would make genuine bargaining possible. . . . Autocratically imposed reform could become part of a process leading at a future stage to compromise and accommodation between freely chosen representatives of all major groups.[2]

In 1985, as more and more U.S. citizens mobilized to support the Free South Africa Movement, Secretary of State George Shultz made a speech calling for an American consensus on U.S. policy toward South Africa. He said:

If we recognize that white opinion holds vital keys to change, then we must also recognize that change must originate in shifts in white politics. In this regard, in the past three years, the white government has crossed a historical divide. . . .[3]

These statements demonstrate that U.S. policy was based on the assumption that white South Africans can and will control the pace and scope of change in

South Africa. Events in South Africa refute this assumption, however. Blacks have organized in growing numbers against all aspects of apartheid. No longer do urban workers, rural groups, community organizations, and students simply object to mounting repression. They have increasingly begun to seize the initiative from the government, to reject its proposed reforms and formulate their own demands for change.

Reagan administration policy makers have also tended to assume that organizations representing black aspirations—like the ANC in South Africa, SWAPO in Namibia, or the MPLA in Angola—are not the legitimate representatives of their peoples, but rather proxies for Soviet expansion in the region. In two secret memoranda written in April and May 1981, Crocker wrote that the Soviet Union and its "surrogates" were trying to thwart the U.S. goals of prosperity, security, and stability in southern Africa, and constructive internal change within South Africa. Furthermore, he requested that the U.S. Secretary of State Alexander Haig tell South African Minister Pik Botha that

We [the United States] share your [South Africa's] view that Namibia not be turned over to the Soviets and their allies. A Russian flag in Windhoek is as unacceptable to us as it is to you.[4]

Crocker added that a top U.S. priority is to stop Soviet encroachment in Africa, and that the United States was exploring ways to remove the Soviet-Cuban presence in Angola in the context of a Namibia settlement. He concluded that a failure of the United States and South Africa to cooperate would encourage further Soviet gains in the region.[5]

As the Reagan administration entered its second term, Shultz again expressed this view when he said:

Our adversaries have no constructive stake in the region, seeing rather in instability their best chance to expand their influence. When the Soviets and Cubans intervene in a part of the world far from their borders, we had better pay attention.[6]

This view is founded on a gross misrepresentation of the source of violence in southern Africa and the nature of the liberation movements there. As Chapter 4 above spells out in detail, the liberation movements have arisen, not as a result of a foreign communist plot, but through the efforts of the inhabitants to throw off the chains of apartheid and the institutionalized poverty inherited from their colonial past. In South Africa, they struggled for a half-century to win full participation in the government through peaceful means. The white minority has systematically used violence in its exercise of state power to repress and exploit the majority. Only when peaceful protest had repeatedly failed, when the state had banned their organizations and jailed their leaders, did the people of South Africa and Namibia turn to armed struggle.

The South African government has repeatedly suggested that the liberation movements, including the United Democratic Front, are communist controlled,

1) Impce·cy region - focal pt. of
   African econ· progress

2)
   Can become a "cockpit" for
   E-W tension - Soviet-Cuban
   military involvement, African
   guerilla operations, & S.A. -
   politically isolated but militarily
   strong -

3) US role = foster regional
   security, counter Soviet
   influence, make possible peaceful
   change -

        Guided change
        Limited change -

Big villain = Chester Crocker
Asst Secy of St ~~state~~ for
African Affairs under Reagan -
His aim was to "undermine" the
efforts in SA + Namibia to end
apartheid -

Responsible for US' "Constructive
engagement" policy =
- ~~no di~~ importance of region
economically + strategically -

SA =   ~~chromium~~
chromium
Manganese
Vanadium pentoxide
Platinum
Uranium
(diamonds)

Other SA STATES =
Copper (Zambia, Namibia,
Zimbabwe, Botswana
diamonds (Botswana,
Namibia)
uranium (Namibia

and that the Soviet Union seeks to dominate the region.[7] Shultz's and Crocker's statements reflect an uncritical acceptance of Pretoria's propaganda. The people of southern Africa aim, not to install another foreign power to rule their land, but to win the right to run their own governments and develop the region's resources to meet their own needs.

There is no reason to suppose that a victory of the South African and Namibian liberation movements would threaten the export of southern African minerals to the United States. It is true that U.S.-based transnational corporations, employing low-paid African labor to develop and manufacture the region's rich deposits, have fostered U.S. dependence on imported southern African minerals. While liberation may ensure improved wages and working conditions for the miners and facilitate increased processing of crude ores, it is unlikely to end the export of minerals to earn foreign exchange. For example, even though the Reagan administration refuses to recognize the Angolan government, the U.S. firm, Gulf Oil, still pumps oil from Angola's Cabinda wells. No matter what kind of post-liberation governments assume power in Namibia and South Africa, they undoubtedly will continue—like other African countries—to try to sell their minerals in the best market.

Despite the inherent fallacies in the Reagan administration's arguments, Constructive Engagement Policy incorporates the two fundamental premises proposed by Crocker:[8]

First, the U.S. government should work with "modernizers" within the South African leadership to implement reforms compatible with the protection of U.S. interests. Gradually, as the blacks attain more say in local government and trade unions, they can negotiate for a greater share of power at the national level. The demands of the majority would thus be gradually modified and then accommodated through compromise.

Second, the U.S. administration should exercise its influence to achieve peace in the region to give the South African minority time to implement these limited reforms.

This chapter discusses:

★ U.S. opposition to international proposals to impose sanctions against South Africa.

★ The ineffectiveness of the Sullivan Principles.

★ The divestiture option.

★ The impact of U.S. policy on efforts to foster limited reform within South Africa, and the nature and probable consequences of U.S. aid to specific groups in South Africa.

★ The growing U.S. support for South Africa's military build-up.

The next chapter explores the extent to which U.S. government policy has tended to undermine the independent southern African states' attempts both to reduce their dependence on South Africa and to support the liberation efforts there.

U.S. Opposition to International Sanctions

Over the years, the independent African states and the majority of the members of the United Nations have repeatedly called for international sanctions to end trade with and investment in South Africa. Although the U.S. government has invoked sanctions against other governments for what it has held to be infringements of human rights,[9] it has repeatedly voted against the U.N. General Assembly resolutions supporting African proposals to impose sanctions against South Africa.

In 1983, Crocker vigorously defended the Reagan administration's position:

The advocates of this approach [supporting sanctions ending U.S. trade and investment in South Africa] would have us disengage and somehow walk away from the issues which southern Africa presents, as if they will magically solve themselves or not affect us if we turn our back on them. I reject that approach; it is basically a "cop-out," cloaked in a fastidious false piety.

Box 5.1

U.S. Votes Against U.N. Resolutions Calling for Sanctions Against South Africa (S.A.)[a]

Year	General Assembly Resolution	Votes of U.N. Members Yes	No	Abstain	U.S. Vote
1981	Sanctions against S.A. (No. 36/172D)	109	18	13	No
	Against military and nuclear collaboration (No. 36/172E)	119	19	4	No
	For the cessation of new foreign investment in S.A. (No. 36/1720)	138	1	7	No
1982	Asks IMF not to grant credits to S.A. (No. 37/2)	121	3	23	No
	Call for international action against apartheid (No. 37/69B)	135	3	8	No
	Sanctions against S.A. (No. 37/69C)	114	10	19	No
	Against military and nuclear collaboration with S.A. (No. 37/69D)	120	8	16	No

Worse, it presumes without a shred of supporting evidence that change in South Africa would be advanced if the United States washed its hands of the problem, leaving the scene to others to work their will. That is not foreign policy; it is "ostrich" policy.[10]

Independent African states and the majority of the U.N. members point out, however, that the people of southern Africa have been working for decades by every means possible to win their own liberation. In desperation, increasing numbers of South Africans have turned to armed struggle. The longer the government can depend on transnational corporations for financial and technological assistance, the longer it is likely to maintain its oppression of the black majority and preserve its influence throughout the region. Effective U.N. sanctions on trade and investment with South Africa would end that support, weaken the regime, and thereby hasten the liberation of black South Africans.

Crocker praised the 1983 white vote for the new Constitution. He claimed the whites' "growing consensus" on the "need for change" was a "milestone in the modern history of South Africa. . . . which opens the way to constructive, evolutionary change toward a system based on the consent of all South African citizens. . . ."[11]

	For the cessation of new investment in S.A. (No. 37/69H)	134	1	9	No
	Oil embargo against S.A. (No. 37/69J)	125	6	13	No
1983	Sanctions against S.A. (No. 38/39D)	122	10	18	No
	Against military and nuclear collaboration with S.A. (No. 38/39G)	122	9	17	No
	For the cessation of new foreign investment in S.A. (No. 38/39I)	140	1	9	No
	Oil Embargo against S.A. (No. 38/39J)	130	6	14	No

Note

a. In 1985, after the Uitenhage killings, the United States did vote to support a U.N. Security Council resolution condemning the killing of blacks and detention of the South African government's opponents, but that resolution did not propose sanctions. (*New York Times*), March 13, 1985).

Source: Prepared by Dan Jamison for the Africa Fund, June 1984.

A similar view was taken by G.W.H. Relly, chairman of the Anglo American Group, the leading mining finance house in South Africa.[12] With Anglo American having reaped about $415 million in profits in 1983—10 percent more than in 1982—Relly apparently regarded the government's reforms as promising. He declared:

> Today I believe most South Africans of all colours desire a more just and equitable society. Mr. P.W. Botha has chosen to set the country now on a course of what might be called decentralised democratization which, while it maintains a substructure of racial self-determination, also appears to envisage a superstructure of national cooperation. If Mr.Botha can maintain the thrust of his policy to embrace the urban black population and then move to some federal system to embrace the country as a whole, we may have reason to hope that these initiatives will evoke the vitality and optimism to bring about a new era, with profound implications for southern Africa as a whole.[13]

This assertion contradicts the stance of the United Democratic Front, the only domestic voice through which the black majority has been able to speak in recent years. They have repeatedly denounced the ethnically divided tricameral legislature established under the Constitution, demanding a political system based on one-person-one-vote.

The Sullivan Principles

A Voluntary Code

Arguing that U.S. investors can help bring about desired changes, the Reagan administration has endorsed the Sullivan Principles, introduced during the Carter administration.[14] Drafted in 1976 by Rev. Leon Sullivan, a black member of the General Motors Corporation's board of directors, these principles embody a voluntary code of conduct for U.S. firms operating in South Africa. They call on U.S. firms to introduce fair-employment practices and non-segregation in the work place. Examination of the application of these Principles suggests that, far from fostering significant improvements in the lives of most black South Africans, they merely serve to justify continued profitable U.S. investment in apartheid.

The Sullivan Code has led to little improvement in the working conditions of black workers employed by U.S. firms in South Africa. The sole enforcement mechanism consists of a voluntary questionnaire sent to signatories, whose responses are then compiled and published in an annual report. Five years after the principles were introduced, only 3 percent of black, coloured, and Asian workers employed by U.S. corporate signatories of the Sullivan Code held management positions. Although blacks, coloureds, and Asians represent 63 percent of the work force of the reporting units, only 0.007 percent are in jobs

Box 5.2

Principles of the Sullivan Code

1. Nonsegregation of the races in all eating, comfort, and work facilities;
2. Equal and fair employment practices for all employees;
3. Equal pay for all employees doing equal work for the same period of time;
4. Initiation and development of training programs that will prepare, in substantial numbers, blacks, coloureds, and Asians for supervisory, administrative, clerical, and technical jobs;
5. Increasing the number of blacks, coloureds, and Asians in management and supervisory positions;
6. Improving the quality of employees' lives outside the work environment in such areas as housing, transportation, schooling, recreation, and health facilities.

Source: Arthur D. Little, Inc., *Seventh Report on the Signatory Companies to the Sullivan Principles*, prepared for Rev. L.H. Sullivan (Cambridge, MA: Arthur D. Little, Inc., 1983). For complete text of Principles, see Rev. Leon Sullivan, "Fourth Amplification of the Sullivan Principles" (Philadelphia: International Council for Equality of Opportunity Principles, Inc., November 1984).

---

where they supervise whites. In 1982 and 1983, the percentage of black employees holding either management or supervisory posts actually declined.[15]

A "Toothless Package"

Black South African workers have rejected the Sullivan Principles. The Motor Assemblers and Components Workers Union of South Africa (MACWUSA), for example, called them a "toothless package" and a "piecemeal reform that allows this cruel system of apartheid to survive."[16]

Furthermore, even if all U.S. firms with investments in South Africa complied with the code, they would have almost no impact on the working conditions of the majority of the black labor force. Because of the relatively capital-intensive nature of their production processes, U.S. firms employ only a small fraction, less than 2 percent, of all black South African wage workers.[17]

Integration of facilities rather than promotion of blacks into management positions or recognition of unions has been a common practice among Sullivan Principle signatories. As the chairman of Union Carbide's South African affiliate explained in 1983, the reform it introduced "has mainly been a matter of integrating the eating facilities and change rooms at our plants."[18] Although it

Box 5.3

Ford Workers' Union Rebuts Sullivan Principles

In January 1982, the Motor Assemblers' and Component Workers' Union of South Africa, one of the unions organizing black workers at Ford, submitted a four-page document on the implementation of the Sullivan Code's fair-employment principles to the company at its request. Ford had received the highest Sullivan Principles rating.

In its document, MACWUSA listed the six principles and the union's comment on each:

★ **Principle 1: Nonsegregation of races:** The union says this has no significance for the needs of black workers, of whom 78 percent are employed in job categories which have no white workers. "The system of job discrimination on the basis of race is being perpetuated in its entirety."

★ **Principle 2: Equal and fair employment practices for all employees:** The union says: Practical experience at Ford shows for a black worker to qualify for a supervisory position he must possess an academic Junior Certificate or undergo a company-offered two-year technical course, while whites with no more than primary school education fill supervisory and even senior positions.

★ **Principle 3: Equal pay for equal work:** The union's comment: 84 percent of the workers in the lowest job categories are black, and 98.5 percent of the workers employed in the top job category are white. Since the black worker does not have job seniority equal to that of the white, the "equal pay for equal work" statement is simply lip service and an empty slogan.

★ **Principle 4: Initiation of and development of training programs for blacks:** MACWUSA claims that over the past five years the company has reported only on the number of black and white employees trained, but has failed to reveal the discriminatory amounts of money spent in training them.

★ **Principle 5: Increasing the number of blacks in supervisory and mangement positions:** The union says the appointment of blacks to managerial positions is "simply tokenism." The company abides by the law that prohibits black supervision over whites, and "as such these black managers have no decision-making power or authority in the company."

★ **Principle 6: Improving the equality of employees' lives outside the work environment:** The union says Ford has failed to address the major question of black housing. Ford gave large sums of money to the East Cape Administration Board (ECAB) for the "improvement" of the Emaplangeni area, subsequently demolished to make way for the new KwaFord township.

The union claims this resulted in exorbitant rents for the original residents, removed by ECAB, who now live in black townships in conditions of squalor. "The new Fordville, with limited houses selling at some R45,000 each, is a window-dressing scheme aimed at promoting a black middle class."

MACWUSA also says "substantial sums of money" from the company are directed toward apartheid organizations and "pro-government" sports bodies.

In summary, MACWUSA says the Sullivan Code "circles around apartheid's basic structures. The Code does not demand apartheid to be abolished, but merely to modernize and ensure its perpetuation."

Source: *Cape Times* (S.A.), January 19, 1982. Ford has since sold a majority of its shares in its South African affiliate. (See Chapter 3.)

has operated in South Africa since 1929, with mining interests in both Bophuthatswana and Lebowa bantustans, Union Carbide has only marginally responded to pressure from concerned shareholders in the United States to introduce reforms.

Even Rev. Sullivan admitted that U.S. firms were introducing changes too slowly.[19] Late in 1984, he reported that some U.S. and British firms planned to violate apartheid laws if necessary to improve workers' conditions. "You can call it organized defiance of the system," Rev. Sullivan stated. A South African publication claimed, however, that the initiative aimed primarily to "head off the divestment campaign."[20]

While the Sullivan Principles have contributed little to improving the working conditions of black workers in South Africa, they have helped deflect criticism of U.S. investment there. Some U.S. institutions called on to divest have sought to use the Principles to judge companies' performance. Some people claim the simple act of signing the Principles constitutes an indication of sufficiently good intentions to eliminate any reason for further action. The number of signatory firms reached 146 in 1982. As a spokesman for one subsidiary of a U.S. firm explained to the Investor Responsibility Research Center, a Washington-based public-interest research group, the company refrained for some time from signing until it realized that "the Principles were being used to pacify critics in the States."[21] By 1983, however, the number of signatory firms had dropped to 120, only a third of the total number of U.S. corporate affiliates operating in South Africa, but the number rose again by June 1985 to 152 as public pressure intensified for divestment.

William Lucy, secretary treasurer of the American Federation of State, County and Municipal Employees (AFSCME), asserted: "Although these Sullivan Principles sound splendid on paper, that is what they essentially remain. Paper principles. Another case of someone's good intentions dashed against the rocks of reality."[22]

Many South Africans, as well as outside critics, reject the U.S. administration's argument that U.S. investments strengthen the economic base from which blacks can organize to negotiate for improved rights. They point out instead that foreign investments strengthen both the minority's rule inside the country and its capacity to dominate its neighbors (see Chapter 3). They add that the South African government has passed legislation that requires key corporations to participate in national plans for military defense of their plants. For example, in event of a national emergency arising in response to mounting black protest, the government could require GM's management to increase its production of military-related equipment.[23]

The Growing Demand for Divestment

South African Support

Supporters of continued U.S. investment in South Africa claim most black South Africans support it. However, expressing opposition to foreign investment is a crime punishable by a minimum of five years in jail and a maximum of the death penality. This renders questionable the outcome of the 1984 Schlemmer poll of 551 workers employed in U.S. companies. The survey, paid for in part by the Reagan administration, claimed 75 percent of those polled opposed divestment. The fact that 25 percent dared to speak in favor, despite heavy punishment if their identities were revealed, suggests instead strong support for divestment. (The survey has also been criticized for poor social science methodology.)[24]

Those few who advocate continued foreign investment generally include members of the small black middle class or employees of a government branch like the bantustan civil service. Dependent on the system, they fear that fundamental change may endanger their privileged positions.

Lucy Mvubelo, secretary general of the National Union of Clothing Workers, and closely associated with the African-American Labor Center (see below), might appear to be an exception. After having been flown to the United States to speak to members of Congress against divestment, she pointed out that her stand was unpopular back home: "[I]n coming here to address you on the question of investment in South Africa, I will once again be labeled . . . a South African government stooge, a 'sell-out,' and I will be denigrated on every possible occasion. . . ."[25]

In spite of government prohibition, most leaders of the trade-union movement, the South African churches, and black political organizations have found ways to call for divestment. Dr. Nthato Motlana of the Soweto Committee of Ten declared: "If I said that the only way to bring change would be total economic sanctions, I would be liable to go to jail. So let's just be cagey. Let's say I support 'pressures,' and leave it at that."[27]

Upon being installed as the first black Anglican Bishop of Johannesburg in February 1985, Nobel Peace Prize Laureate Desmond Tutu asserted, "I give notice that if [within 18 months to two years] apartheid is not being actively dismantled, then . . . I will myself call for punitive economic sanctions [against South Africa] whatever the legal consequences may be for doing so." Earlier, Bishop Tutu had declared:

> Foreign companies in South Africa should stop kidding themselves by saying they are there for our benefit. That's baloney. Whether they like it or not, they are buttressing an evil system.
>
> The Sullivan Principles . . . are there to make apartheid more acceptable, more comfortable; and we do not want apartheid made more comfortable, we want apartheid dismantled . . . These principles are saying nothing more than the kinds of things that a good employer ought to be doing in any case.[28]

Years earlier, Black Consciousness leader Steve Biko had asserted boldly:

> The argument is often made that the loss of foreign investment would hurt blacks the most. It would undoubtedly hurt blacks in the short run, because many of them would stand to lose their jobs. But it should be understood in Europe and North America that foreign investment supports the present economic system of political injustice. . . . If Washington is really interested in contributing to the development of a just society in South Africa, it would discourage investment in South Africa. We blacks are perfectly willing to suffer the consequences! We are quite accustomed to suffering.[29]

Steve Biko died in 1977 while detained by the police under the Terrorism Act. Supporters argue he was tortured and killed by the South African police.[30] Oliver Tambo, exiled president of the African National Congress of South Africa, stated:

> What we in the African National Congress want to see is what the people of South Africa want to see—our people are not only ready and willing to accept the consequences of action against the regime on the economic front, but they have themselves demanded the total political, economic, cultural and military isolation of the racist regime. We demand total isolation of the racist regime—no investment and withdrawal of existing investment.[31]

A Tinderbox

U.S. firms with investments in South Africa have tried to convince their shareholders that their investments are not only profitable, but sound. Yet, as the South African government intensifies its repression, the mounting social tensions within South Africa threaten these very investments. Some years ago, rising black unemployment and underemployment contributed to what *The Economist* called "a time bomb . . . of discontent and revolution-fodder."[32] According to the managing director of the Goodyear Tire and Rubber Company's South African subsidiary, "Foreign companies are going to be the

target. That is where dissident blacks will focus. We are right in the tinderbox."[33]
Ian Leach, general manager of Caterpillar Africa, warned in 1980: "We are secure here for five years. Up to 10 years it is a matter of caution. After than it is anybody's guess."[34] Five years later, some U.S. companies were reducing their operations in South Africa, citing declining profitability.[35]

Divestment to Date

Anti-apartheid groups, churches, universities, and other institutional investors in the United States have organized an extensive campaign to persuade local governments and institutions to divest themselves of shares in companies with investments in or loans to South Africa.

Box 5.4

U.S. Groups Calling for Divestment from South Africa

★ States or territories that have taken action to withdraw funds from firms and/or banks with investments in apartheid include Connecticut, Iowa, Maryland, Massachusetts, Michigan, Nebraska, Wisconsin, and the Virgin Islands. At least 28 cities passed some form of divestment including Atlanta, Boston, Cincinnati, Detroit, Gary, Hartford, Miami, New York, Newark, Philadelphia, San Francisco, and Wilmington. Early in 1984, the congressional committee that oversees Washington, D.C. decided to permit the Washington City Council to block investment of its public funds in firms that do business in South Africa.

★ U.S. unions that have taken funds out of U.S. firms with South African investments include the Service Employees International Union; International Longshoremen's and Warehousemen's Union; United Auto Workers; United Steel Workers; Illinois State AFL-CIO; American Federation of State, Local and Municipal Employees (AFSCME); District 119 National Union of Hospital and Health Care Employees, AFL-CIO; Retail Wholesale and Department Store Workers Union, AFL-CIO; Joint Board, Fur, Leather and Machine Workers Union of the United Food and Commercial Workers International Union, AFL-CIO; and District 31 United Steel Workers of America, AFL-CIO.

★ U.S. churches that have voted to end their links to banking or corporate businesses with interests in South Africa include the National Council of Churches, the American Lutheran Church, the United Methodist Board of Global Ministries, the Reformed Church in America, Union Theological Seminary, and the American Friends Service Committee.

★ More than 50 U.S. universities have partially or fully withdrawn funds from South Africa-linked companies. Those that have sold all their shares in corporations doing business in South Africa include Antioch, Hampshire College, Ohio University, Michigan State, Indiana Central, Western Washington, and the Universities of Massachusetts, Oregon, and New York. Harvard, Dartmouth, Yale, and Brown are among the institutions that partially divested in 1985 in response to increased student demonstrations.

Sources: The American Committee on Africa, "Public Investment and South Africa Newsletter" (1985); "Church and University Action Against Apartheid " (1984); "Questions and Answers on Apartheid" (New York: ACOA, 1984); and "Student Protests Spark South Africa Related Divestment," *American Committee on Africa News* (New York: ACOA, June 10, 1985).

By early 1985, as the anti-apartheid movement grew across the United States, the pressure mounted to persuade U.S. firms to divest from South Africa and for the U.S. government to terminate its Constructive Engagement Policy. In November 1984, Rep. Walter Fauntroy (D-DC), Randall Robinson, Executive Director of TransAfrica, and U.S. Civil Rights Commissioner Mary Frances Berry had launched the Free South Africa Movement by protesting inside the South African Embassy, which they refused to leave until arrested. Thousands of Americans demonstrated against apartheid throughout the country. In the following months, more than 2,000 people submitted to arrest in civil disobedience. They included 18 members of Congress and Senator Lowell Weicker (R-CT), the first senator in U.S. history to be arrested for civil disobedience while in office. Rev. Sullivan, himself, said: "I'm using the companies as a strategy. . . . I think we need the disinvestment campaign to keep the pressure on the companies."[36]

Several congressmen prepared anti-apartheid legislation for the 1985 session of Congress. The congressional Black Caucus played a leading role in putting together a legislative package on South Africa. Several of its members proposed some type of sanction, including a comprehensive bill to end all U.S. ties to the apartheid regime. Another House bill would ban new investment, bank loans to the South African government, and KrugerKands and imports. The export controls bill would prohibit all exports to the South African military and police, as well as the computer and "munitions list" exports to any sector of the government or its agencies. For the first time, several senators, too, initiated major anti-apartheid legislation.

Alternatives

Opponents of apartheid point out there are many opportunities for alternative investments. As Edmund G. Brown Jr., former governor of California, explained:

> There is a mounting consensus that pension fund investments cannot protect retirees' benefits unless they protect employees' jobs and economic interests as well. . . . Investments that create jobs, build houses and return a fair yield could be a model for government pension systems.[37]

Examples of such investment include the Kansas Public Employees' Retirement System program called "Kansas Funds for Kansas Jobs." In the program, the retirement system buys bonds guaranteed by the Small Business Administration. Thus the program makes capital available for small businesses, improving the economy and creating jobs. Other alternative investments include affordable housing, health care and human services, and resource conservation. The interest in public pension-fund investment is growing rapidly, and new alternatives to investments in South Africa are multiplying. Several new investment agencies have emerged which specialize in socially responsible investment portfolios.[38]

Box 5.5

The Financial Implications of Divestment

"We here in Massachusetts are proud to have been the first state in the nation to vote to sell from our public pension fund portfolio all those investments in firms doing business in South Africa. . . . It has been our experience that divestiture makes not only a strong moral statement against apartheid but divestiture has proven to have had no significant impact on our pension earnings. . . . Timely and careful divestiture can result in net increases in pension earnings." (Letter from Michael S. Dukakis, Governor of Massachusetts, August 1983.)

This experience of Massachusetts has been repeated by other states and cities divesting from companies that are involved in South Africa. For instance, the director of the Board of Pensions and Retirement in Philadelphia stated in 1984 that: "We . . . consistently achieved or bettered our assumed actuarial investment return rate of 9 percent in our transactions divesting our portfolio of fixed income securities of firms doing business in South Africa."

The University of Wisconsin Trust Fund found that "divestment of South Africa-related stocks has not hampered or limited our ability to fund suitable sources of investment." Michigan State University found in June 1980, within months of passing divestment resolutions, their portfolio had earned an additional $12 million.

Joan Bavaria, president of Franklin Research Company, has pointed out that fears that divestment will prove costly are groundless. "Rather, [studies] have shown that over time South Africa-free companies have outperformed the restricted stocks with a minimal amount of added risk." This has been borne out by studies conducted by Chemical Bank, the U.S. Trust Co., and Trinity Investment Management Corporation.

Hence, Robert J. Schwartz, Vice President of Shearson/American Express and an expert on socially responsible investment, stressed in 1984; "A decision about divestment should not be cluttered by arguments in regard to investment performance, but be based on the political, moral issues as to whether the decision makers believe that divestment will have an effect on ending the system of apartheid."

In September 1984, the Connecticut state treasurer, Henry Parker, reported that "Connecticut has been able to earn money by selling the holding of socially irresponsible companies. Corporate America must take a strong stand against racism wherever it exists and our divestment law is an important incentive for them to do just that. What is more, we have shown that it is profitable to be socially responsible."

Source: "South Africa: Questions and Answers on Divestment," American Committee on Africa in cooperation with the United Nations Centre Against Apartheid (New York: American Committee on Africa, 1984).

Those who claim that divestiture will have no effect on South African policy tend to ignore the role of foreign investment in reassuring the minority that it can perpetuate its undemocratic rule without fear of sanction. Yet Dr. de Villiers, South African minister of industries, commerce, and tourism, has stated: "If the opposition has doubts about the future of South Africa, I can only say our confidence in our country is borne out by the number of foreign investors."[39] Divestment by U.S. corporations and banks would be a major blow to the confidence of the ruling minority government. Exiled South African editor Donald Woods claimed that "Disengagement . . . will deal a firm psychological blow against the structure and system of apartheid. The white government in South Africa is terribly conscious of world opinon—it affects not to be, but it is extremely conscious of it. . . ."[40]

Important as the psychological-political impact would be, withdrawal of U.S. investments would have another still more important result. U.S. investment in South Africa is centered in the vital sectors of the economy, in areas where

South Africa lacks natural resources and a market large enough to make basic industries viable and the country self-sufficient. This is particularly true, for example, in the oil and electronics industries.

Although South Africa has reduced its oil consumption to as low a level as that of any industrial nation, oil products remain a vital necessity. Because South Africa has not discovered any oil deposits within its borders, it must still import all its crude, mainly from international oil firms. U.S. oil companies ship oil to South Africa, helping the economy there to withstand OPEC's boycott. They own major investments, too, in South Africa's large oil refineries. Complete divestiture would help deprive South Africa of the finance and technology it requires to keep this crucial sector functioning.[41]

South Africa also relies particularly heavily on electronics, especially computers, to stretch the capacity of the skilled white workers to run the economy and its large military machine. According to Jan Timmer, managing director of Philips S.A.: "It is a fallacy that any country other than the U.S. and Japan can ever reach self-sufficiency in electronics. This is because of the sizzling pace of change, the huge sums required for research and the lack of market size."[42] If South Africa could no longer obtain U.S. or other industrialized countries' electronics technology, the ruling minority would find itself seriously handicapped. Computers have played a special role in the repressive machinery. In particular, they facilitate administration of the nationwide passbook and influx control system, that is, control over black migration within South Africa.

Even the South African government's Kleu Commission on Industrial Development Strategy suggested that although successful imposition of sanctions on trade might not be fatal, it would hurt.[43]

Finally, as a major positive consequence of U.S. firms' withdrawal from South Africa, the U.S. government would no longer need to concern itself with U.S. economic interests there. The necessity of maintaining the stability of the present apartheid system would dramatically diminish, considerably broadening U.S. options for supporting meaningful peace and reconstruction in the region.

U.S. GOVERNMENT AID
TO SOUTH AFRICAN GROUPS

Under the Constructive Engagement Policy, the Reagan administration, for the first time in U.S. history, has provided government aid funds directly to South Africans. Critics point out that these funds will, at best, do little to offset the disastrous impact of apartheid on the lives of the African majority. On the contrary, they are more likely to benefit a small elite whose interests coincide with the *status quo*. Thus, in reality, they may strengthen minority rule in South Africa.

Box 5.6

U.S. Aid Funds for South Africa

★ $4 million a year for scholarships to bring approximately 100 black South African students to the United States for graduate and undergraduate studies, mainly in the sciences;

★ More than $1 million in 1983-4 to train South African labor leaders (funds provided in cooperation with the AFL-CIO African-American Labor Center);

★ A $5 million program, implemented through private South African institutions, to provide scholarships for some 400 black South African students each year;

★ $3 million over the next two years to support small businesses, a project administered in cooperation with the National African Federated Chamber of Commerce in South Africa.

Source: Chester Crocker, "Reagan Administration's Africa Policy: A Progress Report," Fourth Annual Conference on International Affairs: U.S.-Africa Relations Since 1960, University of Kansas, Lawrence, Kansas, November 10, 1983; for a critique, see "U.S. Assistance to South Africa," *Washington Notes on Africa* (Washington, D.C.: Washington Office on Africa, Winter 1984).

U.S. Scholarships

Considering the hundreds of thousands of university-age black South Africans denied educational opportunities every year, the U.S. government's $4-million-a-year scholarship program to bring 100 black South Africans to the United States for university study is a drop in the bucket. Likewise, the provision of $2 million over the next two years to tutor black South African high school students will reach only a small percentage of those whose education has been truncated by South Africa's apartheid policy. Critics assert that this aid will serve primarily to train a privileged few, leaving the African majority without access to adequate educational and work opportunities. Two black student groups, the Wits Black Students Society and the Student Representative Council, gave these reasons for their refusal to discuss these educational programs with U.S. congressional subcommittee members during the Americans' 1983 visit to South Africa.[44]

The African-American Labor Center

South African trade unionists have criticized the $1 million the U.S. government is providing to the AFL-CIO African-American Labor Center to initiate training programs for black South African trade unionists. They object that the Labor Center will not help build mass trade-union organizations, but rather train a trade-union elite. "The possibility of excessive American support for certain unions," a South African research group said, "may have the effect of placing control firmly in the hands of leadership rather than rank and file membership." The group also pointed to evidence of past CIA influence in the Center.[45]

When Irving Brown (former head of the Center), Patrick O'Farrell (its current leader), and two other AFL-CIO executive members visited South Africa, local unionists expressed their concerns about the proposed program. Even before the U.S. unionists arrived, MACWUSA and the South African Allied Workers Union (SAAWU) indicated their hositility to the visit. Leaders of the Federation of South African Trade Unions (FOSATU) publicly expressed doubt as to the need for an "external body." An organizer from a Cape Town union declared:

> Although we have agreed to meet the delegation, we have misgivings about the role the United States Government plays in the African-American Labour Center. Its previous courses at Cornell University have had a corrupting influence on South African unionists. Their lavish way of throwing money around is not the way we believe in running a union.[46]

A Scandinavian trade-union official stated:

> The Americans are traveling around offering money independently to trade union leaders. That way of buying friends, goodwill and agents must be directed to the upper structure of the national unions as the goals are mainly political. It is obvious that the (American unions) . . . don't consider trade union assistance from the point of view of giving a hand to the common workers' situation, but as part of U.S. foreign policy. They don't give a damn about the common workers' situation, as you can easily see from their training programmes. They are always geared to trade union leadership training. But if you never train the rank and file members how will they defend their rights, especially against dishonest leadership. . . ?[47]

Supporting Black Businesses

The $3 million the U.S. government provided to support small business in black communities during the next two years appears symbolic at best. Small black businesses will never be able to compete with the South African Anglo American Group or U.S. transnational corporate affiliates whose direct investments run into billions of dollars. Moreover, the National African Federated Chamber of Commerce (NAFCOC), through which the United States is channeling these funds, in no way challenges the apartheid system. The South African government apparently welcomes its initiatives.[48] Many black South Africans view a U.S. grant to that agency, therefore, as yet another measure designed to encourage the growth of an elite black group that will accommodate marginal change rather than support elimination of the entire apartheid system.

These kinds of programs led Sanford J. Ungar, senior associate at the Carnegie Foundation for International Peace, to conclude: "America is 'constructively engaged' with only a small privileged stratum of South African society."[49]

And Franklin H. Williams, president of the U.S.-based Phelps-Stokes Fund, declared: "Constructive engagement has not proved itself capable of anything but illusory progress. In fact, it feeds the bones, muscle and sinew of apartheid."[50]

U.S. POLICY AND SOUTH AFRICA'S MILITARY BUILD-UP

The Reagan administration's Constructive Engagement Policy has gone beyond supporting the limited reforms in South Africa. Building on earlier administrations' initiatives, and sometimes going further, it has contributed to strengthening the South African regime's police-state apparatus and military capacity.

CIA Links

The U.S. government's contacts with Pretoria's police establishment are long-standing. A former CIA agent, John Stockwell, pointed out in 1978: "The CIA has traditionally sympathized with South Africa and enjoyed its close liaison with BOSS [Bureau of State Security]. The two organizations share a violent antipathy toward communism and in the early sixties the South Africans had facilitated the Agency's development of a mercenary army to suppress the Congo rebellion."[51] He added that a "cordial relationship" continued between the two intelligence agencies.

For a few years, following the Soweto uprising, known U.S. contacts with the police diminished. As the information summarized in Box 5.7 shows, however, they have increased again in recent years.

Military Shipments

Although the U.S. government agreed to the 1977 U.N. boycott to stop all shipments of military supplies to South Africa, it continued from the outset to permit the shipment of "grey area" items. Ostensibly for civilian uses, these items can be used for police and military purposes.[52] The Carter administration did, however, reduce the value of licenses for private sales of items actually on the Munitions List to $4.6 milllion in 1978, $25,000 in 1979, and none in 1980.[53]

Box 5.7

Some Known U.S.-South African Police Links

1971:   South African police received U.S. training materials for fixed and moving physical surveillance procedures and techniques.

1975:   Agents of the U.S. Drug Enforcement Administration conducted an intensive course for 130 police in the South African Police College on the "latest investigative methods and techniques," which typically include courses on surveillance, undercover operations, raid planning, interview and interrogation techniques, and the development and use of informers.

1976:   South African police visited the United States to study riot-control methods.

1982:   Chicago police hosted a South African police major in a law-enforcement training course on police-media relations.

1983:   A Detroit police representative visited several police installations in South Africa. South African police representatives attended the Detroit convention of the International Association of Chiefs of Police, which has 31 members from South Africa and Namibia. With U.S. State Department approval, the U.S. Drug Enforcement Administration trained a South African vice and drug officer in the United States.

Sources: NARMIC/American Friends Service Committee, *Automating Apartheid: U.S. Computer Exports to South Africa and the Arms Embargo* (Philadelphia: AFSC, 1982), and "Military Exports to South Africa—a Research Report on the Arms Embargo" (Philadelphia: AFSC, 1984).

Under the Constructive Engagement Policy, the Reagan administration broadened the category of dual-use items that could be sent to South Africa to include trucks, computers, planes, and chemicals banned by previous administrations. In addition, it authorized licenses for $28.3 million worth of items on the Munitions List for 1981-83, more than the total value of commercial military materials shipped to Pretoria over the previous 30 years. By contrast, in the same three-year period, U.S. firms received permission to ship military exports valued at only slightly more than $1 million to each of South Africa's Front Line neighbors. (In the same period, the State Department authorized only $20.3 million worth of commercial arms sales to El Salvador, Honduras, and Guatemala, combined.)

The U.S. military has also maintained its direct ties with the South African military. In 1981, Jeane Kirkpatrick, the chief U.S. delegate to the United Nations, received a visiting South African delegation that included Lt. Gen. T.W. Van der Westhuizan, the head of his country's military intelligence service. Although the U.S. State Department later termed this a regrettable mistake, the relationship between the two countries' military establishments persists. The Silvermine communications intelligence center near Capetown, for example, routinely sends intelligence to the National Security Agency headquarters in Maryland. The United States reportedly also provides South Africa with intelligence on black African governments and organizations in exchange for the use of landing facilities by U.S. intelligence-gathering aircraft.[54]

Nuclear Weapons?

Over the years, despite the fact that South Africa has refused to sign the Nuclear Non-Proliferation Treaty, previous administrations permitted the sale of nuclear technology to South African parastatals.[55] This enabled them to process and utilize the extensive uranium deposits available both in South Africa and Namibia. Many experts have concluded that by the 1970s the Pretoria regime had already taken advantage of this to acquire the capability to produce nuclear weapons.[56]

The Constructive Engagement Policy, however, went further to permit U.S. firms to sell technologies that might contribute directly to South Africa's nuclear-weapons capacity. For example, the U.S. government has approved export licenses to U.S. firms to sell highly sophisticated computer systems to South Africa which could be used in nuclear-weapons production.[57] The State Department has also licensed Westinghouse to provide technical and maintenance services to nuclear-power installations in South Africa, enhancing South Africa's capability to produce such weapons.In 1981, the Reagan administration permitted two U.S. firms, Edlo International Inc. and Swuco, to sell enriched fuel to South Africa.[58]

By contributing to South Africa's capability to process uranium for nuclear uses, the United States has helped South Africa to use nuclear power as a means of reducing its dependence on imported oil and hydroelectricity produced in neighboring countries. In addition, South Africa is in a position to sell processed uranium to would-be powers like Pakistan, Taiwan, Argentina, Israel, and Brazil as a means of influencing them to support South Africa in the arena of international opinion. Such sales would undermine the effect of the Nuclear Non-Proliferation Treaty, which South Africa had refused to sign.

Uranium Sales

The U.S. government has permitted U.S. firms to purchase crude uranium from South Africa, some of which may come from Namibia in violation of U.N. policy, for use in their nuclear power plants. After 1978, the U.S. nuclear industry imported increasing amounts of uranium from South Africa, reaching 3,451 metric tons in 1983.[59] Major buyers included Baltimore Gas and Electric, Yankee Atomic, and Carolina Light and Power. In 1981, the largest U.S. buyer of South African uranium, Baltimore Gas and Electric, purchased 45 percent of the uranium the United States imported from South Africa.[60]

In addition to importing uranium directly from South Africa, U.S. firms purchase it from other countries that do not report the country of origin. Some of these supplies may come from South Africa. For example, in the early 1980s Boston Edison considered purchasing uranium from Rio Tinto Zinc's South African affiliate, Palabora. But a member of the utility's board objected to the use of South African uranium. Boston Edison then signed a contract with another non-South African affiliate of Rio Tinto Zinc for delivery from 1985 to 1990 of approximately 750 tons of U308. But the contract did not specify the origin of uranium; it could be mined in South Africa or elsewhere.[61]

The expansion of U.S. purchases of uranium from South Africa has had two major implications. First, it has provided foreign exchange that South Africa needed to import the expensive technologies required for its military machine, including nuclear weapons. Second, in flagrant violation of U.N. Decree No. 1 on Namibia,[62] South Africa, in collaboration with Rio Tinto Zinc and other transnational corporations, has extracted from Namibia much of the uranium it sells. Thus, U.S. companies by importing uranium sold by firms like Rio Tinto Zinc may be further supporting and legitimizing South Africa's illegal control of Namibia.

Ironically, by contrast, the U.S. government has utilized the Trade with the Enemy Act to deny U.S. private voluntary agencies like Oxfam America permission to ship seeds, medical supplies, and agricultural implements to such countries as Vietnam and Kampuchea, both struggling to overcome the destructive impact of years of war.[63] Meanwhile, the Constructive Engagement Policy in southern Africa has permitted U.S. firms to sell technologies that have contributed to South Africa's military build-up in general and its nuclear capacity in particular.

SUMMARY

In the early 1980s, U.S. foreign policy had the effect of strengthening the South African minority government. On one hand, the Reagan administration refused to support the efforts of black leaders, as well as a majority of the member states of the United Nations, to impose a boycott to end trade with and investment in South Africa. Despite widespread international and domestic criticism, the

U.S. administration continued to oppose divestiture by U.S. firms. Yet the evidence shows that even when they endorse the Sullivan Principles, U.S. firms fail to take significant measures to reduce the negative consequences of apartheid. For the first time, furthermore, the U.S government has granted financial assistance to small numbers of blacks inside South Africa, a measure which may serve to steer the growing popular resistance into a path of accommodation with the *status quo*.

On the other hand, in violation of the U.N. sanctions prohibiting the sale of military equipment to the regime, the U.S. government began to grant licenses to U.S. firms to sell not only military equipment, but also sophisiticated technology that could strengthen the regime's nuclear capacity. And it permitted U.S. firms to purchase uranium, some of which—in violation of U.N. resolutions—may well have come from Namibia.

In short, U.S. government policy toward South Africa has worked contrary to the black majority's efforts to abolish the apartheid system. Rather, it has strengthened the minority's military capacity to enforce apartheid and destabilize its neighbors.

Forty thousand people attended this mass funeral of victims of the Vaal Triangle unrest in South Africa in 1984. (Photo by *Rand Daily Mail* [Johannesburg] Sept. 17, 1984)

Alexandra, on the far outskirts of Johannesburg, is one of the black "townships" where the law requires blacks to live if they have permits to work in white areas (United Nations Photo/151629)

CHAPTER SIX

The United States
and South Africa's Neighbors

U.S. POLICY

The second strand of the Constructive Engagement Policy involved stabilizing
the region to give South Africa's rulers time to accommodate the forces pressing
for change within a framework consistent with U.S. interests.[1] In carrying out
this policy, the Reagan administration has pressured neighboring states to
acquiesce to South Africa's diplomatic initiatives.

Anthony Lewis, writing in *The New York Times*, reported that the United
States had become engaged in "an intricate and ambitious diplomatic venture,
one that could affect all of southern Africa." The United States and South
Africa, he pointed out, were "acting separately but in close coordination" to
seek solutions to a number of regional problems, including that of Namibia.[2]

By 1984, Angola and South Africa had negotiated an agreement by which
Africa, he pointed out, were "acting separately but in close coordination" to
seek solutions to a number of regional problems, including that of Namibia.[2]
SWAPO. The agreement, it was hoped, was a prelude to the long-stalled U.N.
elections. Mozambique and South Africa had signed the Nkomati Accord, by
which Mozambique agreed to ban activities of the African National Congress
(ANC) of South Africa on its soil in return for South Africa's pledge to end
support for the Mozambique National Resistance Movement (MNR).

Some claimed that Nkomati symbolized a new era of peace throughout
southern Africa—the ultimate success of the Reagan administration's Constructive Engagement Policy. Others, with more understanding of the historical
forces at work in the region, considered it little more than a lull in the storm.
This chapter discusses:

★ The Reagan administration's rationale for the regional Constructive
Engagement Policy.

★ The way the Reagan administration has stepped up pressure on the
independent states of the region through pre-existing channels, including the
International Monetary Fund, food aid, radio broadcasts, and the United
Nations.

★ The consequences of the U.S. pressures as applied to three members states
of the Southern African Development Coordination Conference (SADCC).

Like the first strand of the Constructive Engagement Policy described in
Chapter 5, the second is built on a growing involvement of the U.S. government

in the region. As Table 1.2 shows, this is reflected in the expansion of U.S. loans and grants to the southern African states since they achieved independence. In the mid-1970s, after Mozambique and Angola had won independence, the Western powers, led by a succession of U.S. statesmen, starting with then-Secretary of State Henry Kissinger, called for majority rule to install "moderate" black governments in southern Africa. Voicing abhorrence of white racism, they sought to meet the people's demands for freedom without altering the underlying structures that had made the region so profitable for foreign investors.

The Rationale

In 1980, before becoming assistant secretary of state, Dr. Chester Crocker had spelled out the arguments lying behind what would become the Reagan administration's southern African policy:

> U.S. officials correctly insist that the timetable and the blueprint for change in South Africa are not for outsiders to impose. Yet without Western engagement in the region as a whole, it will not be possible to assure that South Africans are permitted to build their own future. The American stance must be firmly supportive of a regional climate conducive to compromise and accommodation in the face of concerted attempts to discredit evolutionary change and to exploit the inevitable ambiguity and periodic "incidents" that will accompany political liberalization.[2]

Three years later, Crocker pointed out the United States was "actively engaged in efforts to reduce and contain crossborder violence in southern Africa, whether that violence comes in the form of terrorist bombs shattering glass and ending lives in South Africa or South African military raids into neighboring states."[4]

Undersecretary of State Lawrence S. Eagleburger said: "The United States categorically reaffirms the principle that all states have a duty to refrain from tolerating . . . organized activities within their territory by guerrillas or dissidents planning acts of violence in the territory of another state."[5]

In 1985, Secretary of State George Shultz declared:

> Peace within South Africa . . . is directly linked to the question of regional peace. A society that feels immensely threatened by outside forces is less likely to loosen the controls at home. Nor can black states normalize their relations with their South African neighbor so long as there is no convincing movement away from apartheid.

These statements fundamentally misrepresent the nub of the conflict between South Africa and its neighbors. They put the South African regime's military destabilization of neighboring countries on a par with the efforts of the South African and Namibian liberation movements to free their own peoples. By focusing on "crossborder" violence, they overlook the fact that the South African and Namibian liberation movements from the outset have had firm support within South Africa and Namibia, as Chapter 4 showed.

Reagan administration officials have expressed concern for "East-West" tensions in southern Africa, citing a need to counter Soviet influence. This has been a major theme of the administration's foreign policy throughout the world. In southern Africa, presumably, the fear is that the Soviets might establish military bases, or gain control over strategic minerals, or threaten the sealanes used by supertankers to carry oil around the Cape.

It is true that several Front Line States have adopted socialist policies. They have taken this approach, not because of Soviet influence, but because they deem these policies the most appropriate for achieving their development goals. This does not necessarily mean that they will become puppets of the Soviet Union. Socialist countries elsewhere have followed their own paths, expanding trade with Western countries and even welcoming Western investments.

Even if "East-West" considerations are taken into account, however, Constructive Engagement is likely to be counterproductive in its own terms. By effectively reinforcing the system of apartheid, the policy fuels the very tensions in southern Africa that the Reagan administration says it wants to alleviate. And because in the long run apartheid is doomed, so is a diplomatic strategy that relies on minority-ruled South Africa as a regional bulwark against Soviet influence. Indeed, the more the United States bolsters South Africa at the expense of the neighboring states, the more acutely these countries are likely to perceive a need for aid from the Soviet Union or Cuba.

Peace?

The white rulers and the transnational corporations based in South Africa seek peace with the neighboring states on terms that permit the continued exploitation of the region's rich resources and low-cost labor. In addition, the neighboring states are an important market for goods manufactured in South Africa. But the anti-apartheid movement within South Africa, coupled with military action by the liberation forces, threatens continued minority rule and the investments of transnational corporate affiliates. The rising costs of South Africa's military campaigns, including the stationing of up to 100,000 troops in Namibia and repeated invasions of Angola, have imposed heavier tax burdens. Growing international demands for an end to trade and investment under conditions of apartheid, together with the international recession, jeopardize the markets for South Africa's exports and raise the costs of its essential imports.

OLD CHANNELS

In line with Crocker's perception of Constructive Engagement, the Reagan administration has endorsed the kind of "peace" in southern Africa which would enable South Africa to carry out diplomatic initiatives designed to preserve its dominant regional status. To implement this policy, the administration has utilized a number of channels developed since the end of World War II.[7]

The International Monetary Fund

One channel of U.S. influence in southern Africa has been the International Monetary Fund (IMF). Several studies have shown the United States plays an important role in shaping IMF decisions.[8] As the largest contributor to the IMF, the U.S. government controls a fifth of the votes governing IMF policy. The United States and the other major Western nations that have important interests in South Africa control 40 percent of the votes in the IMF. This gives them a decisive voice in shaping IMF policy for the region. No independent African state has as much as 1 percent of the vote in the Fund's policy-making fora. The southern African member states, combined with nine other sub-Saharan countries, cast only 2.88 percent of the total IMF votes.[9]

In 1982, M. Peter McPherson, head of the U.S. Agency for International Development (AID), explained to a congressional committee:

> U.S. support for the MDBs [multilateral development banks] should be designed to encourage emphasis on the private sector as a vehicle for growth. . . . U.S. representatives to replenishment negotiations for these kinds of development banks are stressing the importance the U.S. places upon MDB efforts to . . . foster more appropriate LDC [leser developed country] policies toward the private sector.[10]

In the 1970s, the IMF had begun to play a role in pressuring several member states of the Southern Africa Development Coordination Conference (SADCC) to give up their efforts to restructure their economies and to reduce their ties with South Africa. For SADCC member states (as for Third World countries elsewhere), the worsening conditions in the world economy had caused growing balance-of-payments deficits and increasing international debts which led several to request IMF assistance. As a condition for its help, however, the IMF required them to introduce austerity programs.[11] This meant cutting back on the social-welfare expenditures they had begun to make to improve the quality of life for the majority of their citizens.[12] At the same time, the IMF insisted that they reduce state activity designed to foster greater industrial growth to develop more balanced, integrated economies. In the case of Zambia, reports indicated the IMF influenced the government to resume shipping a large share of its exports and imports through South Africa.[13]

In Zimbabwe, according to a press report, IMF pressures to cut costs helped persuade the new government to call a moratorium on further efforts to implement land redistribution—despite the fact that the liberation war had centered on the land question.[14]

Beginning in 1981, Tanzania refused to comply with the IMF conditions. As a result, the IMF and the Western banking community blocked needed additional investment, credit, and aid to Tanzania. This contributed to severe shortages disrupting the national economy.[15]

At the same time, in 1982 the IMF allocated $1.1 billion to South Africa. Many African leaders objected. Some argued South Africa did not qualify for this assistance.[16] As Table 6.1 shows, the allocation raised South Africa's share to almost half of all purchases of IMF funds made by the southern African states since the IMF's inception in 1947.

At the 1984 annual IMF-World Bank meeting, official South African delegates and Western commercial bankers lobbied extensively to boost South Africa's role in the economic development of southern Africa. The South African press reported that the South African delegation was "delighted" with the outcome.[17]

In sum, while providing massive assistance to South Africa, IMF policies have worked against the efforts of independent countries of the region to reform their economies and reduce their dependence on South Africa.

Food Aid

Food aid, especially in the drought years of the early 1980s, provided another channel of U.S. influence in southern Africa. The available evidence suggests this assistance did not flow entirely from disinterested humanitarian motives.

In 1983, Crocker stated:

> Some old shibboleths badly need re-examination, including the notion that a country must physically produce its own food supplies, when in some cases it may be more efficient—and no less self-sufficient—to concentrate on cash crops and [buy] food with the money thus earned.[18]

This is quite a different concept of self-sufficiency from that advocated by the SADCC member states, who seek to reduce their dependence on food imports.

Certainly, their need for food aid made the southern African states more susceptible to pressures. For example, even though South African destabilization tactics and the drought destroyed crops and brought 200,000 southern Angolans to the brink of starvation, Angola (which for years refused to acquiesce to U.S. pressures to oust Cuban forces) received only a tiny and decreasing percentage of the total amount of food aid the United States shipped to southern Africa. Tanzania, after its government refused to curtail its criticisms of South Africa or accede to IMF pressure for "reform," received less than half as much food aid in 1983 as it had in 1981, despite the continuing drought. On the other hand, after Mozambique agreed in 1983 to negotiations that led to the 1984 Nkomati Accord, it began to receive significantly more food aid.

Table 6.1
Southern African States' Purchases of IMF Currencies, 1947-1984[a]
(in millions of SDRs[b] and as a percent of total IMF purchases by southern African states)

	1947-79	1980	1981	1982	1983	1984	Total 1947-84	% of total regional purchases
Lesotho	0.6	–	–	2.0	–	–	2.6	0.1
Malawi	35.9	24.4	30.0	14.7	34.2	37.8	177.0	4.6
South Africa	980.1	–	–	902.2	–	–	1882.3	49.3
Swaziland	1.9	–	–	4.3	10.0	–	16.2	0.4
Tanzania	138.0	40.0	15.9	1.7	6.1	–	202.3	5.3
Zambia	439.0	50.0	359.3	41.5	188.4	147.5	1225.7	32.1
Zimbabwe	c	32.5	37.5	–	153.6	89.9	313.4	8.2
Total Regional Purchases							3819.5	100.0

Notes

a. The principal way the Fund makes its resources available to members to meet balance-of-payments difficulties is by selling them the currencies of other members or SDRs in exchange for their own currencies. A member country to which the Fund sells currencies or SDRs is said to make "purchases" or "drawings" from the Fund. Once a member country has spent its quota of its own currency in the Fund, it must then obtain credit from the Fund to purchase additional currencies of other countries. Since the Fund's resources are of a revolving character to finance temporary balance-of-payments deficits, members must subsequently repurchase their currencies from the Fund with the currencies of other members or SDRs. The Fund reports monthly on each member country's purchases of currency.

   Angola did not join the IMF. Botswana was a member, but made no purchases. Mozambique joined the IMF in late 1984.

b. The IMF created SDRs or Special Drawing Rights in the 1970s to enable member states to purchase additional funds to offset balance-of-payments difficulties. The unit value of an SDR fluctuates with the weighted value of a package of five currencies. Hence, the SDR value of a specific allocation of funds, like that for South Africa in 1982, may vary from its U.S. dollar value.

c. Prior to independence, the minority regime ruling Zimbabwe did not receive IMF credit.

Source: International Monetary Fund, Table: "All Purchases," *International Financial Statistics* (Washington, D.C.: IMF, March 1985).

Table 6.2

U.S. Food (P.L. 480[a]) Aid to SADCC Member States by Fiscal Years, 1981-85
(in millions of U.S. dollars)

	1981	1982	1983	1984	1985
Angola[b]	3.7	2.3	1.2	2.6	1.9
Botswana	5.4	3.0	1.8	2.5	1.4
Lesotho	13.1	5.1	7.3	7.4	6.3
Malawi	2.9	0.1	0.2	0.0	0.0
Mozambique[c]	5.3	4.2	9.7	8.1	25.7
Swaziland	0.6	0.0	0.4	0.0	0.0
Tanzania	14.8	7.6	5.6	3.8	3.9
Zambia	10.0	7.0	12.4	15.1	10.0
Zimbabwe	0.0	4.0	6.8	6.7	9.6

Notes

a. P.L. 480 refers to Public Law 480, under which the United States provides free or low-cost surplus food to nations in need.
b. The figures for Angola for 1981-83 are from *Food For Peace (P.L. 480) Office Statistics* and *U.S. Department of State Report on Human Rights* (Washington, D.C.: February 1984).
c. The figures for Mozambique for 1981-83 are from the same sources as for Angola; but the P.L. 480 office supplied slightly different data: for 1983, $9.2 million and for 1984, $10.6 million (letter to Christ Root, Washington Office on Africa, May 14, 1984).

Sources: Unless otherwise noted, all figures for 1981-83 are from *Agency for International Development (AID) Congressional Presentation, Annex 1, Africa*, Fiscal Years '85 and '86. (Washington, D.C.: AID, 1984 and 1985). Table used for each country: "U.S. Overseas Loans and Grants—Obligations and Loan Authorizations". For 1984-85, U.S. State Department, "U.S. Assistance to Africa," AF/EPS: 2/06/85:1466 G:gg.

Daily Radio Broadcast Reports

In an effort to win regional support for its Constructive Engagement Policy, the Reagan administration increased its use of a third channel of influence, U.S. broadcast reports. Prior to 1982, the U.S. Information Agency's (USIA) daily report on the Middle East and Africa had ignored the releases issued by the South African-supported UNITA (Union for the Total Independence of Angola) and the MNR. In 1982, following President Reagan's appointment of a new director, the USIA began to use these releases, as well as circulating more anti-Zimbabwe reports.[19]

The United Nations

In the United Nations, the U.S. delegation prevented international condemnation of South Africa for its activities designed to destabilize its neighbors. It vetoed a Security Council resolution condemning the 1981 South African invasion of Angola.[20] It intervened to prevent South Africa being named in a

Security Council resolution condemning the 1981 attempted coup against the government of Seychelles. (Trials in South Africa later revealed that South African officials had actively supported the coup attempt.[21])

The United States also voted against the candidacy of Salim Salim, Tanzanian foreign minister, for secretary general of the United Nations although it had been widely assumed that the next secretary general would be African, and the Organization of African Unity had endorsed him.[22] Given Salim Salim's consistently critical position on South Africa's role in the region, as secretary general he undoubtedly would have fostered further criticism.

THREE CASE STUDIES

The U.S. administration engaged in diplomacy to influence several neighboring states to acquiesce to South African diplomatic overtures. Three case studies— Zimbabwe, Angola, and Mozambique—show the impact of these efforts.

Zimbabwe

U.S. aid to Zimbabwe during the three years after it attained independence provides one illustration of how Constructive Engagement worked. In his 1983 address, Crocker emphasized U.S. efforts to "counsel restraint and dialogue between South Africa and other neighbors such as Lesotho and Zimbabwe, complementing and reinforcing their own efforts to arrive at a workable basis of coexistence."[23]

Early Promises
In the Zimbabwean case, these U.S. efforts had a history. In the 1970s, the United States, as well as Britain (whose colony Zimbabwe had been), had promised that a new black Zimbabwean government would receive large sums—the Kissinger Plan proposed $1.5 billion[24]—for reconstruction and resettlement. Those promises apparently helped to persuade the Front Line States and the Zimbabwean liberation forces to accept the Constitution negotiated at Lancaster House.

The Lancaster House Constitution
The Lancaster House Constitution contained many flaws.[25] First, it did not guarantee one-person-one-vote. In an entrenched clause that could not be set aside until 1990, it reserved 20 percent of the seats in Parliament for the white minority that constituted less than 3 percent of the population.

Second, it attempted to preserve the inherited pattern of land ownership by requiring the new government to pay compensation for all the land it acquired for resettlement of the rural black population at a "market price" determined on a willing-seller-willing-buyer basis—as if the liberation war had never occurred. This requirement also applied to efforts to nationalize the holdings of the foreign corporations, which owned about 70 percent of the assets in the "modern" sector.

Third, the Constitution effectively obliged the new government to retain the white civil servants employed by the previous regime. They were to receive full salaries until their normal retirement, as well as the pensions introduced by the former government. All these payments would be remittable in foreign currency. The prospective costs were so high that the government opted to keep most of these civil servants in place.

Thus, the Lancaster House Constitution, negotiated under pressures exerted on the Zimbabwean liberation movement by both Britain and the recalcitrant minority regime, obstructed the new government's efforts to implement the basic reforms required to end institutionalized poverty.

The Mugabe Election Victory

Robert Mugabe and his supporters in ZANU-PF (the Zimbabwe African National Union-Patriotic Front) won a clear majority in the first election with 57 percent of the votes. The other liberation party, Joshua Nkomo's ZAPU (the Zimbabwean African People's Union, which for the election took for itself the name Patriotic Front) won another 23 percent. Despite the constraints inherent in the Constitution, the two parties together had the potential voting power to control the new Parliament and institute sweeping new reforms.

After the Mugabe government took office, it organized ZIMCORD (Zimbabwe Conference on Reconstruction and Development), an international conference at which it hoped the Western powers would fulfill their pledges to provide the large sums required to finance postwar reconstruction. But, in almost all cases, the dollar amounts finally provided fell far short of those promised.[26]

The Reality of U.S. Aid

Although the United States became the largest donor to Zimbabwe, its aid package from 1980 to 1984—including loans—totaled only about $250 million.[27] Moreover, although the major share was directed to agriculture, it was not to be used for resettlement on former commercial farms, despite the mid-1970s pledge of then-Secretary of State Kissinger and the Zimbabwean government's clearly expressed preference for resettling peasants on those lands. Instead, U.S. aid policy focused on encouraging the new government to develop the Communal Areas.[28] These were the former Tribal Trust Lands, the infertile, overcrowded, inadequately watered half of the national land area on which the former government had forced the black peasant population to live. Yet the new government could do little to make most of the Communal Areas viable unless at least half the peasants relocated on the underutilized half of the lands previously allocated to white farmers. The three-year drought underscored this reality when thousands of Zimbabwean peasant families in the Communal Areas struggled to survive on limited relief rations.

The United States provided another major share of its aid to Zimbabwe through the Commodity Import Program.[29] This provided private Zimbabwean firms (including transnational corporations' local affiliates) with U.S. credit to buy U.S. exports of machinery and equipment. On the surface, this appeared laudable. Closer analysis revealed, however, that existing industries in Zimbabwe capable of producing the kinds of machines and equipment being imported under the program now found their markets eliminated.[30] In other words, while the Commodity Import Program created a market for U.S. exports in the early 1980s, it did so by infringing on the markets of existing industries in Zimbabwe itself. This contributed to rising unemployment which further swelled the population of the Communal Lands.

Zimbabwe's new rulers took over an economy burdened by heavy costs of postwar reconstruction. Yet they sought to improve the lot of the black majority by allocating increased funds to long-neglected social-welfare programs. At the same time, in the three years following independence, along with the rest of southern Africa, they faced the combined impact of drought, international recession, and South African destabilization maneuvers. Like their neighbors, they confronted mounting balance-of-payments deficits and growing international debt. They called on the IMF for help. It imposed the typical set of conditions: cuts in government spending and reduced state intervention.[31] The IMF sought to reopen the economy—effectively protected during the 15 years of the Unilateral Declaration of Independence—to the supposed benefits of international market forces. The resulting measures contributed to halting initial efforts at land reform. The government reduced social-welfare expenditures and cut back subsidies and price controls. Doubled interest rates prohibitively raised the costs of borrowing for small, emergent businessmen and peasant farmers. Instead of altering the inherited tax program to increase revenues from the transnational firms' high profits, the government raised general sales taxes to levels even higher than those prevailing under the previous regime. The government introduced a floating devaluation, under which the value of the Zimbabwean dollar plummeted from Z$1.00 = US$1.40 in 1982 to Z$1.00 = US$0.75 in 1984. The resulting rise in the cost of imported machinery, equipment, and materials spurred inflation and reduced real incomes, particularly for peasants, wage earners, and the growing numbers of unemployed.[32]

At the end of 1983, following an official U.S. declaration that it would refuse to aid any country that strongly disagreed with it in the United Nations, the United States cut its aid to Zimbabwe by a third. It took this action shortly after the Zimbabwean government announced its nonaligned position relating to the Soviet downing of a Korean jet, and criticized the U.S. invasion of Grenada.[33] The 1985 U.S. aid pledge to Zimbabwe was 15 percent less than in 1984.[34] This reduction came despite the three-year drought and the influx of tens of thousands of Mozambican refugees.

Thus, far from fulfilling past pledges, U.S. aid to Zimbabwe, together with the IMF's conditions for assistance, served to hamper the new government's attempts to achieve fundamental reform. Despite their nation's extensive natural resources, the people of Zimbabwe, like those of the other independent southern African states, confronted mounting unemployment and falling living standards.

Angola and the Namibian Negotiations

The U.S. Stance

U.S. actions relating to Angola and the liberation struggle in Namibia illuminate other aspects of the impact of the Reagan administration's Constructive Engagemanet Policy in southern Africa. Commenting on Namibia in his 1983 speech, Crocker maintained the administration sought to "bring about conditions that would make it politically possible for South Africa to relinquish control of this territory."[35] In other words, the U.S. government adopted Pretoria's position that the issue in Namibia was not South Africa's refusal to comply with U.N. Resolution 435 (calling for South African withdrawal and elections under U.N. supervision). Crocker added: "The South African Government's position on this issue reflects its assessments of prospects for its own future security in the region."

The Cuban Issue and U.S. Pressures

In the context of Constructive Engagement, the Reagan administration proposed making the withdrawal of Cuban troops from Angola a precondition for Namibian independence. (Former U.S. Ambassador to the United Nations Donald McHenry claimed that South Africa had been on the verge of granting independence to Namibia when the Reagan administration proposed this policy.) The South African government then adopted a more aggressive stance by sending troops in to occupy southern Angola, purportedly to pursue SWAPO forces. When questioned about the Cuban troop issue during a congressional hearing, Crocker stated: "From our standpoint, we made no bones about it, we don't see any reason why there ought to be communist forces in Africa, none whatsoever."[36]

The Cubans had come in response to Angola's request for assistance to defend itself against the first of what became a series of South African invasions. Citing that request, other independent states in the region contended that the issue of Namibian independence should be considered separately from that of the Cubans' withdrawal.[37]

Yet Crocker persisted in arguing that the successful outcome of U.S. negotiations with Angola on the Cuban troop issue "would open the way to South Africa's implementation of the international agreements we have reached for Namibia's transition to independence."[38]

For years, however, South Africa had stalled the international negotiations that aimed to implement the U.N. resolution calling for Namibian independence. Time after time, when an agreement appeared imminent, the South African government broke off talks. As already noted above, France withdrew from the

Western "Contact Group" in 1983, declaring that the issue of Cuban troops prolonged the negotiations and served no useful function.[39]

In early 1984, with its economy disrupted by South African invasions and by sabotage from the South African-supported UNITA, the Angolan government agreed to begin phased withdrawal of Cuban troops on two conditions: 1) South Africa would remove all its troops from southern Angola; and 2) South Africa would grant Namibian independence with free elections as called for by the United Nations.[40] Box 6.1 lists U.S. pressures that preceded the Angolan government's decision to agree to phased withdrawal.

The South African and Angolan governments agreed to cooperate with the United States to create a joint monitoring commission to supervise withdrawal

Box 6.1

Examples of U.S. Pressures on Angola

★ From 1981, the CIA, acting through third parties, began to provide substantial aid to UNITA in Angola, an organization heavily supported by South Africa.[a] The aid has included money, arms, and equipment.[b]

★ Gen. Vernon Walters, a former deputy CIA director, flew to Luanda several times to attempt to persuade Angola to agree to the withdrawal of Cuban troops.[c]

★ In 1981, the United States vetoed a U.N. Security Council resolution condemning South Africa's large-scale armored invasion of Angola and occupation of a large area in the southern provinces.[d]

★ In August 1982, as South Africa sought to extend its military control in southern Angola, President Reagan sent a letter classified as "secret" to President Nyerere of Tanzania, chairman of the Front Line States, urging him to accept the "linkage" of a Namibian settlement to withdrawal of Cuban troops from Angola. He suggested if the "linkage" were not accepted soon, the United States would cease to press for implementation of the U.N. plan for Namibia.[e]

★ "USIA Daily Report: Middle East and Africa" increased by more than 300 percent its broadcast of destabilization-style propaganda from UNITA sources.[f]

★ A former UNITA public relations agent joined the U.S. mission to the United Nations.[g]

★ Crocker met with Jonas Savimbi, UNITA head, and reportedly sought to persuade Angola's MPLA government that UNITA should be included in preparations for a nonaggression pact between South Africa and Angola.[h]

★ In June 1985, a pro-Reagan U.S. lobbying group, Citizens for America, sponsored a meeting in Jamba, Angola, attended by representatives of of South African troops to ensure that SWAPO (the Namibian liberation forces) did not operate out of Angolan territory. Bypassing the United Nations—which remained nominally responsible for the decolonization process—the United States established a liaison office in Windhoek, Namibia's capital, to oversee the process.[41]

But even after this agreement, South Africa stalled on withdrawing its troops from Angola. In early 1985, the United States closed its liaison office in Windhoek and announced it would conduct future monitoring through the U.S. Embassy in Pretoria.[42] Finally, in April 1985, South Africa announced it had withdrawn the last of its troops from Angola.[43] But this announcement did not mark the end of South Africa's military involvement in Angola or its delaying tactics in Namibia. In May 1985, Angolan forces captured a band of South

---

UNITA and of anti-government groups from Nicaragua, Laos, and Afghanistan. The delegates announced the establishment of an alliance called the Democratic International. The organizer, Lewis E. Lehrman, stated that the conference was privately sponsored and that he was not a presidential envoy; but he read to the delegates a letter, supporting the initiative, that he said came from President Reagan.[i]

Sources

a. Gordon Winter, *Inside BOSS* (London: Lane, 1982), p. 540; John Stockwell, *In Search of Enemies* (New York: Norton, 1978), discusses the CIA role in support of UNITA in the 1970s.

b. "Uneasy over secret war," *Time Magazine*, May 16, 1983; "Secret Warriors: The CIA is Back in Business," *Newsweek*, October 10, 1983.

c. Sean Gervasi, interview with African officials, August and November 1983, reported in Sean Gervasi, "Southern Africa: Dr. Crocker's Secret War," paper prepared for Sanctions Working Group (New York: photocopy, 1984).

d. *New York Times*, September 4, 1981.

e. *Jeune Afrique*, October 27, 1982.

f. Elaine Friedland, "The Reagan Administration's Policy Toward the Southern African Development Coordination Conference," paper prepared for delivery at the 1984 annual Meeting of the International Studies Association, March 27-31, 1984, p. 13.

g. Seymour Maxwell Finger, "The Reagan-Kirkpatrick Policies and the United Nations," *Foreign Affairs*, Vol. 62, Winter 1984, p. 444.

h. "Savimbi Had 'Meetings in S. Africa'," *Daily Telegraph* (Britain), June 25, 1984. See also "South Africa seeks full peace pact with Angola," *Guardian* (Manchester), July 4, 1984; "Resisting 'Pax Pretoriana'," *West Africa* (Nigeria), July 9, 1984.

i. Alan Cowell, "Rebel Units Sign Anti-Soviet Pact," *New York Times*, June 6, 1985; *Africa News* (Durham, NC), June 17, 1985.

African commandos who had been sent, their leader reportedly said, to conduct economic sabotage against the installations of the U.S. firm, Gulf Oil.[44]

South Africa's chief of state, P.W. Botha, declared unilaterally in April 1985 that his government was creating an administration to draft a constitution and to administer some of Namibia's internal affairs. South Africa apparently took this initiative without the blessing of the Reagan administration. Bernard Kalb, a U.S. State Department spokesman, asserted: "Any purported transfer of power that might take place now or in the future to bodies established in Namibia by South Africa is null and void." He added that the Botha announcement would not affect Namibian negotiations or agreements achieved so far.[45] As this book went to press, the outcome of further negotiations remained uncertain.

Pressures on Mozambique and the Nkomati Accord

U.S. Food Aid

The United States exerted similar pressures on Mozambique to enter negotiations with South Africa. In 1983, Crocker told an American audience that the United States had "moved to rebuild our relations with Mozambique . . . while responding to that nation's desperate economic situation with food aid." In the course of that effort, he said, "We have quietly encouraged bilateral talks between Mozambique and South Africa . . . [and] sent an Ambassador to

Box 6.2

Details of U.S. Policy Toward Mozambique

*March 1981: The United States revoked food aid after Mozambique expelled U.S. embassy officials for alleged spying attempts. Crocker headed a mission to Mozambique to review U.S.-Mozambique relations.[a]

*June 1982: The U.S. Information Agency began to broadcast MNR propaganda reports on Mozambique.[b]

*1983: Mozambique became one of the largest recipients of U.S. food aid in Africa. Although large numbers of people in Mozambique faced starvation and thousands had already died from lack of food, the Reagan administration did not increase food aid to that country until the Mozambican government had agreed to negotiate a nonaggression pact with South Africa.[c]

*1984: In FY 1984 (beginning October 1, 1983), the United States provided the following food commodities to Mozambique, costing $10 million—$17 million with transport costs—through the P.L. 480 program: 5,160 tons of dairy products

Maputo to help foster this fragile dialogue between our two states."[46]

But Crocker did not tell his audience that South Africa, by its support of the MNR's efforts to destabilize Mozambique, had contributed to the conditions leading to the uprooting and starvation of tens of thousands of Mozambicans.[47]

Mozambique and the ANC

The South Africans claimed that the Mozambican government had permitted the ANC to have military camps in Mozambique. But the ANC denied this:

> Sensitive to matters of security for the People's Republic of Mozambique, we did not ask for and have never had training camps on Mozambican territory. The apartheid regime cannot name a single ANC combatant who has ever crossed into South Africa at any point on the long Mozambique-South African border. The ANC has honoured the agreement reached with the FRELIMO leadership that this border should not be used for crossing either cadres or materials.[48]

On March 16, 1984, Samora Machel, president of Mozambique, and P.W. Botha, prime minister of South Africa, signed what has become known as the Nkomati Accord. The key point of the Accord is contained in Article Three, which reads:

> The High Contracting Parties shall not allow their respective territories, territorial

---

	by government-to-government agreement; 7,000 tons of grain, through the World Food Program; 31,340 tons of grain, by government-to-government agreement.[d]
*1984:	After the signing of the Nkomati Accord, the U.S. Congress lifted its ban on development aid to Mozambique with an initial allocation of $500,000.[e]
*1985:	Projected food aid increased to $25.7 million.[f]

Sources
a. See *New York Times*, March 14, 26, 29, 1981.
b. Elaine Friedland, "The Reagan Administration's Policy Toward the Southern African Development Coordination Conference," op. cit., p. 13.
c. Sean Gervasi, Interviews with Mozambique officials, November 1983, and congressonal sources, January 1984, cited in Gervasi, "Southern Africa: Dr. Crocker's Secret War," paper presented for Sanctions Working Group (New York: photocopy, 1984).
d. Data on U.S. food aid is from letter from P.L. 480 office, Washington, D.C. to Chris Root of the Washington Office on Africa, May 1984.
e. *International Herald Tribune*, June 13, 1984.
f. See Table 6.2

waters or air space to be used as a base, thoroughfare, or in any other way by another state, government, foreign military forces, organizations or individuals which plan or prepare to commit acts of violence, terrorism or aggression against the territorial integrity or political independence of the other or may threaten the security of its inhabitants.[49]

Other Pressures on Mozambique

U.S. pressures were among a number of factors that preceded Mozambique's signing of the Nkomati Accord. The drought, the international recession, and South Africa's direct and surrogate destabilization tactics had taken their toll on Mozambique's economy.[50]

Mozambique had paid a heavy price over the years for its support of the Zimbabwean liberation movement. The estimated cost of its implementation of the U.N. boycott of the Smith regime alone totaled $556 million. (See Table 6.3.) Sabotage by the South African-supported MNR had cost another estimated $3.8 billion. By 1984, Mozambique's debt to Western governments and banks, as well as to international financial organizations, totaled $1.4 billion. In addition, after Mozambique's independence, South Africa had laid off some 80,000 Mozambican mine workers. They returned to Mozambique, adding to the growing numbers of unemployed and reducing remittances of foreign exchange to the country.[51]

Table 6.3
Estimate of Direct Losses and Reduction of Income Suffered by Mozambique Since It Attained Independence in 1975[a]

Description of Action	Costs (US $Million)
1. Rhodesian sanctions and aggressions, March 1976 to February 1980	$556
2. Flood damage, Inkomati, Limpopo, 1977	$34
3. Zambezi flood, 1978	$64
4. Effects of South African destabilization (reduced railway port traffic, $248) (Cancellation of mine agreements, $2,647) (Reduction of mine employment, $568) (Direct and surrogate aggression, $333)	$3,796
5. Drought damage, 1982-3	$154
6. Increased oil prices since 1975	$819
7. Reduced export income due to drought, worsened terms of trade, destabilization	$131
Total	$5,554

Note
a. These estimates exclude the financial consequences of the effects of the colonial economy, war devastation, dependency, and recession, as well as economic sabotage of enterprises, equipment, and vehicles when settlers left after independence.

Source: People's Republic of Mozambique, (untitled) National Planning Commission, 1984.

As a result of the Accord, Mozambique hoped not only for an end to MNR disruption, but also for stepped-up trade through Maputo Harbor, the boosting of its tourist industry, and the sale of its surplus Cabora Bass electricity.[52]

After the Accord was signed, U.S. government agencies and private voluntary organizations using U.S. government funds substantially increased their activities in Mozambique. Critics suggested, however, that this aid might serve to restrict Mozambique's attempts to fundamentally restructure its economy. For example, Joseph Hanlon, author of *Mozambique: The Revolution Under Fire*, argued that the new aid posed new problems for the Mozambican government.[53] He pointed out that U.S. aid agencies directed agricultural assistance only to the larger peasant farmers. These would be more likely to resist the proposed transition toward producer cooperatives.

Hanlon added that the Western governments and transnational banks had refused to grant credit to Mozambique until its government "agreed to a comprehensive package including joining the IMF and negotiating a settlement with South Africa." This, he maintained, had hindered the Mozambican government's implementation of the 1983 Fourth Party Congress decision to provide increased consumer goods in the rural areas, higher agricultural producer prices, and more support for small private business.

South Africa's Need for the Accord

South Africa, too, had reasons for seeking the Accord. Its rulers hoped to relieve pressure on its overcrowded ports, obtain new outlets for its tourist enterprises, and salvage its electric-power grid, the capacity of which had been devastatingly lowered by drought and ANC sabotage inside South Africa. But more importantly, as Finance Minister Owen Harwood stated, South Africa— (caught) "in one of the most difficult phases since the Great Depression"— hoped to gain greater access to markets for its surplus industrial products in Mozambique and neighboring countries.[54] Pretoria probably also hoped to curb Mozambique's vocal support for the liberation of South Africa itself.

The top officials of leading transnational corporations welcomed the Nkomati Accord. Major South African business leaders—Harry Oppenheimer and Gaven Relly of the Anglo American Group, Donald Gordon of Standard Bank, and John Maree of the Barlow Rand Group, among others—attended the signing ceremony. The industrial share prices on the Johannesburg Stock Exchange made a record jump following the Accord. Lonrho, the largest nonmining finance house in South Africa, sponsored a television show praising the Accord. Prime Minister Botha said, "I have a vision of the nations of southern Africa working together in every field of human endeavor . . . a veritable constellation of states."[55]

Inside South Africa

Inside South Africa, anti-apartheid leaders responded to the pact by challenging the government to show its good faith by negotiating with the people of South Africa. Addressing a rally of more than 1,000 people in Laudium, near Pretoria,

Dr. Allan Boesak, a leader of the United Democratic Front, asserted that the signing of the Accord would usher in a difficult period of increased repression for internal anti-apartheid forces:

> But we must be strong. . . . We must tell this government, if you can make agreements with Mozambique and Angola, then why not with the people of this land. If you will not do so now, we will force you to one day. No matter how many deals you make with Mozambique, the final deal must be made with us.[56].

The Uncertain Outcome

Whether the Nkomati Accord would lead to the results either side hoped for, or even to peace of any kind, remained uncertain. Mozambique's government began implementation by requiring most ANC personnel—whether students, diplomatic personnel, or refugees—to leave the country.[57] All other South African refugees were sent to camps supervised by the U.N. High Commissioner for Refugees some distance from Maputo. The government allowed the ANC to retain only a 10-person diplomatic office.

Another immediate consequence of the Nkomati Accord was a more open repression of ANC supporters in neighboring Swaziland. The Swazi government announced that it had reached a similar, but secret accord with South Africa some two years earlier. Swazi police engaged in shootouts with ANC members seeking to escape a general roundup.[58]

Apart from the strong action taken by the Mozambican government against the ANC, however, the Accord did not have much immediate practical effect. South Africa donated 5 million apples to the children of Mozambique. Talk of South African businessmen launching all sorts of ventures in Mozambique flourished briefly, then faded away.[59]

The hoped-for diminution of MNR sabotage did not take place. The day after the Accord was signed, despite South Africa's claims that it had no influence over the MNR, the MNR radio station, operating out of South African territory, closed down. It re-opened shortly thereafter operating out of the Venda bantustan. Observers suggested that South Africa was hoping, thus, to force Mozambique to sign an accord with Venda. This would have constituted a form of recognition which the international community had refused to give. At the same time, inside Mozambique, the MNR attacked and blocked lorries carrying food to starving peasants in Tete Province. A few weeks later, it attacked trains and automobiles within a 50-mile radius of Maputo.[60]

There is little evidence that Pretoria applied the kind of pressure to push MNR members out of South Africa that Mozambique used on ANC members. A week after the signing of the Accord, as MNR activities intensified, the secretary general of MNR, Evo Fernandes, visited South Africa. By October 1984, Mozambique was objecting that South Africa had failed to keep its part of the bargain.[61]

For a year after the signing of the Nkomati Accord, the MNR continued attacking rural development projects in Mozambique. Although the rains came at last, relief agencies reported the main obstacle to recovery was the paralysis of transport, caused by the war and a fuel shortage. The U.N. Disaster Relief Organization reported armed rebels were disrupting emergency aid work in southern Mozambique, where more than 2 million people remained short of food. A Red Cross representative declared: "The war situation is the main cause of the disruption of transport." A British reported added: "And it seems that the situation is deteriorating."[62]

Relief workers reported that when they could get seeds and tools to the peasants, they responded well:

> In Machaze district where six months ago five or six children were dying every day, the maize is above the heads of those who have survived and morale has soared.
> But in other areas where seed is available, the war has prevented it being used in the most effective way. Communal villages for those made homeless by the rebels have to be sited where they can be defended. And that is often not where the best land is to be found.[63]

The U.S. administration continued to voice support for the Nkomati Agreement. The U.S. ambassador to Mozambique, Peter Jon de Vos, stated:

> We considered Nkomati a courageous step in which we served as an intermediary facilitating negotiations and at times pressuring each side.[64]

An American observer pointed out that the unraveling of the Nkomati agreement would "destroy the only modest triumph the Reagan administration could claim from its much heralded policy of 'constructive engagement.' "[65]

Following reports that South Africa, Malawi, and the Comoros Islands had provided the MNR with supplies, the U.S. State Department called on Mozambique's neighbors to cooperate to ensure that the MNR not receive assistance from their territories.[66]

Finally, on its first anniversary, the South African ministers of foreign affairs and defense, R.F. Botha and Magnus Malan, flew to Maputo to try to salvage the Nkomati Accord. Botha announced the dismissal or transfer away from the Mozambican border of members of the South African Defence Force suspected of sympathizing with the MNR. He disclosed that a South African police investigation, initiated in response to Mozambican complaints, had exposed a pro-MNR gang of forgers operating in South Africa, paying counterfeit U.S. dollars and South African rand for goods smuggled from Mozambique. He indicated that the same people flew arms and other supplies to the rebels. He added that the MNR was partly financed by "an international web of bankers, financiers, and businessmen."[67]

Whatever the outcome of these negotiations, the Nkomati Accord fit in with the U.S. Constructive Engagement Policy in that it gave the South African minority government more time to work out its long-term plans.

Africa's Response

The independent governments of the region, on the other hand, objected strongly to the pressures that led to the Nkomati Accord. President Kenneth Kaunda of Zambia termed the Accord a "setback for all of us," and declared: "We would be less than honest if we tried to glorify the situation. We accept we are weak—but if we glorify this [pact] we will be making a tactical error."[68]

The Botswana High Commissioner in London, Sam Mpuchane, pointed out that the Nkomati and Lusaka Accords with Mozambique and Angola were the result of "severe pressure," and added:

> The countries neighboring South Africa continue to experience tremendous economic, military and other forms of pressure aimed at forcing them to accommodate apartheid in one way or another. . . . My own country is known to have come under severe pressure by South Africa to sign an accord of the Nkomati type.[69]

Mpuchane refused to detail the pressures, but it is known that South Africa tried to prevent Botswana from going ahead with a new factory unless it signed, and that South Africa delayed renegotiating the revenue-sharing formula of the South Africa Customs Union to which Botswana belongs. While refusing to sign a nonaggression pact with South Africa, however, Botswana had already made it clear that it would not be used as a base for attacking any neighboring country.

On June 13, 1985, a South African military unit crossed the Botswana border to the capital of Gaborone and killed 16 people in a predawn raid. South African authorities stated that the attack was aimed at ANC insurgents. The dead included three women, a 5-year-old child, and a Sudanese refugee with Dutch citizenship; a 10-year-old child and another Dutch citizen were among six people injured. Botswana President Quett K.J. Masire said he believed the raid was in retaliation for Botswana's refusal to sign a nonaggression treaty with South Africa. The U.S. government, protesting the attack, recalled its ambassador to South Africa for consultations.[70]

In response to the Nkomati Accord, Ambassador Mohammed Sahnoun of Algeria, representing U.N. Special Committee Against Apartheid at a press conference held under the auspices of the Greater London Council, March 21, 1984, asserted:

> The Special Committee considers that, so long as apartheid persists in South Africa, the international community has a duty to impose comprehensive and mandatory sanctions against the racist regime in South Africa and assist the legitimate struggle of the dispossessed and oppressed peoples of South Africa and Namibia for self-determination, independence and freedom. It must condemn the actions of governments, transnational corporations and other interests which, through their collaboration

with the racist regime, encourage it in its racist, repressive, oppressive and aggressive policies. . . .

The Special Committee denounces the propaganda of the racist regime and its friends in favour of a relaxation of international action against apartheid. There can be no relaxation of international action against apartheid. There can be no relaxation so long as the racist regime, with its enormous military machine and nuclear build-up, seeks to perpetrate racist domination in South Africa and establish its hegemony in the region.

The Special Committee recognises that the liberation movements and all those fighting for freedom in South Africa . . . deserve even greater moral and material support at this critical time.

The Special Committee also calls for increased economic and other assistance to the Front Line States and Lesotho to overcome the effects of South African aggression and natural calamities.[71]

Oliver Tambo, president of the ANC, answering a journalist who asked what the ANC planned to do in view of the Nkomati pact, reiterated:

It is not true, it simply is not true, that the African National Congress has been launching attacks on South Africa from Mozambique. There is not a single occasion when we did. Of course, we went through Mozambique, an African country, as we have gone through other African countries to reach our own country. . . . But we launched nothing out of Mozambique.

What are we going to do about this nonaggression pact which forbids Mozambique to allow transit to South Africans going back to their own country? Well, we have had many problems like that in the past and that is how we relate to it—as a problem to be solved. What we do know is that our actions have been planned and staged in South Africa. . . . We will find a way of intensifying those actions. In fact this agreement is a challenge to the victims of the apartheid system. . . . Our people are ready to meet this challenge.[72]

SUMMARY

In implementing its Constructive Engagement Policy, the Reagan administration exerted pressures that served to slow down efforts designed to implement fundamental reconstruction and reduce the independent southern African states' dependence on South Africa.

The IMF, in which the United States exercises a major influence, imposed conditions for needed assistance, undermining SADCC member states' efforts to change inherited structures that institutionalized poverty. At the same time, the IMF allocated the greatest share of its funds in the region to aid the South African regime.

Concurrently, the Reagan administration utilized other pre-existing channels to influence regional policy. In increasing food aid as the drought spread, it favored some countries that followed its "recommendations" and not others pursuing a more independent course. It increasingly included in its daily broadcast reports propaganda emanating from South African-supported UNITA and MNR, and exercised its influence to thwart or reduce U.N. attempts to condemn South Africa's destabilization policies.

Examination of the available evidence from three cases—Zimbabwe, Angola, and Mozambique—illustrates the impact of these increased pressures. As the senior associate of the Carnegie Endowment for International Peace, Sanford Ungar, observed: "[T]he Reagan Administration has emerged as a sponsor—in some instances, a broker—of pacts South Africa has signed with neighboring black-ruled states."[73]

18. An African National Congress college in Tanzania where South African refugees learn the skills needed to rebuild their homeland. The college is named after a young African freedom fighter, who was hanged by the South African regime. (Photo by African National Congress)

CHAPTER SEVEN

Toward An Alternative U.S. Policy

U.S. INTERESTS

For years, the U.S. government has regarded southern Africa as a region of economic and geopolitical significance for the United States. U.S. transnational corporations have made substantial investments there, and the region remains an important source of raw materials for U.S. industry. Reagan administration officials have further characterized southern Africa as a potentially volatile focus of East-West confict and of rising Soviet influence.

As preceding chapters have shown, the administration's Constructive Engagement Policy has served to strengthen the white-minority government of Pretoria, and to impair efforts of independent black-ruled states to reduce their dependence on South Africa. Americans have to ask themselves whether this policy—which in effect has reinforced the system of apartheid—is really in the best interests of the United States and the majority of people in southern Africa. This chapter:

★ Reviews contrasting perspectives on southern Africa, as expounded by the Reagan administration and its critics.

★ Outlines the potential benefits of southern African liberation and development, both for people of the region and for Americans.

★ Proposes an alternative U.S. policy designed to hasten an end to apartheid and foster self-reliant development in southern Africa.

Divergent Perspectives

Asked following the Nkomati Accord for his assessment of Constructive Engagement, Assistant Secretary of State Chester Crocker revealed his perspective on the processes of liberation in southern Africa:

> . . . what has been accomplished in recent months after years of investment is a clear signal that sovereignty is a two-way street—boundaries are two-way things and that if there's to be violence in one direction, there is going to be violence in the other direction. So far so good. . . . [1]

Questioned on future U.S. policy relating to such organizations as the United Democratic Front (UDF) and the African National Congress (ANC) of South Africa, he said:

You cannot get government changes in the right direction unless you have a white majority for change and a power base. I don't think the biggest issue, which is what national political role does the African majority have, has yet moved. . . . I don't know what the next step may be, but it would clearly be consistent with what has already begun to have multiracial cabinet (sic) with groups other than whites. . . .[2]

Ignoring the failure of patient and peaceful protest to halt the imposition of apartheid, Crocker added:

The illusion that armed struggle will solve South Africa's problems has been dealt a body blow. . . . So has the illusion that South Africa faces a total onslaught from its neighbours. . . . In such circumstances, the role of the ANC is for the ANC to define as well as for the South African government to define. . . . We don't dismiss it nor do we endorse it.[3]

By constrast, ANC President Oliver Tambo, on the eve of a tour throughout Europe to explain his organization's efforts to win liberation, asserted: "Our conception of an effective struggle is a combination of political and armed struggle. We cannot rely solely on the gun, but it would be disastrous if we abandoned it. Nonviolence has brought about more, not less apartheid."[4] The ANC, Tambo said, would only negotiate with the regime after ensuring there would be "a serious dialogue, aimed at bringing about an end to apartheid." One condition would be participation in that dialogue by Nelson Mandela and other jailed ANC leaders.

Sanford Ungar, senior associate at the Carnegie Endowment for International Peace, asserted: "[J]udged on the record so far, 'Constructive Engagement' has hardly fulfilled its promises. Things are getting worse, not better, in South Africa, and despite some encouraging signs the region remains a tinderbox."[5]

Many American experts on southern Africa have urged the United States to pursue a policy fundamentally different from that of Constructive Engagement: one of recognizing the ANC and supporting the full liberation of the black majority of South Africa. Thomas G. Karis, professor of political science in the graduate program of the City University of New York, served as a foreign service officer in the American Embassy in Pretoria in the late 1950s. In an article in *Foreign Affairs*, after describing the history of the ANC, he argued:

In pressing South Africa to change direction, the United States cannot be ambiguous on a step that symbolizes such a change: the universal franchise. As recognition of an equal state in society, it has been endorsed by nearly every black leader in South Africa since the end of World War II. It is crucial to any settlement.

So is the role of the ANC. The United States can hardly stigmatize the ANC for its failure to eschew violence so long as the American alternative is unilateral change by a minority government based upon institutionalized violence. . . .

It follows that the United States should maintain contact not only with black groups tolerated by the government but also with the ANC. It should recognize the ANC as a legitimate political force whose guerrillas are freedom fighters entitled to treatment as prisoners of war under the Geneva Convention.[6]

Box 7.1

"South African Blacks Have Started to Rise Up"
By Beyers Naude*

The era of protest politics has been set aside in South Africa, replaced by the first phase of a militant revolutionary era. As one youth leader put it last year: "We are now at war. . . ."

Now the moment has arrived when the people, after decades and decades of silent suffering, have started to rise up—burning Government property, bombing the homes and businesses of black officials and other stooges, killing black police officers. Many of us who oppose the regime have foreseen these developments for years—and we believe that all of it could have been prevented if our pleas had been heard and heeded. But now that this situation has become a bitter reality, what awaits us?

South Africans, both black and white, will now have to agonize on how to resolve the crisis. Yet a serious obligation also rests on the most powerful and affluent country in the world to reconsider its responsibility toward South Africa. The United States must help us to minimize the emerging violence and maximize the chances of peaceful change.

To begin with, it must recognize that its lack of meaningful support for the South African black community and its struggle for liberation has created feelings of deep anger and animosity not only toward Washington and its policy of "constructive engagement," but also toward many American institutions and initiatives in South Africa. A word of serious warning has to be sounded to the American Government and people: Do not be surprised if the anger of black South Africans eventually turns to hatred or rejection of an American presence in Africa. Take cognizance now of these feelings of anger and bitterness and consider active steps to create a better attitude.

Second, Americans must disabuse themselve of the bogus concept that the root cause of the unrest is a Communist onslaught created and manipulated by Moscow. Please recognize that the policy of apartheid is the real threat to peace and stability in my country—and all of southern Africa.

Third, Americans should give more serious attention and weight to the pleas of the churches and other organizations in South Africa known for their opposition to apartheid. Please listen to these groups, which are trying to do everything in their power to bring about fundamental change by peaceful means or, where peaceful change is no longer possible, with a minimum of violence. Americans should also do all they can to support the efforts in their own country—by churches, academic institutions and other organizations—to press their Government to change its disastrous policy toward South Africa.

Fourth, the United States should terminate the policy of "constructive engagement" and initiate more meaningful pressures to hasten fundamental, nonviolent change. The whole disinvestment debate could soon become irrelevant if the current unrest in South Africa continues unabated—for before long it will have created such an unstable economic climate that overseas investors will be frightened to do business here. Before long, they will decide of their own free will not to support any further investment. They will conclude that the risk is too great and will initiate steps toward disinvestment.

Fifth, Washington should encourage Pretoria to ease up. I am convinced that no return to stability is possible here as long as the black leader Nelson Mandela and other political prisoners remain in prison. Americans must understand this, and they should demand the unconditional release of all political prisoners, the right of all exiles to return, the release of all detainees, the unbanning of the banned and the banished. They should also encouarge Pretoria to grant all South African people the freedom to elect their own leaders to initiate the process of negotiated change.

Sixth, the United States must make it clear that it does not want to see things get worse. The situation in South African may eventually become so ungovernable that the authorities would be forced to declare a state of emergency—and this could very easily lead to military rule of some kind. Such a development would have disastrous consequences for the cause of justice and peace in South Africa, fanning the flames of violent revolution and eventually leading the country into civil war. If the United States is sincere in its concern to prevent further violence, it should take effective steps now to prevent the establishment of military rule, with all its serious consequences not only for the black and white South Africans, but also for the rest of southern Africa.

Finally, the American Government and people must reassess their policy toward Namibia, Angola, Mozambique, and Zimbabwe—a policy that is creating increasing frustration, cynicism, and bitterness toward the United States in all these countries. The State Department clearly fears their Marxist tendencies and fears to lend them American support. But the sooner both the United States and South Africa accept that the political change that black South Africans wish to bring about will inevitably involve changes in the capitalist system of free enterprise—a change toward some form of social- ism—the less traumatic and painful the transition toward majority rule will be.

I do not believe that the United States can determine the direction or momentum of change in South Africa, but it can help the South African Government to understand and accept what is happening. It can also enlist the support of other Western countries to prepare South Africa and themselves for the upheaval of fundamental change that is on its way. I share the fears of many here that this process is going to be painful—and bloody. But the sooner the apartheid system is dismantled, the greater the hope of shortening this period of bloodshed and hastening the transition to nonracial democratic rule.

*Beyers Naude is a Minister of the Dutch Reformed Church and secretary general of the South African Council of Churches. This article is adapted from a longer essay in the May-June 1985 issue of *Africa Report* magazine.

Source: *New York Times*, April 12, 1985. Copyright 1985, The African American Institute, reprinted with permission of *Afrca Report.*

U.S Concerns

The continuing struggle for liberation in southern Africa poses complex issues of fundamental importance to people in developed countries. First, it involves basic questions of human rights: the rights of the people of southern Africa to build institutional structures they deem necessary to provide productive employment opportunities and raise living standards. Americans, for whom a revolution and civil war helped shape the foundation of democracy, should understand that the South African majority's struggle for these rights remains a vital concern.

Second, the southern African liberation movements have arisen in the context of a changing international division of labor and social relationships that have direct implications for the people of the United States. Transnational corporations have constructed many factories in South Africa. These relatively capital-intensive industries have squeezed out small-scale handicrafts and artisans' shops and hindered recent industrialization efforts in neighboring states, helping to perpetuate the unemployment that drags down the living standards of tens of thousands of black southern Africans. They have contributed to the white minority's ability to build its industrial capacity without permitting the black majority to acquire a wide range of new skills or assume supervisory positions. Transnationals have provided critical military technologies, especially in the fields of energy, computers, and transport, which the minority requires to maintain its rule at home and its domination of the region. In addition, by building plants in South Africa, U.S. transnationals have contributed to reduced employment in the United States.[7]

Third, by the 1980s, a further danger emerged: South Africa's determination to thwart the liberation movements might lead to a wider war. South Africa's military-industrial build-up had provided a temporarily profitable market for transnationals' capital and equipment; but it also furnished the minority goverment with the arrogance born of possessing the most sophisticated weapons of war, potentially including nuclear weapons. This arrogance lay at the root of tensions and mounting violence throughout southern Africa.

TOWARD PEACEFUL CHANGE AND JOBS FOR ALL

The Fruitful Alternative

Over the years, transnational corporate managers have lobbied the U.S. government to accept continued South African domination of southern Africa. U.S. citizens should consider the implications of the fact that the people of southern Africa are not merely demanding an end to minority rule. They seek the expansion of productive employment opportunities to raise the incomes and living standards of the poor majority of the regions' inhabitants.

Table 7.1 shows that countries characterized by balanced, industrialized development provide far larger markets for the sale of goods produced in factories of core industrial nations like the United States than does the distorted, minority-dominated regional economy of southern Africa. The United States, for example, sells an average of about two times as much for each inhabitant of the developed countries as it sells to South Africa, since, despite the relatively high level of industrialization, the mass of the black South African population remains impoverished. The United States sells almost 10 times as much per inhabitant to the developed market economies as it sells to the grossly impoverished people of the rest of Africa.

These data suggest that if member states of the Southern African Development Coordination Conference succeed in reducing their dependence on South Africa and achieve more balanced, integrated industrial and agricultural development, their people may become far larger customers for U.S. exports. The liberation of South Africa, by raising the incomes of the majority, could increase significantly the size of the South African market. By hastening the industrial transformation of the region, it could speed the day when all southern Africans could participate in world trade on a more equitable basis. Transnational corporate investments that contribute to this goal would benefit not only the people of southern Africa, but also those of the United States. At the same time, more democratic and equitable socioeconomic development in southern Africa would help to eliminate the roots of regional violence.

THE FOUNDATIONS OF AN ALTERNATIVE U.S. POLICY

The American people need to consider the building blocks for shaping an alternative approach in southern Africa: an approach designed to help the inhabitants undertake self-reliant development on national and regional levels,

Table 7.1
Estimated U.S. Trade with Developed Market Economies, South Africa,
and other African States (as a percentage of all their exports and imports,
and in terms of the amount of trade per each inhabitant
of their respective trading partners, 1977)[a]

	In $ millions	As % of total	$ value per each inhabitant of trading partner[b]
U.S. Exports to:			
The World	117,926	100.0	—
Developed Market Economies[c]	73,225	62.1	99
South Africa	1,074	0.9	43
Rest of Africa	4,359	3.6	10
U.S. Imports from:			
The World	145,742	100.0	—
Developed Market Economies[c]	79,932	54.8	108
South Africa	913	0.6	36
Rest of Africa	14,637	10.0	34

Notes
a. *1977, predating the worldwide recession, reflects a more normal trade pattern than that of the early 1980s.*
b. Dollar value of trade with trading partner, divided by population of trading partner.
c. Includes Canada, South Africa, United Kingdom, Belgium, Denmark, France, Federal Republic of Germany, Ireland, Italy, Austria, Finland, Iceland, Norway, Portugal, Sweden, Switzerland, Greece, Malta, Spain, Yugoslavia, Israel, Japan.
Source: Calculated from United Nations, *Yearbook of International Trade Statistics, 1979/80* (New York: 1981).

as well as at the grassroots level. By implication, the body of this book has suggested two sets of such building blocks:

I. Toward Political Self-Determination and Self-Reliant Development

A. Full support inside and outside the United Nations for the complete liberation of Namibia in line with U.N. Resolution 435. This implies:

1. Full support for an end to South African rule, and fair and free elections under U.N. supervision based on one-person-one-vote.

2. Elimination of U.S. support for the South African requirement that Cuban troops withdraw from Angola as a precondition for implementing U.N. Resolution 435.

3. U.S. governmental support, until Namibia gains independence, for enforcing the U.N. ban on the extraction of natural resources from Namibia by transnational corporations.

B. Full support for the independent southern African states' efforts to achieve effective national and regional independence from South Africa through strengthening the Southern African Development Coordination Conference (SADCC). This implies:

1. An end to all U.S. measures that pressure South Africa's independent neighbors to accommodate Pretoria's goals.

2. U.S. financial assistance for development of essential infrastructure required to achieve integrated national and regional development and to reduce dependence on the network of roads, railroads, and energy sources based in South Africa.

3. U.S. government incentives—including Export-Import Bank credit and double taxation agreements—to encourage U.S. transnational corporations to invest within the context of southern African states' own national and regional development plans.

4. An end to U.S. support for IMF and World Bank austerity "conditions" that reinforce external dependence and South African domination; and support instead for policies permitting SADCC member states to implement planned institutional changes promoting national and regional self-reliant development.

II. Toward Ending Apartheid

A. Recongition that meaningful change will not, indeed cannot, come about exclusively through the minority South African government; and hence, insistence on negotiations with the leaders of the liberation movement for the institutionalization of one-person-one-vote. This implies:

1. Support for the complete elimination of all aspects of the apartheid system, including an end to bantustanization and constitutional "reforms" designed to mask the continued extension of that system.

2. Support for full protection of and financial assistance to South African refugees through the U.N. High Commissioner for Refugees.

B. Until the complete elimination of apartheid, implementation of measures designed to exert pressure on the minority government to achieve that end through:

1. Full U.S. enforcement of the U.N. sanctions on trade in military hardware with South Africa, including a ban on exports of all "gray" area materials and equipment; and support for the extension of those sanctions to prohibit all trade with South Africa in the fields of uranium sales and nuclear technology.

2. Prohibition of further expansion of trade and investment by U.S. firms in South Africa, including an end to all existing incentives such as

Export-Import Bank credit, double-taxation agreements, and use of U.S. funds for IMF assistance.

3. A requirement that U.S. firms divest from key sectors of the South African economy, particularly banking and finance, computers, military technology, nuclear and other energy-related activities.

SUMMARY

The architects of Constructive Engagement insist that, to protect U.S. interests in southern Africa, the U.S. government should accept the South African minority's initiative toward gradual "reform" based on ethnic divisions among the population. Under this approach, the U.S. government should exert pressure to slow the essential institutional transformation required to enable South Africa's neighbors to reduce their dependence on Pretoria.

The evidence compiled in this Impact Audit shows that Constructive Engagement flies in the face of history, the determined opposition of the majority of South Africans, and the expressed disagreement of the leaders of the politically independent southern African states. Implementation of this policy essentially undermines basic principles of human rights and self-determination that most Americans believe in.

Constructive Engagement serves the narrow interests of a handful of giant U.S. transnational corporations. By encouraging them to invest in South Africa, it permits them to strengthen the minority-controlled, military-industrial complex which has fostered the persistent underdevelopment that impoverishes the majority of the region's inhabitants. Their relatively capital-intensive technologies aggravate unemployment in southern Africa.

On balance, the evidence gathered in this book argues for an alternative approach. It proposes strong U.S. support for the full liberation of the people of Namibia and South Africa, and for the integrated development of southern Africa. These steps would provide a sounder foundation for improved trade relations with the United States, while contributing to peace and the fulfillment of the human rights and basic needs of the great majority of people in southern Africa.

South African refugees digging a 3 mile trench for a water pipe for the African National Congress Development Center at Dakawa, Tanzania (Photo: African National Congress)

Appendixes

APPENDIX I
Southern Africa Country Profiles*

ANGOLA
Date of independence: 1975
Area: 481,351 sq. mi. (1,246,699 sq. km.)
Population (1983): 8 million
Life expectancy (1983): 42 years
Percent literacy among adults (1983): Males, 35%; females, 19%
Percent of population urban: 20-30%
Gross Domestic Product (1979): $2.9 billion
Per capita income (1979): $419
Main exports: Crude oil (68%); coffee (14%); diamonds (11%)
Manufacturing, as percent of GDP: 18-20%; employment: 81,900

Angola, a relatively large country with rich and varied agricultural and mineral resources, was the home of relatively developed economic and state structures prior to colonization by the Portuguese. But Portugal extracted as much wealth from Angola as possible, often working with transnational firms based in more developed countries. It settled its own surplus population on lands taken from the Africans who were forced to provide labor. The colonial administration grossly neglected the basic needs of the African population, leaving health and educational standards among the lowest on the continent. Large estates in the northwest grew coffee, Angola's main export until, shortly before independence, oil was discovered and developed by the U.S. firm, Gulf Oil. The German firm, Krupp, mined Angolan iron ore for shipment to its mills in Europe. De Beers, of the South African Anglo American Group, opened a diamond mine. The Anglo American Group, as well as Barclays and Standard Bank, owned shares in the major commercial bank. Portuguese firms, sometimes in cooperation with European and South African interests, established import-substitution manufacturing industries to meet settler and modern sector requirements. As the liberation war dragged on, the Portuguese established closer economic and military ties with South Africa.

In 1975, after more than a decade of guerrilla warfare, the people of Angola won liberation from the Portuguese. The new government, headed by the Popular Movement for the Liberation of Angola (MPLA), confronted attacks by internal opposition groups: the National Front for the Liberation of Angola (FNLA), and the National Union for the Total Independence of Angola (UNITA), both covertly supported by the United States. The young Angolan government requested Cuban troops to help defeat the first outright invasion of South African armed forces. Although most of the governments of Europe and Africa recognized the new government, the United States did not.

*This appendix draws on sources used throughout the book to provide background information on the independent countries of southern Africa. South Africa is not included in this appendix because it is covered at length in Chapter III.

The MPLA announced its intention, over time, to implement a transition to socialism along Marxist-Leninist lines. The flight of skilled Portuguest workers and the abandonment of farms and factories by Portuguese owners and managers, however, forced the government to take over far more sectors of the economy than originally planned. It reached an agreement with Gulf Oil, leaving management and marketing in the U.S. firm's hands, but retaining a significant share of the profits—the major source of government finance. Cuba—with whom the MPLA had developed close ties during the liberation war—provided medical personnel and teachers who could speak Portuguese to help overcome the overwhelming lack of skilled personnel. South Africa's lengthy occupation of southern provinces and repeated attacks, directly through incursions of its own troops and indirectly through its aid to UNITA, disrupted the fledgling government's efforts to carry out its development plans.

The new Angolan government became a leading Front Line State, offering assistance to the liberation movements of both Namibia and South Africa. It was a founding member of the Southern African Development Coordination Conference (SADCC), and assumed responsibility for formulating a regional energy program.

BOTSWANA
Date of independence: 1966
Area: 220,930 sq. mi. (570,000 sq. km.), landlocked
Population (1983): 900,000
Life expectancy (1983): 50 years
Percent literacy among adults (1983): Males, 61%; females, 61%
Gross Domestic Product (1981): $956 million
Per capita income: $1,124
Main exports: Diamonds (56%), copper/nickel (13%), beef (18%)
Manufacturing employment: 4,150

Botswana covers a large land area, but because much of it is desert, the population remains small. In the 19th century, as the white settlers spread up through what is now South Africa, the Botswana king asked for British protection. The territory became a much-neglected colony. The Batswana people largely retained their traditional economy, based primarily on herding cattle. For years, their main export was migrant labor to South African mines and farms. After attaining independence in 1966, the government became a parliamentary democracy, with the king becoming the first elected president.

Shortly after independence, De Beers of the Anglo American group opened the world's second largest diamond mine, Orapa. This raised Botswana's per capita income to the highest in independent southern Africa. Further exploration led De Beers to open a second diamond mine in the 1980s. Anglo American and American Metal Climax (AMAX) also began to mine copper-nickel at Selebi-Pikwe, in which the government acquired a small share.

Most Batswana still engage in agriculture, centered around cattle holding. The injection of wealth into the economy from the mines, however, has distorted access to resources and income distribution. The numbers of households owning no cattle rose to more than a third by the mid-1970s. In 1975, a new land-tenure system, the Tribal Grazing Land Policy, introduced commerical leasing of land which threatened to dispossess large numbers of families who owned no cattle.

The growing civil service, financed by mineral revenues, has become the largest wage employer. The capital-intensive mining sector employs relatively little labor. In part because of its membership in the South African Customs Union, Botswana is unable to compete with South African-based factories, and has established relatively little manufacturing industry. Barclays and Standard banks have long provided the country's major banking facilities.

Despite its extensive economic dependence on South Africa, Botswana joined SADCC in 1979.

LESOTHO
Date of independence: 1966
Area: 11,716 sq. mi. (30,227 sq. km.), landlocked
Population (1983): 1,400,000
Life expectancy (1983): 52 years
Percent literacy among adults (1983): Males, 58%; females, 81%
Gross Domestic Product (1979): $300 million
Per capita income (1979): $214
Main exports: Diamonds (56%); mohair (11%); wool (9%)
Manufacturing, as percent of GDP: 2.2%; employment: 6,582

Lesotho is a small mountainous nation surrounded by South Africa. In the 19th century, having fought a guerrilla war against the advancing Europeans, the Basotho people gradually withdrew to the rugged mountains, finally calling for British protection which ultimately became colonial status, with the economy dominated by South Africa.

In 1966, upon attaining independence, Lesotho established a Westminster-type parliamentary government. The king remained little more than a figurehead.

Independence did little to change the political economy or the lives of most of the people. The overcrowded farming areas of the country had been denuded of trees and eroded by heavy rains. Some Basotho grow sheep and sell the wool, almost entirely in crude form, for spinning and weaving in Southern African factories; a few people dig for diamonds in the northern mountains. In the 1970s, Anglo-De Beers opened a medium-sized mine, in which the government acquired a 25 percent holding. Barclays and Standard provide commercial banking facilities, and the currency is linked directly to the South African rand. As a member of the South African Customs Union, Lesotho has been unable to establish many industries, although a few foreign firms established small-scale last-stage assembly and processing plants in cooperation with the Lesotho National Development Corporation. Most men between the ages of 18 and 40 years—up to 70 percent of the male labor force—migrate to work in South Africa.

Lesotho joined SADCC in 1980. As long as it remains surrounded by minority-ruled South Africa, however, Lesotho seems unlikely to be able to do much to realize meaningful economic cooperation with the other members.

MALAWI
Date of independence: 1964
Area: 45,483 sq. mi. (117,801 sq. km.), landlocked
Population (1983): 6.5 million
Life expectancy (1983): 47 years
Percent literacy among adults (1983): Males, 48%; females, 25%

Percent of population urban (estimated): 15%
Gross Domestic Product (1981): $1.3 billion
Per capita income (1981): $203
Main exports: Tobacco (41%); sugar (27%); tea (13%)
Manufacturing, as percent of GDP: 12%; employment: 33,379

Malawi is small and relatively overpopulated compared to its neighbors, although it has rich, well-watered soils along the banks of Lake Malawi. A former British colony (Nyasaland), it became a member of the Federation of Rhodesia and Nyasaland (1953-63), which was dominated by the settler-controlled Southern Rhodesia (now Zimbabwe) government. Although some estate agriculture was developed, Malawi served primarily as a labor reserve providing low-cost migrant labor, especially for the mines and farms of Southern Rhodesia and even South Africa.

In 1964, after African complaints finally led to the break-up of the Federation, Malawi (along with Zambia, formerly Northern Rhodesia) attained independence. After a conflict in the leadership of the new government, President Hastings Banda assumed essentially dictatorial powers, and the opposition fled into exile. The government established close relations with South Africa. Malawi is one of the few independent African countries north of the Zambezi to accept financial assistance from Pretoria. With the help of the World Bank and the British American Tobacco Company, the government established extensive small-scale peasant tobacco cultivation. The government also encouraged foreign investment in import-substitution industries, although these remained capital-intensive and contributed little to restructuring the national economy. The per capita income remains the lowest in the region.

Malawi joined SADCC in 1980.

MOZAMBIQUE
Date of independence: 1975
Area: 303,769 sq. mi. (786,367 sq. km.)
Population (1983): 12.9 million
Life expectancy (1983): 47 years
Percent literacy among adults: Males, 44%; females, 23%
Percent of population urban: 10%
Gross Domestic Product (1979): $2.5 billion
Per capita income (1979): $243
Main exports (1981): Cashews (16%); shrimp (15%); sugar (12%); tea (9%); cotton (7%)
Manufacturing, as percent of GDP (1973): 14%; employment: 99,500

In the 16th century, the Portuguese, using force of arms, disrupted centuries of Arab trade with the peoples who lived in what is now Mozambique, and established outposts through which they gradually came to dominate the entire country. By the end of the 19th century, at the time of the scramble for Africa, however, Portugal had declined to a relatively backward European nation, barely retaining its colonies as the British and Germans divided southern Africa between them. Unable to fully subdue the African populations or to finance development of Mozambique's mineral and agricultural resources, the Portuguese authorities granted concessions to large foreign companies employing forced labor in central and northern Mozambique, and negotiated to provide low-cost migrant labor to South African mines in exchange for the diversion of South African trade through Lourenco Marques (now Maputo) harbor. The colonial government obtained most of its revenues in the form of gold paid by South Africa out of a fixed percentage of the wages withheld from the Mozambican mine workers, and payments for trade through its ports from South Africa, landlocked Southern Rhodesia (Zimbabwe), and Nyasaland (Malawi).

As the liberation struggle mounted, the Portuguese, seeking to bolster their economic and military strength, established closer ties to the white-minority South African regime. In cooperation with South African parastatals and transnational corporations, they constructed the huge Cabora Bassa hydroelectric project, which South Africa planned to incorporate into its regional power grid. Barclays, Standard, and Anglo American helped handle much of the trade through the Lourenco Marques harbor.

By the time Mozambique achieved independence, the destruction of the pre-existing economy and the exploitation of the people had left it with per capita incomes, education, and health standards that were among the lowest in the region.

In 1975, following more than a decade of guerrilla warfare, the Mozambican people, along with Angola, won independence with the collapse of the Portuguese dictatorship. FRELIMO, the governing party, sought initially to promote national integration and to achieve political mobilization of its scattered population. Massive flight by the Portuguese, who destroyed much capital equipment before they left and took with them critical skills, imposed immense difficulties in recovering from the war. Nevertheless, in 1977, at its third Congress, FRELIMO declared its intention to implement what it termed a "Popular Democratic Revolution," seeking to build socialism along Marxist-Leninist lines. At the same time, it intensified its support of the Zimbabwean liberation forces and enforced strict sanctions against the Smith regime at considerable cost in terms of revenue lost and destruction of its own infrastructure through Rhodesian attacks.

The new Mozambican government not only played an important role as a Front Line State in supporting the liberation of Zimbabwe, but also in founding and developing SADCC. It assumed responsibility for developing the infrastructure and transportation networks of the region.

By the beginning of the 1980s, on top of worsening terms of trade, mounting foreign debt, and severe drought, Mozambique suffered repeated attacks by the South African-supported Mozambican National Resistance Movement (MNR), which disrupted internal production and distribution of food, as well as hampering the efforts of SADCC member countries to shift their trade from South Africa to Mozambican ports.

SWAZILAND
Date of independence: 1968
Area: 6,700 sq. mi. (17,400 sq. km.), landlocked
Population (1983): 600,000
Life expectancy (1983): 47 years
Percent literacy among adults (1983): Males, 64%; females, 58%
Gross Domestic Product (1977): $313 million
Per capita income (1977): $614
Main exports: Sugar (38%); wood pulp (14%); fertilizer (11%)
Manufacturing, as percent of GDP: 16% (primarily processing agricultural products); employment: 6,500

Swaziland is a small mountainous kingdom situated between South Africa and Mozambique. In the 19th century, Swaziland was forced to defend itself, first from the threat of invasion from the south in the aftermath of the Zulu wars of expansion; then, later, against the Europeans' amibtions for its resources and access from the Transvaal to the sea. In the latter half of the century, the king granted concessions to both the Boers and British for land and mineral rights covering the entire country. At the end of the Boer war in 1902, after becoming involved in efforts to adjudicate the conflicting claims to concessions, Britain assumed the role of protector over Swaziland.

The British administration, imposing taxes, police powers and the laws of the Transvaal on Swaziland, coerced the majority of Africans to farm less fertile, rocky lands, or to work for the companies and settlers owning Swazi concessions and on South African mines and farms. The queen regent accelerated the process by urging young Swazi men to seek work in the South African gold mines and contribute a fourth of their earnings—five pounds sterling a year—to a fund to buy back the land and pay the costs of the royal household, including the young king's education.

By World War II, the Native Areas had become grossly overcrowded. Only then, as part of an effort to retain the support of the colonized people, did the British contribute funds to buy back some European land and turn it over to the Swazi Crown. After the war, foreign investments multiplied. The South African mining finance house, Anglo American Group, acquired a growing interest in a vast timber pulp mill, and began operating the only iron-ore mine and the largest coal mine in the country. The British Commonwealth Development Corporation capitalized extensive irrigation projects that laid the foundation of the fruit and sugar plantations eventually established by the U.S. firm, Del Monte, and the British companies, Tate & Lyle and Lonrho.

By the time Swaziland attained independence in 1968, the king had parlayed his circumscribed royal establishment in the colonial scheme of indirect rule into a position of relative power and prestige which he carried over into the post-independence era. By the 1970s, mounting discontent, demonstrations and strikes among growing numbers of youth, workers, and unemployed led the king to abolish Parliament and rule by decree. The reconstituted Parliament, blending Westminster and Swazi traditional rule, remained essentially under the king's control until he died in 1982.

Swaziland joined SADCC in 1980, and was assigned responsibility for coordinating regional educational programs.

TANZANIA
Date of independence: 1962
Area: Mainland: 362,688 sq. mi. (939,362 sq. km.); Zanzibar and Pemba: 1,020 sq. mi. (2,641 sq. km.)
Population (1983): 19.8 million (plus about 500,000 who live on Zanzibar and Pemba)
Life expectancy: 52 years
Percent literacy among adults: Males, 78%; females, 70%
Percent of population urban: 10%
Gross Domestic Product (1981): $4.5 billion
Per capita income (1981): $228
Main exports: Coffee (34%); cotton (16%); cloves, almost entirely grown on Zanzibar (10%); diamonds (6%)
Manufacturing, as percent of GDP: 9%; employment: 60,226

As a nation, Tanzania came into being after independence in 1962 through the merger of Tanganyika and Zanzibar. After World War I, Tanganyika, a former German colony, had been taken over by the British as a protectorate. A large coastal land area with many resources, it had nevertheless been neglected by the British in favor of the neighboring settler-dominated colony, Kenya. Until World War II, Tanganyika's main export was sisal produced on large estates. After synthetics reduced sisal's value, coffee, half grown on estates and half by peasants, and peasant-grown cotton became the leading exports. The Anglo American Group's De Beers took over the Williamson diamond mine. Zanzibar, for centuries an Arab island trading center, had developed cloves as its primary agricultural export, mostly for sale in Asia.

After independence, the government expanded health, education, and social-welfare expenditures in an effort to raise living standards. Over the years, it achieved improvements in the quality of rural life.

In line with World Bank advice, the government initially sought to stimulate peasant production of export crops to raise incomes and revenues to finance its programs. In 1967, however, after confronting worsening terms of trade which reduced its foreign-exchange earnings and revenues, the Tanzanian government, at Arusha, declared its intention of implementing a transition to ujamaa socialism, that is, socialism built around village-level cooperation. It took over the banks and financial institutions, increased its direct control over foreign trade, and purchased a majority of shares of the few large factories and some estates. The government failed, however, to implement an effective long-term development strategy designed to render Tanzania less dependent on exports to uncertain world markets.

In the 1970s, under Idi Amin, Uganda invaded Tanzania. Ultimately Tanzania won the war, but at considerable expense. Prolonged drought, combined with the mounting international recession, aggravated balance-of-payments difficulties. By the end of the decade, deeply in debt, the government requested International Monetary Fund assistance. The IMF proposed conditions which the government rejected because they would require dismantling its socialism and sharply reducing living standards. Tanzania suffered severe shortages of fuel, spare parts, and materials which disrupted its continued development efforts. Tanzania has provided significant assistance to the liberation movements, particularly of Mozambique and South Africa. It became a leading Front Line State, and the first meeting of SADCC took place at Arusha. Tanzania assumed responsibility for formulating a SADCC-wide industrial strategy.

ZAMBIA

Date of independence: 1964
Area: 290,724 sq. mi. (752,975 sq. km.), landlocked
Population (1983): 6.0 million
Life expectancy (1983): 50 years
Percent literacy among adults (1983): Males, 79%; females, 58%
Percent of population urban (1983): 40%
Gross Domestic Product (1981): $3.8 billion
Per capita income (1981): $638
Main exports: Copper (85%); cobalt (10%)
Manufacturing, as percent of GDP: 19%; employment: 45,510

The British South Africa Company, coming north from South Africa in the 19th century in search of mineral riches, carved out Zambia and Zimbabwe as colonies named after Cecil Rhodes, Northern and Southern Rhodesia. Zambia's economy was shaped around four giant mines on what became known as the Copper Belt, developed by the South African-based Anglo American Group and the U.S. firm, American Metal Climax (AMAX). The African peasants were pushed off a 20-mile-wide strip on both sides of the railway that ran from the Copper Belt down to South African ports. About 1,000 white settler farmers, many of them from South Africa, employing tens of thousands of low-paid African workers, produced most of the basic foodstuffs consumed by the growing migrant mine labor force.

The colonial authorities neglected the remainder of the country. In the 19th century, for example, the Lobatse people in what is now the Western Province of Zambia had created an integrated crop and cattle complex based on irrigation channels drawing water from the Zambezi. The great explorer-missionary, Livingstone, called it a land of milk and honey, unlike anything he had seen elsewhere in Africa. Negotiating with the king to impose taxes on the people, the British South Africa Company created conditions which forced men to work on the mines and farms of the region (some walking as far as South Africa). The loss of their labor led to the neglect of the irrigation network, and gradually the whole pre-colonial agricultural complex fell into decay. Today, the per capita income in the Western Province is the lowest in Zambia.

The white-settler government of Southern Rhodesia (now Zimbabwe) dominated the post World War II Federation of Rhodesia and Nyasaland (1953-63), taxing the mine profits of Zambia which might have otherwise been directed to developing Zambia's rural areas. The sale of Southern Rhodesia manufactures throughout the Federation's common market blocked construction of factories in Zambia.

After the break-up of the Federation and the attainment of independence in 1964, Zambia's new government taxed the mines to finance roads, schools, and hospitals. Growing numbers of people, unable to find employment in the neglected rural areas, crowded into the squatter compounds that mushroomed at the outskirts of all the cities along the line-of-rail. The urban population increased to 40 percent of the total, swelling the numbers of the un- and underemployed.

Early after attaining independence, Zambia joined Tanzania in obtaining Chinese assistance to build the TanZam Railroad to provide a route to the sea other than that through South Africa. (The Western governments and the World Bank refused to fund it, they said, because the existing routes were adequate.)

Complying with U.N. sanctions, the Zambian government cut off imports of manufactured goods from Southern Rhodesia (see discussion of Zimbabwe below). This created the conditions for private firms, in cooperation with government parastatals, to construct last-stage assembly and processing import-substitution industries. These were typically located along the already relatively developed line-of-rail, used capital-intensive machinery, and imported parts and materials to produce luxury and semi-luxury items. (Beer and cigarettes provided 40 percent of these industries' value-added.) As a result, they only marginally altered the inherited dualistic economy and provided relatively little new employment.

At the same time, the government ministries, still largely manned by excolonial civil servants, failed to adequately alter the marketing, credit, and extension education facilities—originally shaped to service the line-of-rail estates—to increase the output and sales of crops produced by the peasants in the hinterlands.

In 1969, hoping to influence the mine companies to expand their output, thus increasing employment, foreign-exchange earnings, and government revenues, the government purchased a majority of their shares. Due to the shortage of trained Africans, however, the companies continued to manage the mines and market the copper. In the process, taking advantage of the contract negotiated with the government, they siphoned out of the country—untaxed—a much larger share of the profits, reducing government revenues required to finance growing public expenditures.

In the mid-1970s, because of an oversupply of copper aggravated by recessions in the developed countries, the world copper price fell. Zambia could no longer afford to import the materials, equipment, and foodstuffs on which its import-substitution industries and swollen urban population remained dependent. Nor could it continue to finance the current expenditures required to keep its extended education, health, and other government facilities operating. Its balance-of-payments and budget deficits soared, forcing it to borrow heavily both internally and abroad. By the 1980s, it was spending more than 40 percent of its foreign-exchange earnings to pay off its overseas debts. It received assistance from the International Monetary Fund, but at the expense of reducing government employment and social services; eliminating subsidies and devaluing its currency, thus raising the cost of living, especially for the urban poor; re-opening its trade routes to South Africa; and ending its intervention to reshape its inherited dualistic economy.

Zambia, under President Kenneth Kaunda, also became a leading Front Line State, providing regional offices for the liberation movements of Angola, Zimbabwe, Namibia, and South Africa. The Zambian government was a founding member of SADCC and assumed responsibility for formulating proposals for regional financial institutions.

ZIMBABWE
Date of independence: 1980
Area: 150,866 sq. mi. (390,759 sq. km.), landlocked
Population (1983): 7.5 million
Life expectancy (1983): 53 years
Percent literacy among adults (1983): Males, 76%; females, 71%
Percent of population urban: 20%
Gross Domestic Product (1981): $5.9 billion
Per capita income (1981): $786
Main exports: Tobacco (28%); gold (9%); iron products (15%); sugar (7%); nickel (5%)
Manufacturing, as percent of GDP: 25%; employment: 180,500

Zimbabwe, along with Zambia, was colonized by the British South Africa Company under Cecil Rhodes, after whom both colonies were named, Southern and Northern Rhodesia. When the British South Africa Company failed to find significant mineral deposits in Southern Rhodesia, however, it decided to develop the colony's agricultural potential. It turned over the better half of the land to fewer than 7,000 white settler farmers and corporations, squeezing the Africans into infertile, dry "Tribal Trust Lands." The settler farms, employing hundreds of thousands of low-paid African farm laborers, and favored by extensive subsidies, marketing, research, and credit facilities funded by the government, produced 95 percent of the country's agricultural exports as well as most of its internally marketed foodstuffs.

During the Federation of Rhodesia and Nyasaland era (1953-63), the settler government taxed the profits of Zambia's mines to develop essential infrastructure in Zimbabwe to attract industries. These produced a growing range of manufactures for sale within the protected Federation market, rapidly creating the largest manufacturing sector of any country in sub-Saharan Africa except South Africa. At the same time, the Anglo American Group moved its headquarters within the Federation from Zambia to Zimbabwe. It invested some of its copper profits to finance its acquisition and development of the Hwangwe coal mines, which sold coal at government-guaranteed prices; used the profits of that to finance the Bindura nickel mine; and expanded its ownership and control of sectors of the national economy, including timber, beef, and sugar. To do so, it became an active partner in the nation's interlocked financial institutions—banks, insurance firms, pension funds, and building societies—that helped it to accumulate and reinvest the growing national surplus. By the time of independence, transnational corporations, headed by the Anglo American Group, held an estimated 70 percent of the assets in the "modern" sector.

When the Federation broke up and Malawi and Zambia became independent, the settler minority (less than 3 percent of the population) unilaterally declared independence (UDI) from Britain. Imposing apartheid-style racist policies, the government announced that white rule would last a thousand years. When the United Nations imposed sanctions, urging member states to stop all trade with and investments in the white-ruled state, the regime retaliated by prohibiting transnational corporate affiliates from shipping their profits out of the country. Instead, until the mid 1970s, they reinvested in expanding local industries to meet the needs largely of the settler farmers, mining companies, and high-income minority, achieving an 8-10 percent annual growth rate, centered around domestic industrial growth. The country boasted a relatively high per capita income, but the distribution was sharply skewed, with less than 5 percent of the population receiving roughly 75 percent of the cash income.

After the minority regime unilaterally declared independence, the black majority, despairing of achieving change through peaceful means, began a guerrilla war lasting 15 years through which they sought to win majority rule and land redistribution. The Front Line States provided substantial assistance to the guerrillas, who, by the late 1970s, had liberated much of the countryside and essentially brought the minority-run economy to a standstill. In 1979, seeking to end a conflict that threatened to further radicalize the peoples of the region, Britain, the United States, and South Africa persuaded the minority regime to meet with the leaders of the liberation forces at the Lancaster House in London. Under the resulting compromise Constitution, the black majority overwhelmingly voted for the ZANU-PF party.

ZANU-PF declared, as its aim, a transition to socialism along Marxist-Leninist lines. The new government did not, however, fundamentally restructure the inherited institutions. Instead, it increased expenditures on education, health, and social welfare, and shifted about 10 percent of the population from the former Tribal Trust Lands—now called "Communal Areas"—to unutilized lands purchased from white settler farmers. The impact of drought and the international economic crisis sharply reduced export earnings and government revenues. Unwilling to tax the significant investable surpluses held in the private corporate and financial sector, the government raised the sales tax and borrowed heavily at home and abroad. It called on the International Monetary Fund for assistance, accepting as conditions the need to cut its social expenditures and devalue its currency, resulting in sharp increases in the cost of living for the poor majority.

In 1980, Zimbabwe's new government joined SADCC and assumed responsibility for food security in the region, appointing as head of the program the white minister of agriculture, formerly a commercial farmer.

Mozambique refugees after their long trek into Zimbabwe (Oxfam America staff photo by Barbara Kaim)

APPENDIX II - A

Southern African Production of Selected Minerals and Their Uses[a], 1983 (in metric tons unless otherwise specified; and as a percentage of total world production)

Mineral (in metric tons unless specified)	South Africa		Angola		Botswana		Namibia		Zambia		Zimbabwe	
	volume	%	volume	%	volume	%	volume	%	volume	%	volume	%
Asbestos	221,111	5.3	—	—	—	—	—	—	—	—	153,000	3.7
Chromite ('000 tons)	2,232	25.0	—	—	—	—	—	—	—	—	431	4.8
Copper	220,000	2.7	—	—	24,000	0.2	50,447	0.6	868,251	10.8	20,400	0.2
Diamonds (gem '000 carats)	3,760	28.6[b]	775	3.3	740[c]	2.7[b]	915	2.9	—	—	—	—
Gold ('000 troy ounces)	21,847	49.1	—	—	—	—	—	—	—	—	—	—
Manganese ore ('000 tons)	2,886	11.6	—	—	—	—	7,460	16.7	10	—	453	1.0
Platinum ('000 troy ounces)	2,600	40.1	—	—	—	—	—	—	—	—	—	—
Vanadium	4,468	14.8	—	—	—	—	—	—	—	—	3	—
Vermiculite	153,034	30.9	—	—	—	—	—	—	—	—	—	—
Uranium oxide	7,128	16.5[d]	—	—	—	—	4,450	10.8[d]	—	—	—	—

Notes

a. The primary uses of these minerals are:

   Asbestos: As protection against sound, heat. (Health hazards have led to declining consumption in the United States; environmental concerns, which South African mining companies have not had to consider, have required increased expenditures to protect U.S. miners.)

   Chromite: Principally used in stainless steel; also refractory bricks and in the chemicals industry.

   Copper: For electrical wires and electronic equipment, and as a component in brass.

   Manganese: For making steel.

   Platinum: To control automobile exhaust emissions and upgrade the octane rating of gasoline; as a catalyst to produce acids and organic chemicals; in electrical contacts; and dental alloys.

   Vanadium: Mainly for making steel, some use in titanium alloys for airplanes.

   Vermiculite: For concretes, plasters, and increasingly for thermal insulating; some agricultural uses.

   Uranium: For nuclear energy.

b. Percent of total gem and industrial diamonds.

c. 1981 data.

d. Used 1982 data, since 1983 world output statistics not yet available.

Sources: U.S. Department of Interior, *Minerals Yearbook*, Vol. I, *Metals and Minerals* (Washington, D.C.: Government Printing Office, 1984); and Vol. III, *Area Reports: International, 1983* (Washington, D.C.: Government Printing Office, 1985); also United Nations, *Energy Statistics Yearbook* (New York: United Nations, 1984).

APPENDIX II - B

Selected South African Mineral Exports[a], By Destination, 1982
(in metric tons unless otherwise specified, and as percentage of exports to U.S. and other major buyers)

Mineral	Total Exports (Metric tons)	To Us (%)	To Other Buyers (%)
Asbestos	120,934	9.4	Japan (41.5); Italy (14.4); Taiwan (10.2)
Chromite (thousand tons)	852	29.4	Japan (36.6); West Germany (16.5); Austria (4.7)
Diamonds - gem (thousand carats)	392,203	70.2	Belgium-Luxemburg (13.5); United Kingdom (11.2)
Gold (thousand ounces)	630	b	West Germany (47.6); Japan (28.7); Hong Kong (17.4)
Manganese			
Ores & concs., metal-lurgical grade (thousands of tons)	2,170	5.5	Japan (47.7); Norway (13.2); West Germany (12)
Oxides	531	—	Austria (33.8); Italy (18.1); Finland (16.9)
Metal, including alloys	9,582	47.7	West Germany (35.1); Sweden (9.4)
Platinum Group			
Ore & concs ($000)	$3180	96.8	West Germany (3.2)
Metals including alloys (troy ounces)			
Paladium	675,425	67.5	Japan (31.1)
Platinum	1,177,386	47.8	Japan (49.7)
Rhodium	51,190	81.3	Japan (18.6)
Iridium, etc.	34.586	—	Japan (100.0)
Unspec. ($000)	159,845	2.2	United Kingdom (86)
Uranium			
Ores & Concs. ($000)	$52,367	—	NA
Oxides, compounds	3,451[c]	100.0	—
Vermiculite	146,094[d]	—	Italy (14.9); Belgium-Luxemburg (1.5)

Notes
a. Includes Namibia, Botswana, Lesotho, and Swaziland.
b. Insignificant.
c. Almost half South Africa's total uranium oxide output, almost a third of Namibia's and South Africa's output, combined.
d. Figures are shipments by producers for export, and not necessarily the actual exports.
Source: Calculated from U.S. Department of the Interior, *Minerals Yearbook*, Vol. III, *Area Reports: International, 1983* (Washington, D.C.: Government Printing Office, 1985).

APPENDIX III - A

Top 200 U.S. Companies in South Africa & Namibia - Ranked by Number of Employees[a]

Rank	Company	SA/Nam. Employees
1	Newmont Mining#	9,850+
2	Ford Motor	6,673
3	U.S. Steel#	5,688+
4	General Motors	4,949
5	Coca Cola	4,765+
6	Mobil Corp.	3,342+
7	U.S. Gypsum (Masonite)	2,631+
8	Goodyear Tire & Rubber	2,510
9	Allegheny International	1,922+
10	General Electric#	1,892+
11	R.J. Reynolds Industries	1,807
12	IBM	1,793
13	Johnson & Johnson	1,663+
14	Minnesota Mining & Manufacturing	1,590
15	Union Carbide#	1,457+
16	Norton Co.	1,342+
17	United Technologies	1,253+
18	Colgate-Palmolive	1,234+
19	Emhart Corp.	1,159
20	Owens-Illinois Fiberglas#	1,100+
21	Chevron Corp.[b]#	1,076+
21	Texaco#	1,076+
23	Nestle [Swtz] (Carnation)	1,046
24	American Cyanamid	1,025
25	Nabisco Brands	983+
26	Dun & Bradstreet (Nielsen)	963
27	Borg-Warner	958
28	CPC International	934
29	ITT#	913+
30	Joy Manufacturing	907
31	Phelps-Dodge Corp.#	893+
32	Xerox	770
33	Dresser Industries	767+
34	Tenneco	736+
35	Baker International	706
36	Kimberly-Clark	704
37	British Petroleum [UK] (Sohio, Kennecott)#	649
38	Firestone Tire & Rubber	615
39	Price Waterhouse & Co.#	600

Rank	Company	SA/Nam. Employees
40	H.H. Robertson Co.	585
41	NCR Corp.	584
41	Swiss Aluminum [Swtz.] (Maremont)	584
43	Eastman Kodak	567
44	Burroughs	563
45	PepsiCo Inc.	556
46	Chesebrough-Pond's	529+
47	Sperry Corp.	529
48	International Harvester#	526+
49	Crown Cork & Seal	525
50	Warner-Lambert Co.	515+
51	Exxon Corp.	509
51	Sentry Insurance	509
53	Gencorp Inc. (General Tire)**	504
54	American Home Products	503
55	CBI Industries	500
55	Rheem Manufacturing	500
57	Mine Safety Applicances	496
58	National Education Corp.	495
59	Deere & Co.	490
59	Rexnord Inc.	490
61	Ingersoll-Rand	477
62	Arthur Young & Co.	475
63	VF Corp.#	470
64	UAL Inc.#	461
65	Marriott Corp.	460
66	Merck & Co.	443+
67	Columbus McKinnon	438
68	Revlon Inc.	437
69	Sterling Drug	401
70	Ernst & Whinney Intl.*	400
70	Ted Bates Worldwide	400
72	Eaton Corp.	388
73	Readers Digest Assoc.	380
74	AM International	370
75	Baxter Travenol Labs.#	354
76	Marmon Group	350+
76	Fruehauf#	350
78	Marsh & McLennan#	347
79	Bristol-Myers	346
80	BBDO International	340
81	Borden	338
82	Kellogg Co.	333
83	Heinemann Electric#	330

Rank	Company	SA/Nam. Employees
84	Echlin Inc.	320
84	Hoover Co.	320
86	Control Data	313+
86	Air Products & Chemicals	313
88	Oak Industries	299
89	Gillette	296
90	Alexander & Alexander Services	291
91	Schering-Plough	285
92	Foster Wheeler	281
93	Precision Valve Corp.	280
94	Richardson-Vicks	278+
95	MCA Inc.	270
96	Pfizer	267
96	SmithKline Beckman	267
98	Interpublic Group of Cos.	260+
99	Assoc'd Metals & Minerals	260
100	Beatrice Cos.	255+
101	Timken Co.	251
102	Arthur Andersen & Co.*	250
102	J. Gerber & Co.*	250
102	Motorola	250
105	Hewlett-Packard Co.	247
106	Eli Lilly & Co.	240
107	Citicorp#	237
108	Intl. Minerals & Chemical	234
109	Henkel [WG] (Amchem)	231
110	American Brands	211+
11	Olin Corp.#	210
112	Ferro Corp.#	209
113	Upjohn Co.	208
114	Allied Corp.	200+
114	Dart & Kraft	200+
114	Dow Chemical#	200+
117	Surveilance Hldg. [Swtz] (SGS Control)	200
118	Nalco Chemical	199
119	Honeywell	192
120	Grey Advertising	190
121	Squibb	189
122	ACCO World	185
123	Fluor Corp.	182+
124	Phillips Petroleum	178
125	Bandag Inc.	173
126	Harnischfeger Corp.	170

Rank	Company	SA/Nam. Employees
127	S.C. Johnson & Son	168
128	Warner Communications	166
129	American International Group	160
129	Dominion Textile [Can] (DHJ)	160
131	Cooper Industries	153
132	Tidwell Industries	150
133	National-Standard Co.	149
134	Donaldson Co.	147
135	W.R. Grace & Co.	143
136	Abbott Labs	141
137	Chicago Pneumatic Tool	138
138	Broken Hill Pty. [Aust] (Utah Intl.)	135
139	Scovill Inc.	130
140	Monsanto	125
141	Bell & Howell	122
142	Johnson Controls	121+
143	Union Camp	119
144	CIGNA Corp.	113+
145	Federal-Mogul Corp.	112+
146	Computer Sciences Corp.#	110
147	Rohm & Haas	104
148	Parker Pen	102+
149	Preformed Line Products	102
150	D'Arcy-McManus & Masius	101
151	Ashland Oil	100
151	Bundy Corp.#	100
151	Estee Lauder Inc.	100
151	Houdaille Industries	100
151	Robbins Co.	100
151	Singer Co.	100
157	Armco	96+
158	Champion Spark Plug	92
158	Mohawk Data Services	92
160	Allis-Chalmers	90
160	Sandoz [Swtz] (Master Builders)	90
162	IMS International	87
163	FMC Corp.	81+
164	Libbey-Owens-Ford	80+
165	Caterpiller Tractor	76
166	Gates Corp.	74
167	Engelhard Corp.	72+
168	GTE Corp.	70+
168	Wilbur-Ellis Co.	70+
170	Groller Inc.	70

Rank	Company	SA/Nam. Employees
170	G.D. Searle & Co.	70
170	Unilever [UK] (Natl. Starch)	70
173	Black& Decker	63
174	Ogilvy & Mather Intl.#	62+
175	American Standard (Trane)	62
176	Harper Group	60
177	Parker Hannifin Corp.	59
178	Phibro-Salomon Inc.	57+
179	Amdahl Corp.	56
180	Solvay [Belg] (Salisbury Labs)	55
181	Tokheim Corp.	54
182	Midland-Ross Corp.	53
183	Tambrands Inc.	52
184	Albi International	50
184	Canadian Pacific [Can] (Koehring)	50
184	Celanese Corp.	50
187	CBS	46
188	Air Express International	45
189	Butternick Co.	44
189	Franklin Electric	44
191	McGraw Hill	43
192	General Signal (Leeds & Northrop)	42+
193	Lubrizol Corp.	42
194	Balkinds Agencies [SA]	40
194	Carman Industries	40
194	Hanson Trust [UK] (U.S. Industries)	40
194	National Utility Service Inc.	40
194	C.J. Petrow & Co. [SA]	40
199	Saatchi & Saatchi [UK] (Hay Assocs.)	39
200	Loctite Corp.	38
200	Stauffer Chemical	38

Notes

\# Company data prorated by ownership percentage.

* Company claims no equity ownership.

a. Data as of April 1985. The numbers of employees, the amounts invested, and the amounts loaned by each company, and hence their ratings, vary considerably from year to year.

b. Chevron was formerly Standard Oil of California.

Source: *Unified List of U.S. Companies With Investments or Loans in South Africa or Namibia*, compiled by Pacific Northwest Research Center, Inc. (New York: ACOA, 1985). The list draws primarily on the following sources: Investor Responsibility Research Center, *Foreign Investment in South Africa and Namibia* (Washington, D.C.: IRRC, 1984); U.S. Consulate General (Johannesburg) list of U.S. firms (1982); and Dun & Bradstreet, *Principal International Businesses, 1983.*

APPENDIX III - B

Top U.S. Companies in South Africa & Namibia -
Ranked by Direct Investment (Assets)

Rank	Company		SA/Namibia Assets ($ million)
1	Phibro-Saloman Inc.	LT	$420.0
2	Mobil Corp.		400.0
—	Caltex (joint venture of Standard Oil of California and Texaco)		334.0
3	Ford Motor		230.0
4	Chevron Corp.	GT	167.0
4	Texaco#	GT	167.0
6	U.S. Steel#		158.9
7	Burroughs	GT	150.0
8	Brit. Petrol [UK] (Sohio, Kennecott)#		144.9
9	General Motors		140.0
10	General Electric	GT	120.0
11	Goodyear Tire & Rubber		97.0
12	IBM		88.6
13	Newmont Mining		86.0
14	Coca Cola	GT	60.0
15	Deere & Co.	LT	58.0
16	Union Carbide#		54.5
17	CPC International	LT	50.0
18	Dresser Industries	GT	45.0
19	Control Data	GT	44.0
20	International Harvester		43.0
21	Johnson & Johnson		42.0
22	Xerox		42.0
23	NCR Corp.	LT	40.0
24	Phelps-Dodge Corp.#		37.0
25	Sperry Corp.		33.0
26	Dow Chemical#		32.0
27	Ingersoll-Rand		31.0
28	CIGNA Corp.	GT	29.0
29	Borg-Warner		29.0
30	Baker International	GT	28.2
31	FMC Corp.	LT	28.0
32	Joy Manufacturing		27.5
33	Minnesota Mining & Manuf.		26.0
33	Norton Co.		26.0
35	Revlon Inc.	LT	26.0
36	Honeywell	LT	25.0
37	Merck & Co.		23.0

Rank	Company		SA/Namibia Assets ($ million)
38	Caterpiller Tractor		22.0
39	United Technologies		21.0
40	Rexnord Inc.		20.1
41	Warner-Lambert Co.	GT	19.3
42	Colgate-Palmolive	GT	18.3
43	Alexander & Alexander Services		18.0
44	Warner Communications	LT	18.0
45	R.J. Reynolds Industries	GT	17.3
46	Air Products & Chemicals		17.0
46	Sentry Insurance		17.0
48	Dart & Kraft		16.0
48	Interpublic Group of Cos.		16.0
48	U.S. Gypsum (Masonite)		16.0
51	PepsiCo		15.0
52	American International Group		14.3
53	Bristol-Myers		14.2
54	Chesebrough-Pond's[1]	GT	14.0
55	Lubrizol Corp.		14.0
55	Phillips Petroleum		14.0
57	Borden	LT	14.0
58	Pfizer		13.0
59	Firestone Tire & Rubber#	GT	12.5
60	Cooper Industries		12.0
60	SmithKline Beckman		12.0
62	Hewlett-Packard Co.		11.8
63	American Home Products	GT	11.7
64	Owens-Illinois Fiberglas#		11.0
65	Allis-Chalmers	LT	11.0
66	ITT	GT	10.0
67	Eaton Corp.		10.0
67	Exxon Corp.		10.0
67	Rohm & Haas		10.0
67	Swiss Aluminum [Swtz] (Maremont)		10.0
71	Schering-Plough		9.5
72	Fluor Corp.	GT	9.0
73	Abbott Laboratories	LT	6.5
74	Nabisco Brands	GT	5.5
75	Celanese		5.5
76	Baxter Travenol Laboratories#		5.2
77	Chicago Pneumatic Tool		5.2
78	American Standard (Trane)	GT	5.0
79	Armco		5.0
79	W.R. Grace & Co.		5.0

Rank	Company	SA/Namibia Assets ($ million)	
81	Dun & Bradstreet (Nielsen)	GT	4.7
82	Sybron Corp.	LT	4.7
83	Kimberly-Clark#		4.3
83	Motorola		4.3
85	Oak Industries		3.9
86	Gillette		3.3
87	Champion Spark Plug	LT	3.1
88	Scovill Inc.	LT	3.1
89	Kidde & Co.#		3.0
89	Peabody International#		3.0
91	Parker Pen	LT	3.0
91	Tidwell Industries	LT	3.0
93	Grolier Inc.		2.8
94	Beatrice Cos.	GT	2.4
95	Parker Hannifin Corp.	LT	2.4
96	Franklin Electric		2.3
96	Stauffer Chemical[1]		2.3
98	Ashland Oil		2.1
99	Loctite Corp.	LT	2.1
100	Eli Lilly & Co.		2.0
100	Monsanto		2.0
102	American Cyanamid	GT	1.8
103	D'Arcy-McManus & Masius		1.8
104	Fruehauf#	LT	1.8
105	John Fluke Manufacturing		1.7
106	Engelhard Corp.		1.5
106	Wilbur-Ellis Co.		1.5
108	American Hospital Supply		1.3
108	Stanley Works		1.3
110	Fuqua Inds. (Simplicity Patterns)		1.1
110	Koppers Co.		1.1
112	Johnson Controls		0.9
113	Marriott Corp.	LT	0.6
114	Fuji Bank [Japan] (Heller Overseas)	GT	0.5
115	CBS		0.5
116	A.H. Robins Co.		0.4
116	West Point-Pepperell#*		0.4
118	Flow General		0.3
119	Citicorp#		0.2
120	Aries Resources		0.1
120	Diamond Shamrock		0.1
120	Dana Corp.		0.1

(Notes on next page.)

Notes

\#   Company data prorated by ownership percentage.
*   Company claims no equity ownership.
LT   = Less than.
GT   = Greater than.
1.   Chesebrough-Pond's is acquiring Stauffer Chemical
See notes and source for Appendix III - A.

APPENDIX III - C

U.S Banks Participating in Loans to South Africa - Ranked by Outstanding Loans in Which Participated (1972-May 1984)

Rank	Bank	Outstanding Loans ($ millions)
1	Citicorp	$ 1,594.7
2	First Boston, Inc.	956.4
3	Kidder, Peabody & Co.	938.8
4	Goldman, Sachs & Co.	784.5
5	Manufacturers Hanover Corp.	736.4
6	Merrill Lynch & Co.	704.7
7	Morgan Stanley & Co.	635.3
8	Smith Barney Inc.	632.2
9	Prudential Insurance (Bache)	620.4
10	American Express (Shearson/Lehman)	546.3
11	J.P. Morgan & Co.	541.7
12	Arnhold & S. Bleichroder Co.	454.7
13	PaineWebber Group Inc.	427.1
14	Chase Manhattan (Lincoln First)	397.3[1]
15	Dillon, Read & Co.	371.6
16	Drexel Burnham Lambert	354.1
17	Aetna Life & Casualty (Montague [UK])	248.1
18	Phibro-Salomon (Saloman Bros.)	229.1
19	Chemical New York Corp.	192.0
20	Sears Roebuck (Dean Witter Reynolds)	182.2
21	Bear, Stearns & Co.	180.6
22	Private Export Funding Co. (PEFCO)	175.8
23	Continental Illinois Corp.	170.2[2]
24	Dresdner Bank [W.Germ.] (ABD Securities)	164.0
25	Lazard Freres & Co.	162.7
26	New York Hanseatic Corp.	148.0
27	CoreStates Financial (Philadelphia Natl.)	120.5[3]
28	NCNB Corp.	GT 101.5[4]

Rank	Bank	Outstanding Loans ($ millions)
29	InterFirst Corp.	100.0
30.	BankAmerica (Seafirst)	84.4
31	Irving Bank Corp.	78.5
32	Bank of Boston (First National Bank of Boston)	50.0[5]
32	Bankers Trust New York Corp.	50.0
32	Dow Chemical Co.	50.0
32	Fidelcor	50.0
32	First Chicago Corp.	50.0[6]
32	First Washington Securities Corp.	50.0
32	E.F. Hutton Group	50.0
32	Rothschild Inc. (New Court Securities)	50.0
40	PNC Financial (Provident Nat'l.)	38.9[7]
41	European American Bancorp	25.0
42	Midland Bank [UK] (Crocker National)	16.0
43	First Wisconsin Corp.	4.7
44	Centran Corp.*	4.6
45	Society Corp.*	2.4
46	National City Corp. (National City Bank/Cleve)	0.2
—	Texas Commerce Bancshares Inc.	GT 0.0[8]
—	Maryland National Corp.	GT 0.0[9]
—	Bank of New York Co.	GT 0.0[10]
—	United Banks of Colorado Inc.	GT 0.0[11]
—	First Bank System (Banks of Iowa)	GT 0.0
—	First Interstate Bancorp.	GT 0.0
—	Fleet Financial Group Inc.	GT 0.0
—	Northern Trust Corp.	GT 0.0
—	Peoples Bancorp.	GT 0.0

Notes

These rankings are based on the outstanding amounts of those loans in which the banks participated during 1972-May 1985, where data on such loans were publicly available; it is probable that banks have participated in more loans to SA borrowers than have been made public. The rankings are not based on a bank's own share of these loans (which is usually not known) nor on the known amount of its own loan to S.A. borrowers (on which data are very sparse). Sources on loan participation are the studies by Beate Klein and others published by the U.N. Center Against Apartheid and Corporate Data Exchange. Sources on banks' own loans (shown in notes below) are IRRC, *Foreign Investment in South Africa and Namibia*, recent issues of *The Wall Street Journal*, and various banks' announcements.

"Outstanding" loans are loans not yet fully repaid.
GT = Greater than.
* Society Corp. is acquiring Centran Corp.

(Notes continued on next page.)

1. Chase subsidiary LincolnFirst had $10.0 million of its own outstanding to S.A. borrowers as of 12/83.
2. Continental Illinois had $315-420 million of its own outstanding to SA borrowers as of 12/83.
3. CoreStates subsidiary Philadelphia National had $20.7 million of its own outstanding to SA borrowers as of 12/83.
4. NCNB had $217.0 million of its own outstanding to SA borrowers as of 12/83; another $130.0 million of its own was loaned to SA borrowers in 1984 (maturity dates of 1984 loans unknown).
5. Bank of Boston had $75.0 million of its own outstanding to SA borrowers as of 3/85. [See footnote 40 of Chapter 3 for Bank of Boston's new policy in 1985.]
6. First Chicago says it had none of its own outstanding to SA borrowers as of 3/85.
7. PNC Financial had $1.8 million of its own outstanding to SA borrowers as of 3/84.
8. Texas Commerce Bankshares had $33.5 million of its own outstanding to SA borrowers as of 3/84.
9. Maryland National had $17.9 million of its own outstanding to SA borrowers as of 12/83.
10. Bank of New York had $11.5 million of its own outstanding to SA borrowers as of 12/83.
11. United Banks of Colorado had $170,000 of its own outstanding to SA borrowers as of 12/83.

Source: See Appendix III-A.

APPENDIX III - D

U.S. Banks Participating in Loans to South Africa - Ranked by Total Amount of All Loans in Which Ever Participated, 1972-May 1984

Rank	Company	Toal Loan Participation ($ million)
1	Citicorp	2,623.0
2	Manufacturers Hanover	1,414.9
3	First Boston Inc.	1,309.4
4	Kidder, Peabody & Co.	1,154.6
5	Chase Manhattan (Lincoln First)	1,027.5
6	J.P. Morgan & Co.	963.9
7	Smith Barney Inc.	857.7
8	Goldman, Sachs & Co.	850.0
9	Merrill Lynch & Co.	804.7
10	Prudential Insurance (Bache)	670.4
11	Morgan Stanley & Co.	660.3
12	American Express (Shearson/Lehman)	639.0
13	PaineWebber Group Inc.	517.6
14	Arnhold & S. Bleichroder Co.	495.2
15	Dillon, Read & Co.	437.1
16	Drexel Burnham Lambert	354.1
17	Continental Illinois Corp.	GT 327.0[1]
18	Aetna Life & Casualty (Montague [UK])	323.1
19	Chemical New York Corp.	310.4
20	BankAmerica (Seafirst)	284.3
21	Phibro-Salomon Inc. (Saloman Bros.)	269.6

Rank	Company	Total Loan Participation ($ million)
22	Sears Roebuck (Dean Whitter Reynolds)	267.5
23	First Chicago Corp.	248.8
24	Lazard Freres & Co.	227.9
25	Dresdner Bank [WG] (ABD Securities)	204.5
26	InterFirst Corp.	200.0
27	Bear, Stearns & Co.	180.6
28	Private Export Funding Co. (PEFCO)	175.8
29	New York Hanseatic	148.0
30	European American Bancorp.	138.1
31	CoreStates Financial (Philadelphia National)	128.7
32	Irving Bank Corp.	125.0
33	Midland Bank [UK] (Crocker Natl.)	121.7
34	RepublicBank Corp. (Houston Natl.)	101.9
35	NCNB Corp.	GT 101.5[2]
36	Bankers Trust of New York Corp.	100.0
37	PNC Financial (Providence Natl.)	99.8
38	Dow Chemical Co.	62.0
39	Bank of Boston (First National Bank/Boston)	GT 57.5[3]
40	Wells Fargo & Co.	54.0
41	Fidelcor	53.0
42	Maryland National Corp.	51.2
43	Exchange Intl. (Central Natl/ Chicago)**	50.5
44	First American Bank (Northern States)	50.0
44	First Empire State Corp.	50.0
44	First Kentucky National Corp.	50.0
44	First Pennsylvania Corp.	50.0
44	First Washington Securities Corp.	50.0
44	E.F. Hutton Group	50.0
44	Merchants National Corp.	50.0
44	Rothschild Inc. (New Court Secs.)	50.0
44	United Virginia Bankshares Inc.	50.0
53	First Wisconsin Corp.	34.7
54	Centran Corp.*	16.7
55	Citizens & Southern Georgia Corp.	8.1
56	Riggs National Corp.	7.5
57	First Bank System (Banks of Iowa)	6.1

Rank	Company	Total Loan Participation ($ million)
58	Society Corp.*	5.7
59	Arizona BancWest	3.0
60	AmeriTrust Corp.	2.9
61	Norwest Corp. (NW Natl Bk, Minneapolis)	2.5
62	First Atlanta Corp.	2.0
63	Security Pacific Corp.	1.7
64	Bank of Montreal [Can] (Harris Trust)	1.4
65	National City Corp. (Natl City Bk/Cleve)	0.8
66	Mellon Bank Corp.	0.5
67	Huntington Bancshares Inc.	0.4
67	Northern Trust Corp.	0.4
69	First City Bancorp of Texas	0.3
69	First Interstate Bancorp.	0.3
69	Midlantic Banks (New Jersey Bank)	0.3
72	Banc One Corp. (Winters Natl)	0.1
72	Northeast Bancorp (Union Trust)	0.1
—	Texas Commerce Bancshares Inc.	GT 0.0[4]
—	Bank of New York Co.	GT 0.0[5]
—	United Banks of Colorado Inc.	GT 0.0[6]
—	Fleet Financial Group Inc.	GT 0.0
—	Peoples Bancorp.	GT 0.0
—	Ranier Bancorp.	GT 0.0

Notes

These rankings are based on the totals of both repaid and outstanding loans in which the banks participated during 1972-May 1984, where data on such loans were publicly available; it is probable that banks have participated in more loans to SA borrowers than have been made public. The rankings are not based on a bank's own share of these loans (which is usually not known) nor on the known amount of its own loans to SA borrowers (on which data are very sparse). Sources on loan participation are the studies by Beate Klein and others published by the U.N. Centre Against Apartheid and Corporate Data Exchange. Sources on banks' own loans (shown in the notes below) are IRRC, *Foreign Investment in South Africa and Namibia*, recent issues of *The Wall Street Journal*, and various banks' announcements.

*   Society Corp. is acquiring Centran Corp.
**   Bank claims it has had no involvement in any SA loans.
1.   Continental Illinois had $315-420 million of its own outstanding to SA borrowers as of 12/83.
2.   NCNB had $217.0 million of its own outstanding to SA borrowers as of 12/83; another $130.0 million of its own was loaned to SA borrowers in 1984 (maturity dates of 1984 loans unknown).
3.   Bank of Boston has $75.0 million of its own outstanding to SA borrowers as of 3/85.
4.   Texas Commerce Bankshares had $33.5 million of its own outstanding to SA borrowers as of 3/84.
5.   Bank of New York had $11.5 million of its own outstanding to SA borrowers as of 12/83.
6.   United Banks of Colorado had $179,000 of its own outstanding to SA borrowers as of 12/83.
See source for Appendix III -A.
Source: See Appendix III-A.

APPENDIX IV

Resources

A. Organizations

Africa Network
P.O. Box 59364
Chicago, IL 60659
(312) 328-9305

Africa Resource Center
464 19th Street
Oakland, CA 94612
(415) 763-8011

American Committee on Africa/
Africa Fund
198 Broadway, Suite 401
New York, NY 10038
(212) 962-1210

American Friends Service Committee
Peace Education, Southern African
Program
1501 Cherry Street
Philadelphia, PA 19102
(215) 241-7169

Black Vanguard Resource Center
P.O. Box 6289
Norfolk, VA 23508
(804) 623-7785

Clergy and Laity Concerned
198 Broadway
New York, NY 10038
(212) 964-6730

Episcopal Churchpeople for a Free
Southern Africa
339 Lafayette Street
New York, NY 10012
(212) 447-0066

International Defense and Aid Fund
for Southern Africa
P.O. Box 17
Cambridge, MA 02138
(617) 491-8343

Madison Area Committee on Southern
Africa (MACSA)
Pres House
731 State Street Mall
Madison, WI 53703
(608) 251-3667

Mozambique Resource Center
P.O. Box 2006
Madison Square Station
New York, NY 10159

New World Resource Center
1476 West Irving Park Road
Chicago, IL 60613
(312) 348-3370

Southern Africa Task Force
P.O. Box 88128
Houston, TX 77288

Toronto Committee for the Liberation
of Southern Africa
427 Bloor Street West
Toronto, Ontario, Canada
(413) 967-5562

TransAfrica, TransAfrica Forum
545 8th Street SE, Suite 200
Washington, DC 20003
(202) 547-2550

The United Nations Centre
Against Apartheid
c/o The United Nations Information
Center
1889 F Street NW, Ground Floor
Washington, DC 20006

The U.N. Special Committee Against
Apartheid
U.N. Secretariat
New York, NY 10017
(212) 754-5295

United Nations Council for Namibia
United Nations Plaza
New York, NY 10017
(212) 754-5399

Unity in Action Network
251 W. 125th Street, Suite 12
Harlem, NY 10027

Washington Office on Africa
110 Maryland Avenue NE
Washington, DC 20002
(202) 546-7961

B. Liberation Movement Representatives in the United States

African National Congress of South Africa
J.M. Makatini
801 Second Avenue
New York, NY 10017
(212) 490-3487

Pan Africanist Congress of Azania
Ahmed Gora Ebrahim
211 E. 43rd Street, Suite 703
New York, NY 10017
(212) 986-7378

Black Consciousness Movement
of Azania
Andrew Lukele
410 Central Park West, 3C
New York, NY 10025

South West African People's Organization
Theo-Ben Gurirab
801 Second Avenue
New York, NY 10017
(212) 557-2450

C. Periodicals

Africa News, P.O. Box 3851, Durham, NC 27702 ($25/year).
AIM Bulletin, P.O. Box 896, Maputo, Mozambique ($15/year).
ANC Weekly News Briefing, 801 Second Avenue, New York, NY 10017 ($15/year).
Angola Information, 34 Percey Street, London W1P 9FG, England (approx. $25/year).
Facts and Reports, Holland Cmt., O.Z. Achteburgwal 173, 1012 DJ Amsterdam, Holland ($40/year, airmail add $11).
Mozambique Information, 34 Percey Street, London W1P 9FG, England (approx. $25/year).
Namibia Today, SWAPO Office, P.O. Box 953, Luanda, Angola ($20/year).
Register, COWSAR, BM Box 2190, London WC1N 3XX, England ($10/year).
Sechaba, ANC, 801 Second Avenue, New York, NY 10017 ($10/year).
Solidarity News Service, Box 1076, Gaborone, Botswana ($25/year).
Zimbabwe Project News Bulletin, P.O. Box 4590, Harare, Zimbabwe (free).

D. Audiovisuals

Africa: A New Look
Produced by International Films. 30 minutes. Available from Film Library, Boston University, 565 Commonwealth Avenue, Boston, MA 02215. An introduction to the continent and the challenges it faces.

Amandla!
Produced by the Washington Office on Africa Educational Fund. Slide-tape, 35 minutes. Available direct, or through Oxfam America. A stirring attempt to inform Americans

about the history of the black resistance movement in South Africa.

Another Face of Africa
Produced by the Presiding Bishop's Fund, 815 Second Avenue, New York, NY 10017-4594. Slide-tape. Focuses on the role of the Episcopal Church in supporting development efforts in Kenya and Liberia.

Beginning Changes
Produced by Oxfam America. 16mm. 27 minutes. Rental Fee: $10. Introduction to the overseas work of Oxfam America, with examples from Zimbabwe and Mozambique.

Habbanaae: The Animal of Friendship
Produced by Oxfam America. Slide-tape, 25 minutes. Rental Fee: $15. A documentary of the Wodaabe Fulani, a tribe of nomadic herders whose way of life in Niger was nearly destroyed by the severe drought of the early seventies. The issues remain relevant to the current situation.

We Carry A Heavy Load: The Work of Rural Woman in Zimbabwe
Produced by the Zimbabwe Women's Bureau. Slide-tape, 20 minutes. Available from Oxfam America. Rental Fee: $15. An examination of the issues facing women in Zimbabwe and many other parts of Africa.

E. Audiovisual Resources

Africa Film Library
Icarus Films
200 Park Avenue South #1319
New York, NY 10003

Films on Africa: An Educator's Guide to 16mm films in the Midwest.
Madison, WI: African Studies Program, University of Wisconsin, 1974.

The Southern Africa Media Center
California Newsreel
630 Sonoma Street
San Francisco, CA 94103

APPENDIX V

For Further Reading

A. Southern Africa

Association of Concerned African Scholars. *United States Military Involvement in Southern Africa*. Boston: South End Press, 1978.

Mittleman, J.H. *Underdevelopment and the Transition to Socialism: Mozambique and Tanzania*. New York: Academic Press, 1981.

Parsons, Neil. *A New History of Southern Africa*. New York: Holmes and Meier, 1983.

176

Seidman, Ann, and Makgetla, Neva. *Outposts of Monopoly Capitalism: Southern Africa in the Changing Global Economy*. Westport, CT: Lawrence Hill, 1980.

Selwyn, P. *Industries in the Southern African Periphery: A Study of Industrial Development in Botswana, Lesotho and Swaziland*. London: Croom Helm in association with Institute of Development Studies, Sussex, 1975.

Thompson, Carol. *Challenge to Imperialism: The Front Line States in the Liberation of Zimbabwe*. Boulder, CO: Westview Press, forthcoming.

B. Angola

Bender, Gerald J. *Angola under the Portuguese: The Myth and the Reality*. Berkeley: University of California Press, 1978.

Bhagavan, M.R. *Angola, Prospects for Socialist Industrialization*. Uppsala: Scandinavian Institute of African Studies, 1980.

Davidson, Basil. *In the Eye of the Storm: Angola's People*. Garden City, NY: Doubleday, 1972.

El-Khawas, Mohamed A. *Angola: The American-South African Connection*. Washington, D.C.: African Bibliographic Center, 1978.

Harsh, Ernest and Thomas, Tony. *Angola: The Hidden History of Washington's War*. New York: Pathfinder Press, 1976.

Minter, William. *Imperial Network and External Dependency: The Case of Angola*. Beverly Hills, CA: Sage Press, 1972.

Stockwell, John. *In Search of Enemies: A CIA Story*. New York: Norton, 1978.

Wolfers, Michael and Begerol, Jane. *Angola in the Frontline*. London: Zed Press, 1983.

C. Botswana

Colclough, Christopher and McCarthy, Stephen. *The Political Economy of Botswana: A Study of Growth and Distribution*. New York: Oxford University Press, 1980.

Harvey, Charles, ed. *Papers on the Economy of Botswana*. London: Heinemann Educational Books, 1981.

Oommen, M.A., Inganji, F.K., and Ngcongco, L.D., eds. *Botwana's Economy Since Independence*. New Delhi: McGraw Hill, 1983.

D. Lesotho

World Bank. *Lesotho: A Development Challenge*. Washington, D.C.: International Bank for Reconstruction and Development, 1975.

E. Malawi

Williams, T. David. *Malawi: The Politics of Despair*. New York: Cornell University Press, 1978.

F. Mozambique

First, Ruth. *Black Gold: The Mozambican Miner, Proletarian and Peasant*. New York: St. Martin's Press, 1983.

Hanlon, Joseph. *Mozambique: The Revolution Under Fire*. London: Zed Press, 1984.

Isaacman, Allen F. and Barbara. *Mozambique: From Colonialism to Revolution, 1900-1982*. Boulder, CO: Westview Press, 1983.

Machel, Samora. *Establishing People's Power to Serve the Masses*. Dar es Salaam: Tanzania Publishing House, 1977.

Munslow, Barry. *Mozambique: The Revolution and Its Origins*. New York: Longman, 1983.

G. Namibia

Catholic Institute for International Relations and British Council of Churches, *Namibia in the 1980s*. London: Russell Press, 1981.

Cronje, Gillian and Suzanne, *The Workers of Namibia*. London: International Defense and Aid Fund for Southern Africa, 1979.

Green, R.H. *From Sudwestafrika to Namibia: The Political Economy of Transition*. Uppsala: Scandinavian Institute of African Studies, 1981.

Hovey, Gail. *Namibia's Stolen Wealth: North American Investment and South African Occupation*. New York: Africa Fund, 1982.

Liberation Support Movement, ed., *Namibia: SWAPO Fights for Freedom*. Oakland, CA: LSM Information Center, 1978.

Moorsom, Richard. *Agriculture - Transforming a Wasted Land*. London: Catholic Institute for International Relations, 1982.

Namibia in the 1980s. London: Catholic Institute for International Relations, 1981 (one of a series titled, *A Future for Namibia*).

Namibia: The Facts. London: International Defense and Aid Fund for Southern Africa, 1980.

Roberts, Alun. *The Rossing File - The Inside Story of Britain's Secret Contract for Namibian Uranium*. London: Namibian Support Committee (CANUC), 1980.

A Trust Betrayed: Namibia (New York: United Nations, 1974). The United Nations Council for Namibia publishes current documents on the social and economic conditions in Namibia, as well as the role of transnational corporations there.

H. South Africa

Automating Apartheid: U.S. Computer Exports to South Africa and the Arms Embargo. Philadelphia: NARMIC/American Friends Service Committee, 1982.

Biko, Stephen. *Black Consciousness in South Africa*. M. Arnold, ed. New York: Vintage Books, 1979.

Bissell, Richard E., and Chester A. Crocker, eds. *South Africa into the 1980s*. Boulder, CO: Westview Press, 1979.

Carter, Gwendolen M. *Which Way is South Africa Going?* Bloomington: Indiana University Press, 1980.

Clarke, Duncan G. *Policy, Issues, and Economic Sanctions on South Africa*. Geneva: International University Exchange Fund, 1980.

Houghton, D. Hobart. *The South African Economy*. New York: Oxford University Press, 1976.

Human Rights in the Homelands: South Africa's Delegation of Repression.
New York: A Fund for Free Expression, 1984.

Innes, Duncan. *Anglo American and the Rise of Modern South Africa.* New York: Monthly Review Press, 1984.

Magubane, Bernard. *The Political Economy of Race and Class in South Africa.* New York: Monthly Review Press, 1980.

"Military Exports to South Africa - A Research Report on the Arms Embargo." Philadelphia: NARMIC/American Friends Service Committee, 1984.

Nelson Mandela, The struggle is my life. London: International Defense and Aid Fund for Southern Africa, 1978.

Ntantala, Phyllis. *An African Tragedy: The Black Woman Under Apartheid.* Detroit: Agascha Productions, 1976.

Nyangoni, Wellington. *The OECD and Western Mining Multinational Corporations in the Republic of South Africa.* Boston: University Press of America, 1982.

Nyangoni, Wellington. *United States Foreign Policy and South Africa.* New World Research Committee of the Society for Common Insights Press in association with the African Institute for the Study of Human Values, 1981.

Richard, Leonard. *South Africa at War: White Power and the Crisis in Southern Africa.* Westport, CT: Lawrence Hill, 1983.

Schmidt, Elizabeth. *Decoding Corporate Camouflage: U.S. Business Support for Apartheid.* Washington, D.C.: Institute for Policy Studies, 1980.

Seidman, Ann and Seidman, Neva. *South Africa and U.S. Multinational Corporations.* Westport, CT: Lawrence Hill, 1978.

Seidman, Judy. *Face-Lift Apartheid: South Africa after Soweto.* London: International Defense and Aid Fund for Southern Africa, 1980.

South Africa: Time Running Out, The Report of the Study Commission on U.S. Policy Toward Southern Africa. (Chaired by Franklin A. Thomas, president of the Ford Foundation). Berkeley: University of California Press and Foreign Policy Study Foundation, 1981.

Survey of Race Relations in South Africa. Johannesburg: South African Institute of Race Relations, annual.

Tutu, Desmond. *Crying in the Wilderness: The Struggle for Justice in South Africa.* Grand Rapids, MI: W.B. Eberdmans Publishing Co., 1982.

Zdenck, Cervenka, and Rogers, Barbara. *The Nuclear Axis: Secret Collaboration Between West Germany and South Africa.* New York: Times Books, 1978.

I. Swaziland

Booth, Alan R. *Swaziland - Tradition and Change in a Southern African Kingdon.* Boulder, CO: Westview Press, 1983.

Fransman, Martin. *Development and Underdevelopment in Southern Africa: A Case Study.* Botswana: National Institute for Research in Development and African Studies, University of Botswana, 1976.

J. Tanzania

Coulson, Andrew. *Tanzania: A Political Economy.* New York: Oxford University Press, 1982.

Hyden, Goran. *Beyond Ujamaa in Tanzania: Underdevelopment and an Uncaptured Peasantry.* Berkeley: University of California Press, 1980.

Nyerere, Julius K. *Crusade for Liberation.* New York: Oxford University Press, 1979.

Resnick, Idrian N. *The Long Transition: Building Socialism in Tanzania.* New York: Monthly Review Press, 1982.

Rweyemamu, J.F. *Underdevelopment and Industrialization in Tanzania: A Study of Perverse Capitalist Industrial Development.* New York: Oxford University Press, 1973.

Saul, John S. *The State and Revolution in East Africa: Essays.* New York: Monthly Review Press, 1980.

K. Zambia

Bhagavan, M.R. *Zambia, Impact of Industrial Strategy on Regional Imbalance and Social Inequality.* Uppsala: Scandinavian Institute of African Studies, 1978.

Bratton, Michael. *The Local Politics of Rural Development: Peasant and Party-State in Zambia.* Hanover, NH: University Press of New England, 1980.

International Labour Organization/JASPA Basic Needs Mission to Zambia. *Basic Needs in an Economy Under Pressure.* Addis Ababa, Ethiopia: International Labour Office, Jobs and Skills Programme for Africa, 1981.

Kandeke, Timothy Katongo. *Fundamentals of Zambian Humanism.* Lusaka: NECZAM, 1977.

Martin, Anthony. *Minding Their Own Business: Zambia's Struggle Against Western Control.* London: Hutchinson, 1972.

Mhone, Guy C.Z. *The Political Economy of a Dual Labor Market in Africa: The Copper Industry and Dependency in Zambia, 1929-1969.* Rutherford, NJ: Fairleigh Dickinson University Press, 1982.

Shaw, Timothy. *Dependency and Underdevelopment: The Development and Foreign Policies of Zambia.* Athens, OH: Ohio University, Center for International Studies, Africa Program, 1976.

Sklar, Richard L. *Corporate Power in an African State: The Political Impact of Multinational Mining Companies in Zambia.* Berkeley: University of California Press, 1975.

Turok, Ben, ed. *Development in Zambia: A Reader.* London: Zed Press, 1981.

L. Zimbabwe

Clarke, Duncan G. *Foreign Companies and International Investment in Zimbabwe.* London: Catholic Institute for International Relations, 1980.

Lake, Anthony. *The "Tar Baby" Option: American Policy Toward Southern Rhodesia.* New York: Columbia University Press: A Study from the Carnegie Endowment for Peace, 1976.

Martin, David, and Johnson, Phyllis. *The Struggle for Zimbabwe: The Chimurenga War.* Boston: Faber and Faber, 1981.

Ndlela, Daniel. *Dualism in the Rhodesian Colonial Economy.* Lund, Sweden: Department of Economics, University of Lund, 1981.

Stoneman, Colin, ed. *Zimbabwe's Inheritance.* New York: St. Martin's Press, ;1982.

Utete, Charles Munhamu Botsio. *The Road to Zimbabwe: The Political Economy of Settler Colonialism, National Liberation and Foreign Intervention.* Washington, D.C.: University Press of America, 1979.

Zimbabwe—Towards a New Order—an Economic and Social Survey. New York: United Nations Development Programme and United Nations Conference on Trade and Development, 1980.

REFERENCES

Chapter One—Introduction: The Crisis in Southern Africa

1. See Chapter Two for more detailed analysis and sources of information relating to the independent countries of southern Africa.
2. Oxfam America and OXFAM (U.K.) are independent organizations, but they work collaboratively in some overseas projects and frequently share resources and information.
3. Barbara Kaim, Report to Oxfam America from Zimbabwe, February 17, 1984. A year and a half later, several thousand Mozambicans remained in camps established by the Zimbabwean government and private voluntary organizations, while several thousand more continued to work on communal farms. The Zimbabwean government sought to encourage as many as possible to return to Mozambique, but the continued MNR destabilization tactics hindered this effort.
4. Chester Crocker, prepared statement before the Subcommittee on Africa, Committee on Foreign Affairs, U.S. House of Representatives, hearing on "United States Policy Towards Southern Africa: Focus on Namibia, Angola and South Africa," September 16, 1981 (Washington, D.C.: U.S. Government Printing Office, 1983).
5. Economist Intelligence Unit, *Quarterly Economic Review of South Africa, Annual Supplement, 1984.*
6. *South Africa: Time Running Out*, The Report of the Study Commission on U.S. Policy Toward Southern Africa (Berkeley: University of California Press, 1981).
7. In the early 1960s, as the first sub-Saharan African states attained independence, less than 10 percent of colonial Africa had been geologically explored; only after independence have many strategic deposits been discovered in several countries; for example, uranium in Gabon and Niger, and oil in several north African states, Angola and Nigeria.
8. See Chapter 3 below for details and sources.
9. In 1981, British firms held about 55 percent of direct foreign investment in South Africa; U.S. firms, about 18 percent. The latter figure does not, however, include U.S. investments in U.K. firms like British Petroleum (listed on the New York Stock Exchange) or Canadian firms like Falconbridge which invest heavily in South Africa. West German firms held about 10 percent of direct foreign investment in South Africa. See Anne Newman and Cathy Bowers, *Foreign Investment in South Africa and Namibia—A Directory of United States, Canadian, and British Corporations Operating in South Africa and Namibia, With a Survey of the 100 Biggest U.S. Bank Holding Companies and Their Practices and Policies on Lending to South Africa* (Washington, D.C.: Investor Responsibility Research Center, December 1984).
   Japan, Switzerland, and the United Kingdom, in that order, had become South Africa's next largest buyers in 1981; together they purchased nearly a fifth of South Africa's exports. West Germany, Japan, and the United Kingdom are the next largest sources of South Africa's imports, together providing almost 40 percent of South Africa's purchases abroad. (South Africa's export and import data include the data for Botswana, Swaziland, Lesotho, and Namibia.) See Economist Intelligence Unit, *Quarterly Economic Review of South Africa*, No. 2, 1985.
10. Chester Crocker, "Reagan Administration's Africa Policy: A Progress Report," Fourth Annual Conference on International Affairs, U.S.-Africa Relations Since 1960, University of Kansas, November 10, 1983.
11. Numerous press accounts appeared in the spring of 1981 reporting that a formal review of policy toward southern Africa was under way, including articles by Anthony Lewis, "Conservative Reality," *New York Times*, June 11, 1981, and Henry Trewhitt, "Reagan must juggle a mix of ideologies and politics in southern Africa," *The Baltimore Sun*, Jun 4, 1981.
12. Chester Crocker, "South Africa: Strategy for Change," *Foreign Affairs,* Winter 1980-81.
13. Ibid.

Chapter Two—Institutionalized Poverty in Southern Africa

1. The Great Zimbabwe Ruins stand mute testimony to the kingdom that straddled the trade route from what is now Botswana down to the Sabi River and thence to the coast. Among items discovered in the ruins are artifacts showing that the kingdom carried on trade with faraway China and India long before the first European settler arrived. See Peter S. Garlake, *Great Zimbabwe* (London: Thames & Hudson, 1983).
2. Robin Palmer, *Land and Racial Domination in Rhodesia* (Berkeley: University of California Press, 1977).
3. For more detail and specific sources for the information presented here relating to the Zimbabwean land issue, see Roger C. Riddell, *From Rhodesia to Zimbabwe: The Land Question* (London: Catholic Institute for International Relations, 1978).
4. For discussion of colonial development in Zambia, see R.E. Baldwin, *Economic Development and Export Growth, A Study of Northern Rhodesia 1920-1960* (Berkeley and Los Angeles: University of California Press, 1966).
5. *The Transitional National Development Plan, 1982/83-1984/85 of the Republic of Zimbabwe* reported that "about 2.5 million people in the communal areas suffer from a critical energy shortage." (Vol. 1, November 1982, p. 13.) Not only did they lack electricity, but high population growth and density of settlement had led to a severe shortage of wood for fuel.
6. In 1981-2, interviews with bankers by University of Zimbabwe students confirmed that they still held this opinion. See student reports, Economics Department, University of Zimbabwe (mimeo) 1981. For a discussion of the problem of rural credit in Zimbabwe, see Daniel B. Ndlela, *Dualism in the Rhodesian Colonial Economy* (Lund, Sweden: Department of Economics, University of Lund, 1981), Chapter 6.
7. For example, in Zimbabwe prior to independence, the marketing boards charged a levy of 15 percent of the selling price on African peasants' produce; see A.J.B. Hughes, *Development in Rhodesian Tribal Areas: An Overview* (Tribal Areas of Rhodesia Research Foundation, 1974), p. 259.
8. H. Johnstone, *Trade and General Conditions Report* (Nyasaland: 1895-96).
9. For discussion, see Allen Isaacman and Barbara Isaacman, *Mozambique: From Colonialism to Revolution, 1900-1982* (Boulder, CO: Westview Press, 1983).
10. For example, for Zimbabwe see A.T. Stubbs, "The Tribal Trust Lands in Transition: Land Use," paper presented at the Natural Resources Board Symposium, June 2, 1977 (mimeo). The carrying capacity of these lands was discussed fully in V. Vincent and R.G. Thomas, *An Agro-Ecological Survey in the Federation of Rhodesia and Nyasaland, An Agricultural Survey of Southern Rhodesia* (Salisbury: 1960).
11. See for example, P. Raikes, "Report on a tour of regions in Tanzania," (Dar es Salaam, Tanzania: Economic Research Bureau Seminar, mimeo, 1969).
12. For detailed examples of this process, see Robin Palmer and Neil Parsons, eds., *The Roots of Rural Poverty in Central and Southern Africa* (Berkeley, CA: University of California Press, 1977).
13. For example, for Zimbabwe see C. Stoneman, *Zimbabwe Inheritance* (New York: St. Martin's Press, 1981); for Mozambique see J. Hanlon, *Mozambique: The Revolution under Fire* (London: Zed Press, 1984).
14. For example, in northeastern Zambia as many as 40 to 60 percent of adult men migrated to work on the mines. In Lesotho, an even higher proportion of men migrate to South Africa for cash employment. See Colin Murray, *Families Divided: The Impact of Migrant Labour in Lesotho* (Cambridge: Cambridge University Press, 1981); Carol Kerven, *Migration in Botswana: Patterns, Causes, and Consequences* (Gaborone, Botswana: Central Statistical Office, 1980, Vol. III); A.K.H. Weinrich, "Changing Position of Women in Zimbabwe," Economic Commission for Africa, Mulpoc Conference, Lusaka, 1978 (mimeo); A. Michell, "Labor Migration in Southern Africa: Its Impact on Women Left Behind," South/South Conference, Montreal, 1985.

15. For a survey of the literature relating to women in southern Africa, particularly Tanzania, see Ophelia Mascarenhas and Marjorie Mbilinya, *Women in Tanzania, An Analytical Bibliography* (Uppsala: Swedish International Development Agency, 1983).

16. In southern Africa, the Poverty Datum Line, used to define the poverty level, is usually measured as the income necessary to support the average African family at a minimum subsistence level. A detailed study of pre-independence wages in Zimbabwe showed that sub-Poverty-Datum-Line wages were the norm in all sectors for African workers, with wages in the mines being "inadequate for almost all employees"; and in agriculture, "almost 95 percent receive less than $20 a month . . . $25 less than the income needed by a family of six to live at the PDL." See Roger Riddell and Peter S. Harris, *The Poverty Datum Line as a Wage Fixing Standard—An Application to Rhodesia* (Gwelo: Mambo Press, 1975), p. 71. In other countries shortly after independence, household budget surveys conducted by the national Central Statistical Offices show that the average worker earned less than enough to support himself and his family at a level of health and decency; e.g. Central Statistical Bureau, Tanzania, *Household Budget Survey of Wage Earners in Dar es Salaam*, May 1967; Central Statistical Office, Zambia, *Consumer Price Index—Low Income Group, New Series*, Lusaka, 1970 (mimeo) and charts from the Central Statistical Office showed income and expenditure patterns of the African population. In the economic crisis of the late 1970s and early 1980s, real incomes deteriorated further.

17. For the Portuguese colonial educational policies, see Isaacmans, op. cit., pp. 49-52.

18. The minority regime declared independence from Britain without British agreement in order to avoid giving the black majority the right to vote.

19. Government of Zimbabwe, *National Manpower Survey* (Harare: Ministry of Manpower Planning and Development, 1981), Vol. 1, p. 51.

20. The literature relating to these debates is too extensive to cite fully, but the following will give some idea of the main issues. For Malawi: T. David Williams, *Malawi—The Politics of Despair* (Ithaca, NY: Cornell University Press, 1978); Carolyn McMaster, *Malawi: Foreign Policy and Development* (London: Julian Friedman, 1974). For Mozambique: Barry Munslow, *Mozambique: The Revolution and Its Origins* (Essex, England: Longman House, 1983); Joseph Hanlon, *Mozambique: The Revolution Under Fire* (London: Zed Press, 1984). For Tanzania: Ann Seidman, *Comparative Development Strategies in East Africa* (Nairobi: East African Publishing House, 1972); Andrew Coulson, *Tanzania, A Political Economy* (Oxford: Clarendon Press, 1982); *The Agricultural Policy of Tanzania* (Dar es Salaam: Ministry of Agriculture, 1983); John S. Saul, *The State and Revolution in Eastern Africa: Essays* (New York: Monthly Review Press, 1979); Philip Raikes, *Ujamaa Vijijini and Rural Socialist Development* (Copenhagen: Institute for Development Research, 1974). For Zambia: A. Seidman, ed., *Natural Resources and National Welfare: The Case of Copper* (New York: Praeger, 1975); Richard Sklar, *Corporate Power in an African State* (Berkeley: University of California Press, 1975); J. Zulu, *Zambian Humanism: Some Major Spiritual and Economic Challenges* (Lusaka: NECZAM, 1970). For Zimbabwe: *Towards a New Order: An Economic and Social Survey—working papers* (United Nations, 1980); A. Seidman, "Development Strategy for Zimbabwe" in *Zambezia* (Inaugural Lecture), (Harare: University of Zimbabwe, 1983); Andre Astrow, *Zimbabwe, a revolution that lost its way* (London: Zed Press, 1983).

21. An extensive literature supports the argument for more balanced industrial-agricultural development: See United Nations Economic Commission for Africa Studies: *Industrial Growth in Africa* E/CN.14/IN R/1/Rev 1, 1962; *Iron and Steel in Africa* E/CN.14/27, 1963; *East and Central Africa Industrial Mission* E/CN.14/247; *Report of ECA Mission for Economic Cooperation in Central Africa, 1965*. The requirements of an industrial strategy and the consequences of alternative approaches on a national level have been considered in A. Seidman, *Planning for Development in Sub-Saharan Africa* (New York: Praeger, 1974), Chapters 6 and 7. The possible consequences for stimulating rural development are considered in *Progress in Land Reform, Fifth Report* (New York: U.N. Food and Agriculture Organization, 1970), especially Part V.

22. See *International Financial Statistics, Country Reports* (Washington, D.C.: International Monetary Fund), for current consequences for imports, exports, and balance of payments of southern African states.

23. *Accelerated Development in Sub-Saharan Africa* (Washington, D.C.: The World Bank, 1981), Table 3.1, p. 17.

24. For a critique of IMF policy as it affects Third World countries like those in southern Africa, see *'Monetarism' and the Third World* (Institute of Development Studies, Sussex, December 1981), Vol. 13, No. 1.

25. By 1980, Tanzania collected 43 percent of its tax revenue from sales taxes (IMF, *Government Statistics*, 1982). By 1983, the Zimbabwean government had raised sales taxes to 18 percent on all but a very few basic necessities. (Harare: Minister of Finance, Economic Planning and Development, "Financial Statement to Parliament," 1983).

26. For information on the devaluation of currencies by individual southern African states, see *International Financial Statistics* (Washington, D.C.: International Monetary Fund), by country, by year.

Chapter Three—Apartheid, Transnational Corporate Investments, and South African Domination of the Region

1. Gail Hovey, "Apartheid's New Clothes," (The Africa Fund: New York, NY, 1983).

2. Chester Crocker, "Reagan Administration's Africa Policy: A Progress Report," Fourth Annual Conference on International Affairs: U.S.-Africa Relations Since 1960, University of Kansas, November 10, 1983.

3. The Report of the Study Committee on U.S. Policy Toward Southern Africa, *Southern Africa: Time Running Out*, Foreign Policy Study Foundation, Inc. (Commission chair: Franklin A. Thomas, president of the Ford Foundation), (Berkeley: University of California Press, 1981); for background discussion on the bantustans, see B. Rogers, *Divide and Rule: South Africa's Bantustans*, revised edition (London: International Defense and Aid Fund for Southern Africa, 1980); M. Horrell, ed., *Race Relations as Regulated by Law in South Africa, 1948-1979,* revised edition (Johannesburg: South African Institute of Race Relations, 1982).

4. *Forced Removals in South Africa* (Capetown: The Surplus People Project, 1983), Vol. 1, p. 5; see also, *Cape Argus*, February 11, 1983.

5. Allister Sparks, "South African Black Village Uprooted," *Washington Post*, May 4, 1984, p. A1. See also Alan Cowell, "Homes Go Up and Down in Daily Cape Town War," *New York Times*, July 31, 1984.

6. Richard Bernstein, "South Africa Drops a Barrier To Relations Between Races," *New York Times*, April 21, 1985.

7. Judy Seidman, *Face-Lift Apartheid* (London: International Defense and Aid Fund for Southern Africa, 1980).

8. Donald Woods, "Letter to the Editor," *New York Times*, June 10, 1984. Under the new Constitution, P.W. Botha's title changed from prime minister to state president in September 1984.

9. *Survey of Race Relations in South Africa, 1982* (Johannesburg: South African Institute of Race Relations, 1983), p. 334.

10. *Apartheid—The Facts* (London: International Defense and Aid Fund for Southern Africa, 1983), p. 28. This is the source of data relating to education of South African blacks in this section, unless otherwise cited.

11. "South Africa: 1980 School Boycott," International Defense and Aid Fund Briefing Paper No. 1, 1983.

12. *Solidarity News Service* (Botswana), No. 4/84; February 22, 1984.

13. Calculated from Afrikaanse Handelsinstituut estimates of average annual earnings and employment, reported in *Survey of Race Relations in South Africa, 1982*, op. cit., p. 63.

14. For example, the Sullivan Code signatories (see Chapter 5) have promoted Africans to become 3 percent of their managerial staffs. (Arthur D. Little, Inc., *Sixth Report on the Signatory Companies to the Sullivan Principles*, November 1, 1982, pp. 27-28.)
15. *Rand Daily Mail* (South Africa), September 17, 1982; *House of Assembly Debates* (Hansard), South Africa, September 8, 1981; *Survey of Race Relations in South Africa, 1982*, op. cit., p. 120.
16. For discussion of wages and working conditions of domestic workers, see *Survey of Race Relations in South Africa, 1982*, op. cit., pp. 123-4.
17. *1983 Midway Report from the Second Carnegie Study of Poverty in South Africa*, papers presented at a conference in South Africa, April 1984.
18. C. Simpkins, "The Demographic Demand for Labour and Institutional Context of African Unemployment in South Africa: 1960-1980," South African Labour and Development Research Unit, Working Paper No. 39, August 1981.
19. *Star* (S.A.), November 16, 1982.
20. *1983 Midway Report from the Second Carnegie Study of Poverty in South Africa*, op. cit.
21. *Star* (S.A.), *Rand Daily Mail* (S.A.), April 15 and 19, 1982; *Argus* (S.A.), August 3, 1982; *Pretoria News* (S.A.), August 5, 1982; and *Rand Daily Mail* (S.A.), May 27, 1982.
22. *Nedbank* (S.A.), 1983, p. 33, 240; *Star* (S.A.), May 14, 1983; and *Financial Mail* (S.A.), April 23, 1982.
23. U.S. Department of Commerce, *Survey of Current Business*, August 1983; Board of Governors of the Federal Reserve System, Federal Financial Institutions Examination Council, *Statistical Release*, E.16(26) of June 1, 1983.
24. The percent of U.S. direct investments is reported in Anne Newman, "The U.S. Corporate Stake in South Africa," *Africa News*, May 20, 1985, Vol. XXIV, No. 10. Newman is co-author of the IRRC study, *Foreign Investment in South Africa and Namibia* (1984). All other information is from U.S. Department of Commerce, *Survey of Current Business*, which reports on U.S. foreign investments in Africa and South Africa in manufacturing and other sectors. It also reports the rates of return by sector, although in some cases because so few firms are involved—oil is a case in point—it does not report the data because it does not wish to reveal the status of the individual firms. Indirect investments are shares owned by U.S. individuals or corporations in predominantly South African firms. Since figures on U.S. investments in South Africa through U.S. subsidiaries based in Europe or Canada are not available, a complete estimate of all U.S. indirect investments in South Africa is not available.
25. This history has been thoroughly documented elsewhere: Leonard Thompson and Monica Wilson, eds., *The Oxford History of South Africa* (Oxford: Oxford University Press, 1969); N. Parsons, *A New History of Southern Africa* (New York: Holmes and Meier, 1983); J. and R. Simons, *Class and Colour in South Africa, 1850 to 1950* (Harmondsworth: Penguin African Library, 1969); D.H. Houghton, *The South African Economy* (New York: Oxford University Press, 1976).
26. The story of this strike and subsequent reinforcement of the Colour Bar in the mines is detailed in F.A. Johnston, *Class, Race and Gold: A Study of Class Relations and Racial Discrimination in South Africa* (Boston: Routledge & Kegan Paul, 1976).
27. Houghton, *The South African Economy*, op. cit., describes the role of the South African state in its efforts to stimulate foreign investment.
28. Information on Minorca is drawn in part from *Forbes Magazine*, July 7, 1984, p. 117.
29. "Affiliate" or "affiliated company" refers to a company which is partly or wholly owned by another company; it is a related company. "Subsidiary" refers to a company of which more than half the share capital is owned by another compay, called either a holding company or a parent company. Two subsidiaries of the same parent company are affiliated.
30. The names of corporations with contracts with ARMSCOR are unpublished. Information on ARMSCOR is drawn in part from *The Guardian* (Manchester), December 5, 1973.
31. Elizabeth Schmidt, *One Step in the Wrong Direction, An Analysis of the Sullivan Principles as a Strategy for Opposing Apartheid*, revised edition (New York: Episcopal Churchpeople for a Free Southern Africa, January 1985), p. 4.

32. Schmidt, op. cit., pp. 4 and 18. See also "Unified List of U.S. Companies with Investments or Loans in South Africa or Namibia," Appendix III. Although Ford merged its motor interests in South Africa with those of Anglo American, and agreed to remain a signatory of the Sullivan Principles (see Chapter 5 below), Ford continued to contribute in terms of technology and capital to South Africa's production of transport equipment. Ford's director of international affairs said Ford, along with the rest of South Africa's motor industry, had suffered losses in 1984. Ford proposed to close the Neave plant, which employed 1,550 hourly paid and 200 salaried staff, in early 1986. The U.S.-based Investor Responsibility Research Center, a nonpartisan corporate monitoring group, said Ford's decision to merge with Anglo American would not remove the firm from the divestment movement's list. ("Sullivan Hails Ford-Anglo Deal as Breakthrough," *Rand Daily Mail*, February 2, 1985). Other companies, too, reported reduced involvement in South Africa, but publicly cited declining profitability as the reason. (N.D. Kristoff, "U.S. Companies Begin to Cut Some Links to South Africa," *New York Times*, April 29, 1985.) But John Chettle of the South African Foundation, a foe of divestment, admitted in the *Financial Mail* (South Africa, February 1, 1985): "In one respect at least, the divestment forces have already won. They have prevented—discouraged, dissuaded whatever you call it—billions of dollars of new U.S. investment in South Africa."

33. American Committee on Africa, "U.S. Corporations in South Africa: A Summary of Strategic Investments" (New York: ACOA, 1980).

34. Ann and Neva Seidman, *South Africa and U.S Multinational Corporations* (Westport, CT: Lawrence Hill, 1978), p. 100.

35. Schmidt, op. cit., p. 18.

36. Anne Newman, "The U.S. Corporate Stake in South Africa," *Africa News*, May 20, 1985, Vol. XXIV, No. 10.

37. Schmidt, op. cit., p. 19.

38. Newman, op. cit.

39. Schmidt, op. cit., pp. 19-20.

40. Ibid., p. 21. Seidmans, op. cit., pp. 113-16. Several U.S. banks decided not to lend directly to South African government agencies, but continued to lend to the private sector, particularly locally based banks. Anti-apartheid groups pointed out, however, that local banks could lend to government agencies; and in any case, loans to the private sector still provided needed foreign exchange for the national economy that could be used to purchase oil and military equiment. For example, in 1985, the Bank of Boston declared it would no longer lend any funds, not only to the South African government, but to private firms in South Africa. It would only "occasionally execute foreign exchange transactions or confirm a letter of credit for a bank customer exporting to South Africa if the nature of the underlying transaction will not, in the judgement of the Bank, conflict with this policy." (Bank of Boston, "Bank of Boston Adopts a Policy to End All Remaining Lending in South Africa," News Release—Corporate Communications Department, received by Oxfam America, April 1985.)

41. *Business Week*, October 20, 1980.

42. U.S. Department of Commerce, *Survey of Current Business*, August 1982, 1983, and 1984. For a list of U.S. firms with investments in South Africa, see Appendix III.

43. "Dow Chemical here to grow," *The Star* (S.A.), October 28, 1984. For earlier expansion of U.S. investment see, *Financial Times* (S.A.), February 7, 1983.

44. *The Star* (S.A.), September 24, 1973.

45. Prof. J. Keenan, *Black Earnings: Changing Contemporary Patterns* (African Studies Institute: University of the Witswatersrand, 1982).

46. That the South African government, itself, recognizes this problem has been reflected in its efforts to provide incentives to persuade investors to establish new plants in less-developed areas near the growing pools of unemployed labor in the bantustans. (See, for example, the South African government's White Paper, *The Promotion of Industrial Development: An Element of Coordinated Regional Development Strategy for Southern Africa* (Department of Foreign Affairs and Information, 1982).

47. For a summary of the main provisions of the U.S.-South African double-taxation agreement

which has been in effect since 1950, see "Republic of South Africa, Income Tax Treaty," in *Federal Taxes*, Vol. 10 (Englewood Cliffs, NJ: Prentice Hall, 1985) pp. 42, 401-42, 904.

48. See Table 2.1 in Chapter 2.

49. South African Reserve Bank, *Quarterly Bulletin of Statistics*, September 1979; *South African Digest* (Pretoria: Government Printer, September 30, 1977); *Financial Mail* (S.A.), April 7, 1979.

50. *Solidarity News Service* (Botswana), "South Africa—The Militarism of a Society" (SNS special paper), March 1984.

51. *Corporate Activity in South Africa: General Motors Corp. Sales to Police and Military, 1979* (Washington, D.C.: Investor Responsibility Research Center, May 1, 1979), Analysis 6, Supplement No. 16.

52. *Survey of Race Relations in South Africa, 1982*, op. cit., pp. 57-59.

53. The consumer price index (April 1970 = 100) reached 210 by May 1978 [as reported in *Financial Mail* (S.A.), June 30, 1978]; and by 1984 (1980 = 100) had risen another 188 points. (See *International Financial Statistics*, March, 1985, Washington, D.C.: International Monetary Fund, 1985).

54. Official statistics partially conceal these relationships. U.S. and European statisticians follow the lead of South Africa, which after the 1960s incorporated Namibian data with those of South Africa. In addition, after the United Nations declared a boycott of the illegal Rhodesian regime, transnational firms concealed their activities there. Finally, South African trade figures include, without identification, the trade of the politically independent countries of Botswana, Lesotho, and Swaziland, which remain members of the South African Customs Union.

55. *Survey of Race Relations in South Africa, 1982*, op. cit., p. 85 following.

56. For data, see Republic of South Africa, *Foreign Trade Statistics, Imports and Exports*, annual.

57. See discussion in Chapter 2.

58. U.N. Department of Political Affairs, Trusteeship and Decolonization, *Decolonization, Issue on Namibia*, No. 9/Revised edition, December 1977, p. 5.

59. In 1966, the United Nations passed Resolution 2145 (XXI) by 114 votes to 2 (Portugal and South Africa), with three abstentions (France, Malawi, and the United Kingdom), to terminate South Africa's mandate. In 1971, the International Court of Justice gave an Advisory Opinion holding the termination of the mandate was legal (*International Court of Justice Reports, 1971*).

60. The South African government imposed Namibia's "homelands" starting in 1962-3 in accord with the Odendaal Report, which accelerated the systematic program, begun a half century before, of removing the black population from the best farming and mining lands of the country. For a detailed report, see *All Options and None—The Constitutional Talks in Namibia* (London: International Defense and Aid Fund for Southern Africa, August 1976), Fact Paper No. 3.

61. U.N. Council for Namibia, Decree No. 1 for the Protection of the Natural Resources of Namibia, enacted September 27, 1974; U.N. General Assembly Resolution 3295 (XXIX) of 1974.

62. *A Trust Betrayed: Namibia* (New York: United Nations, 1974).

63. Report of the U.N. Council for Namibia (A/10024) (New York: United Nations, 1976), Vol. 1.

64. Company profits are estimated at 44 percent of gross domestic product, compared to total black wages of 9.3 percent of GDP and peasant income of 2.6 percent of GDP. See H.S. Aulatsch and Wilfred W. Asombang, *Towards Economic Development Strategy Options for Independent Namibia* (Lusaka, Zambia: Economics Division, U.N. Institute for Namibia, 1982), Working Paper, p. 30.

65. *Namibia—the Facts* (London: International Defense and Aid Fund for Southern Africa, 1980), p. 27.

66. Ibid., p. 28.

67. Brien Wood, *The Militarization of Namibia's Economy*, U.N. Council of Namibia Seminar on

188

the Military Situation in and Relative to Namibia, SMS/CRP No. 1982/13, June 9, 1982, p. 2.

68. Ibid., p. 7.
69. *Windhoek Advertiser*, April 20 and 21, 1982.
70. *Financial Mail* (S.A.), March 10, 1979.
71. U.N. Document, Anti-Apartheid Committee, A/AC. 115; SR. 361, p. 7; M. Bailey and B. Rivers, *Oil Sanctions Against South Africa, Notes and Documents* (New York: Center Against Apartheid, U.N. Department of Political and Security Council Affairs, June 1978).
72. *Accelerated Development in Sub-Saharan Africa, An Agenda for Action* (Washington, D.C.: The World Bank, 1983), p. 18.
73. See Anglo American Group, *Annual Report*, 1971, p. 77.
74. Houghton, *The South African Economy*, op. cit., describes the founding of ISCOR in South Africa; and D.G. Clarke, *Foreign Companies and International Investment in Zimbabwe* (London: Catholic Institute for International Relations, 1980) gives the basic information about the structure of the Rhodesian Iron and Steel Corporation (RISCO), set up as a parastatal to produce steel in then-Rhodesia (now Zimbabwe).
75. United Republic of Tanzania, *Second Five Year Plan* (Dar es Salaam: 1969), Vol. 1, p. 86.
76. A. Seidman, ed., *Natural Resources and National Welfare—The Case of Copper* (New York: Praeger, 1976) provides the details concerning the copper industry in southern Africa and the Third World.
77. Estimated from Beijer Institute, *Issues in SADCC Energy Planning: Usage Patterns, Resource Potential and Regional Possibilities*, Draft Discussion Document, November 1982, p. 41, following.
78. "Electricity charges may increase by further 60%," *Financial Gazette* (Harare), June 24, 1983.
79. A. Seidman, *The Have-Have Not Gap in Zambia* (Lusaka: University of Zambia, mimeo, 1979).
80. R.H. Green, "Namibia in Transition: Towards a Political Economy of Liberation?" in T. Shaw, ed., *The Future(s) of Africa* (Boulder, CO: Westview Press, 1980), Table 5.
81. For discussion of this process, see R. Murray, *Multinationals Beyond the Market* (New York: Wiley, 1981).
82. These countries, at independence, remained members of the South African Customs Union, a common market arrangement which prohibits member countries from erecting tariff barriers to protect their industries from goods manufactured by other member states. They receive from South Africa a stipulated share of the customs duties on goods they import from outside the Union.
83. U.S. Assistance to International Development, "Malawi," *Development Needs and Opportunities for Cooperation in Southern Africa* (Washington, D.C.: U.S. Agency for International Development, 1979).
84. For details, see A. Seidman, "Distorted Import Substitution Industry: The Zambian Case," in the *Journal of Modern African Studies*, 12, 4/1974.
85. *Financial Mail* (S.A.), March 24, 1978; see also Zambia, *Statistical Digest,* subsequent years.
86. For example, see S.M. Wangwe, "Economic Stabilization Policies in the Industrial Sector," Workshop on Economic Stabilization Policies, Economics Department, University of Dar es Salaam, 1983 (mimeo). First-hand observations from Oxfam America grassroots projects in Tanzania, Zambia, and Zimbabwe; and reports from studies in universities in these countries: e.g. from the Workshop on *Economic Stabilization Policies*, University of Dar es Salaam, Economics Department, 1983; Workshop on *The Zambian Economy: Problems and Prospects*, organized jointly by the Department of Business and Economics, University of Zambia, and the International Development Research Centre of Canada, April 27-29, 1984.
87. *Survey of Race Relations in South Africa, 1983*, op. cit., p. 132, following.
88. The numbers of foreign workers employed in South Africa dropped from 646,504 in 1975 to 301,758 in 1981, according to official South African data; National Manpower Commission,

Annual Report, 1981, p. 252, cited in *Survey of Race Relations in South Africa, 1982*, op. cit., p. 85.

Chapter Four—Toward Regional Independence

1. For details, see D.G. Clarke, *Foreign Companies and International Investment in Zimbabwe* (London: Catholic Institute for International Relations, March 1980).
2. "The MNR and the Pretoria Connection," *Sunday Express* (Britain), August 7, 1983.
3. Zimbabwe Information Group (London), Summer 1980, No. 14.
4. For the American role, see Jeffrey Davidow, *A Peace in Southern Africa: The Lancaster House Conference on Rhodesia, 1979* (Boulder, CO: Westview Press, 1984), pp. 20-22, 78, 86-7; and David Martin and Phyllis Johnson, *The Struggle for Zimbabwe: The Chimurenga War* (Boston: Faber & Faber, 1981), pp. 234-6, 268, 311.
5. For the brief history of South African resistance as recounted here, unless otherwise cited, see International Defense and Aid Fund for Southern Africa, *Apartheid—The Facts*, in cooperation with the United Nations Centre Against Apartheid (London: IDAF, 1983).
6. Donald Woods, *Biko* (New York: Paddington Press, 1978).
7. *Solidarity News Service* (Botswana), December 24, 1983. This news agency is an excellent source of current information about resistance activities in South Africa, as well as more general information concerning South Africa. Another useful source is *Facts and Reports*, edited by Holland Committee on Southern Africa, Amsterdam, Holland.
8. "S. Africa Poll," *International Herald Tribune*, August 30, 1984.
9. "SA poll protestors whipped," *The Guardian* (Manchester), August 29, 1984.
10. *New York Times*, September 24, 1984.
11. "S. African Blacks Use Funerals to Defy Political Curbs," *Washington Post*, September 9, 1984.
12. International Defense and Aid Fund for Southern Africa, *Apartheid—The Facts*, op. cit., Section 6; "Human Rights in the Homelands—South Africa's Delegation & Repression," A Fund for Free Expression Report (New York: 1984).
13. Ben Whitaker, *A Bridge of People—A Personal View of Oxfam's First Forty Years* (London: Heineman Educational Books, 1983), p. 84.
14. *Human Rights in the Homelands—South Africa's Delegation of Repression, A Fund for Free Expression Report* (New York: The Fund for Free Expression, 1984).
15. In December 1982, the International Commission of Jurists published jointly with the Catholic Institute for International Relations and the Human Rights Forum of the British Council of Churches a 45-page pamphlet titled "Torture in South Africa," containing a memorandum on security-police abuses of political detainees, prepared by the Detainees' Parents Support Committee, and other documents testifying to torture practices.
16. "Black Workers Under Siege: The Repression of Black Trade Unions in South Africa" (New York: Africa Fund, 1984).
17. Michael Hornsby, "Violence mars ending of strike by black gold miners in South Africa," *Times* (London), September 19, 1984; and "Police disperse miners," *The Guardian* (Manchester), September 10, 1984.
18. *Solidarity News Service* (Botswana), October 25, 1984.
19. Alan Cowell, "Toll Rises to 16 in South African Rioting," *New York Times*, November 7, 1984.
20. Michael Hornsby, "Catholic Bishops Assail Policy Conduct," *Times* (London), December 7, 1984.
21. Allister Sparks, "S. Africa Show Trial Could Last 18 Months," *Observer* (Britain), December 16, 1984; Patrick Laurence, "Transvaal Strike Men Charged," *Guardian* (Manchester),

190

December 8, 1984; and "Treason Charges Against Durban Pair," *Times* (London), December 14, 1984.

22. AZAPO (the Azanian African People's Office) grew out of a faction of the Black Consciousness movement which persisted in rejecting all efforts to work with progressive whites. The size of its membership is unknown.

23. "From the Frontline," *Solidarity News Service* (Botswana), March 19, 1985 is the source of the story in this and the next paragraph, unless otherwise cited.

24. Allister Sparks, "Tens of Thousands Turn S. Africa Funeral into Political Rally," *Washington Post*, April 14, 1985. Black residents of the area claim 43 were killed, and that the police withheld 14 bodies to falsify the figures. Police insist only 19 were killed, and that the subsequent funeral for 29 included 10 killed elsewhere in the townships.

25. Sparks, ibid.

26. A. Cowell, "Dismissed Blacks Balk at Gold Mine," *New York Times*, April 29, 1985; for details see *Solidarity News Service* (Botswana) April 28, 1985.

27. A. Brooks and J. Brookhill, *Whirlwind Before the Storm: The Origins and Development of the Uprising in Soweto and the Rest of South Africa from June to December 1976* (London: International Defense and Aid Fund for Southern Africa, 1980), pp. 150-157.

28. Martin Welz, "SA Hardens Its Foreign Policy with a Page from U.S. History," *The Sunday Express* (London), October 10, 1982.

29. *Apartheid—The Facts*, op. cit., p. 100-102.

30. *Rand Daily Mail* (S.A.), January 21, 1982.

31. Kevin Danaher, "Government-Initiated Reform in South Africa and Its Implications for U.S. Foreign Policy," in *Politics and Society* 13, No. 2, 1984. See also *Rand Daily Mail* (S.A.), August 22, 1981; *Financial Mail*, January 15, 1982.

32. *Solidarity News Service* (Botswana), December 24, 1983. For analysis of ANC's capacity for armed struggle, see Stephen M. Davis' book, *Season of War: Insurgency in South Africa* (New Haven, CT: Yale University Press, 1985).

33. *Solidarity News Service* (Botswana), December 24, 1983.

34. *Solidarity News Service* (Botswana), October 25, 1984.

35. Gillian and Suzanne Cronje, *The Workers of Namibia* (London: International Defense and Aid Fund for Southern Africa, 1979), p. 101. See also U.N. Council for Namibia, *Compendium of Major Resolutions, Decisions and Other Documents Relating to Namibia*, (A/AC.131/1984/CRD.17, March 29, 1984) for all U.N. resolutions and U.N. voting records concerning Naimbia.

36. Theo-Ben Gurirab, United Nations Emergency Conference on Namibia, March 1981.

37. Early in 1983, Dick Mudge, chairman of the Council of Ministry, resigned to protest the South African administration's pressures in support of the white minority, and the entire Council resigned to support him. See *New York Times*, January 12 and 18, 1983. Late in 1983, the South African-appointed Thirion Committee reported that the multilayered system of racial and ethnic governments was mismanaged, inefficient, and corrupt. See *New York Times*, September 11, 1983.

38. *International Herald Tribune*, June 7, 1984.

39. "Rewards of Coddling South Africa," editorial, *New York Times*, January 5, 1984.

40. "Namibia's financial legacy," *African Business* (Britain), October 1984. By the end of 1984, Namibia's external debt totaled $580 million, on which the government had made four annual payments of more than $50 million, an amount expected to rise to $82 million by 1985. Pretoria guaranteed the debt, but undoubtedly it would press for any independent government to take over the repayment, despite the 1971 International Court of Justice advisory opinion that any obligations and treaties established after the U.N. 1966 revocation of South Africa's mandate would be void. As in the case of the new Zimbabwean government in 1980, international financial agencies will probably require the incoming Namibian government to finance repayment of this debt. If the new government repudiates the debt, it risks the danger that it will

be unable to borrow further-needed funds from international banks.

41. For an overview of SADCC, see Joseph Hanlon, *SADCC: Progress, Projects and Prospects— The Trade and Investment Future of the Southern African Development Coordination Conference*, Special Report No. 182 (London: The Economist Intelligence Unit, 1984).

42. Declaration of the Front Line States made at Arusha, July 3, 1979, "Southern Africa: Toward Economic Liberation," (Arusha: Southern Africa Development Coordination Conference, July 1979).

43. Ibid.

44. Estimate of conventional railroad costs provided by spokesperson for Alcan Company, based on experience in tropics, in interview with A. Seidman in 1979. Tazara railroad cost calculated from overall cost of Tazara Railroad with an estimated inflationary factor included.

45. Cost of building roads in Guinea Bissau, Ministry of Natural Resources, Guinea Bissau, 1978.

46. The Angolan government commissioned the Beijer Institute to provide a background document for the SADCC meeting on energy in Harare, Zimbabwe. *Issues in SADCC Energy Planning: Usage Patterns, Resource Potential and Regional Possibilities* (Harare: SADCC, November 1982). This is the source of information in this section on energy unless otherwise cited.

47. Eastern African Environmental Trends Projects Program for International Development, *Fuelwood and Energy in Eastern Africa* (Worcester, MA: Clark University, 1978).

48. For discussion of advantages of planned regional cooperation, see R.H. Green and A. Seidman, *Unity or Poverty? The Economics of PanAfricanism* (Harmondsworth: African Penguin Library, 1968).

49. If governments end the outflow of the gross national product annually drained out of the economies of southern Africa (see Chapter 2), it should be possible to invest at least 25 percent of the regional GDP as recommended by the World Bank. See World Bank, *World Development Report, 1980* (Washington, D.C.: International Bank for Reconstruction and Development, 1980).

50. Meeting of heads of state of the Front Line States, Maputo, Mozambique, 1982. AIM Mozambique Information Bulletin No. 69 (Maputo: 1982).

51. *South African Digest*, April 27, 1979.

52. J. Stockwell, *In Search of Enemies: A CIA Story* (New York: Norton, 1978).

53. *New York Times*, December 28, 1983; January 6 and 8, 1984.

54. "Savimbi Had 'Meetings in S. Africa'," *Daily Telegraph* (Britain), June 25, 1984. Barry Street, "Angola numbers off," *The Guardian* (Manchester), November 16, 1984.

55. "Destabilization in Southern Africa," *The Economist*, July 16, 1983.

56. Joseph Hanlon, "A grisly form of target practice and a warning," *Sunday Tribune* (London), May 29, 1983.

57. An unnamed U.S. State Department official said that the MNR "receives the bulk of its support from South Africa," quoted in *Africa Report* (U.S.). January-February 1983, p. 48. Prime Minister P.W. Botha agreed with the statement, *Sunday Tribune*, February 6, 1983. About MNR atrocities, see Joseph Hanlon, *Mozambique: The Revolution Under Fire* (London: Zed Press, 1984), pp. 229-30.

58. "Mozambique—The Violent Peace," *The Financial Mail* (S.A.), April 22, 1983.

59. "Destabilization in Southern Africa," *The Economist*, July 16, 1983.

60. Jennifer Davis, "South Africa: Destabilizing the Region" (New York: American Committee on Africa, 1983).

61. *News Notes*, International Defense and Aid Fund for Southern Africa (Cambridge, MA), October 1983; The Economist Intelligence Report, *Quarterly Economic Review of Zimbabwe, Malawi, 3rd Quarter, 1983.*

62. "Pretoria's Secret War Against Zimbabwe," *The Guardian* (Manchester), April 30, 1984.

63. Alan Cowell, "Major Maneuvers Held by Pretoria—South African Show of Might is Expected to be Seen as Hostile by Neighbors," *New York Times*, September 13, 1984.

64. Prepared statement before the Subcommittee on Africa, Committee on Foreign Affairs, U.S.

House of Representatives, hearing on "United States Policy Towards Southern Africa: Focus on Namibia, Angola and South Africa," September 16, 1981 (Washington, D.C.: U.S. Government Printing Office, 1983).

Chapter Five—Constructive Engagement in South Africa

1. "United Nations Policy Toward Southern Africa: Focus on Namibia, Angola and South Africa," Hearing before the Subcommittee on Africa of the House Committee on Foreign Affairs, House of Representatives, September 16, 1981 (Washington, D.C.: U.S. Government Printing Office, 1983).
2. Chester Crocker, "South Africa: Strategy for Change," in *Foreign Affairs*, Winter 1980-81.
3. George Shultz, "Southern Africa: Toward an American Consensus," address before the National Press Club (Washington, D.C.: April 16, 1985).
4. U.S. State Department memorandum of conversations between Assistant Secretary-designate Crocker, South African Foreign Minister Pik Botha, and Defense Minister Magnus Malan on April 15 and 16, 1981, in Pretoria; State Department Scope Paper prepared by Assistant Secretary of State Crocker to brief Secretary of State Alexander Haig for May 14, 1981, meeting with South African Foreign Minister Pik Botha in Washington. Both secret documents were obtained and released by TransAfrica (Washington, D.C.) in June 1981. Parts of the documents were quoted in Kevin Danaher, "Secret Documents: Reagan Leans Right, SWAPO Left Out," *Southern Africa Magazine*, Vol. XIV, No. 4, July-August 1981, pp. 7-9.
5. Ibid.
6. Shultz, op. cit., p. 5.
7. For example, see *South Africa Digest*, April 5, 1985; *The Citizen* (S.A.), March 13, 1985.
8. Chester Crocker, "South Africa: Strategy for Change," op. cit. (See Chapter 1.)
9. In the spring of 1985, the Reagan administration imposed an embargo against Nicaragua. Other countries against which the United States currently maintains sanctions include Cuba, Vietnam, and Kampuchea.
10. Chester Crocker, "Reagan Administration's Africa Policy: A Progress Report," Fourth Annual Conference on International Affairs: U.S.-African Relations Since 1960, University of Kansas, November 10, 1983.
11. Ibid.
12. For a discussion of Anglo American Group's role in South and southern Africa, see Chapter 3.
13. *The Economist*, July 21, 1984, p. 67.
14. Lawrence S. Eagleburger, undersecretary of state for political affairs, before the National Conference of Editorial Writers, San Francisco, California, June 23, 1983: "Southern Africa: America's Responsibility for Peace and Change"; Crocker also emphasized the Sullivan Principles in "Reagan Administration's Africa Policy," op. cit., and the U.S. Ambassador to South Africa, Herman W. Nickol, declared: "We believe very strongly that the U.S. companies here are a positive force for peaceful change in this part of the world." (Speech: "Constructive Engagement at Mid-Term," American Chamber of Commerce, Johannesburg, February 16, 1983).
15. Arthur D. Little, Inc., *Seventh Report on the Signatory Companies to the Sullivan Principles*, October 25, 1983. This and earlier reports are the source of the analysis of the signatories' performance. Note that Britain, under the European Economic Community (EEC) Code, requires firms owning 50 percent or more of the shares of South African companies employing 20 or more workers to report on the progress made in recognizing their employees' rights to organize in unions; the numbers of migrant Africans employed and their benefits; Africans' wages, training and advancement; desegregation in the workplace; and community programs benefiting Africans. See Anne Newman and Cathy Bowers, *Foreign Investment in South Africa and Namibia* (Washington, D.C.: Investor Responsibility Research Center, December 1984).

16. "Union Reviews Sullivan Code," *The Cape Times* (S.A.), January 19, 1982.
17. In 1983, U.S. firms and affiliates operating in South Africa employed 127,000 individuals, only 1.5 percent of the total South African labor force. Of those employees, however, only 69,000 worked for Sullivan Code signatories that submitted reports on their activities in the preceding reporting period. See statement by Rep. Frank G. Wisner before Subcommittee on Financial Institutions of the House Committee on Banking, Finance, and Urban Affairs, 97th Congress, 1st Session, June 8, 1983. Because 36 percent of the Sullivan signatory workforce is white, the actual number of black workers affected by the Principles totals less than 50,000. See Elizabeth Schmidt, *One Step—In the Wrong Direction, The Sullivan Principles as a Strategy for Opposing Apartheid* (New York: Episcopal Churchpeople for a Free Southern Africa, March 1983). See also American Committee on Africa, *The Sullivan Principles: No Cure for Apartheid* (1980); and Arthur D. Little reports on signatory companies, op. cit.
18. *Solidarity News Service* (Botswana), January 25, 1984.
19. *Rand Daily Mail* (S.A.), March 21, 1981.
20. "U.S. Companies Will Defy S.A. Law-Sullivan," *S.A. Report*, (South Africa: December 1984). See also "U.S. investors in S. Africa vote to fight apartheid," *Guardian* (Britain), December 14, 1984.
21. Africa Fund, "The Sullivan Principles: A Critical Look at the U.S. Corporate Role in South Africa," (New York: ACOA, 1981).
22. *ACOA Action News* (New York: American Committee on Africa, 1981), No. 10.
23. Africa Fund, *General Motors in South Africa: Secret Contingency Plans, "In the Event of Civil Unrest"*, (New York: ACOA, 1978); see also "South Africa's Foot-Dragging Vexes U.S. Companies," *Business Week*, October 20, 1980.
24. "Foes of Apartheid Disputed in Poll," *New York Times*, September 23, 1984. A thorough critique of the Schlemmer poll appears in Michael Sutcliffe and Paul Wellings, University of Natal (Durban, S.A.: mimeo, 1985).
25. *Rand Daily Mail* (S.A.), April 2, 1984.
26. *New York Times*, April 4, 1978.
27. FOSATU, *International Policy Statement*, June 1984.
28. "Tutu Slams Foreign Investment," *Washington Notes on Africa* (Washington, D.C.: Washington Office on Africa, Winter/Spring 1985).
29. *Canadian Forum*, December-January 1977-78.
30. For details, see Donald Woods, *Biko* (New York: Paddington Press, 1978).
31. *Guardian* (Manchester), March 24, 1980.
32. *The Economist*, June 10, 1978, p. 108.
33. *Business Week*, October 20, 1980.
34. Ibid.
35. N.D. Kristof, "U.S. companies begin to cut some links to South Africa," *New York Times*, April 29, 1985. At least one pro-investment spokesperson held the U.S. divestment campaign responsible. (J. Chettle, South Africa Foundation, cited in *Financial Times* (London) February 1, 1985.)
36. "Seizing the Moment: the Free South Africa Movement," *Washington Notes on Africa* (Washington, D.C.: Washington Office on Africa, Winter/Spring 1985). Rev. Sullivan quoted in *Washington Post*, February 3, 1985.
37. "Public Investment Policy" address delivered to the first meeting of the Governor's Public Investment Task Force, Los Angeles, July 30, 1980.
38. These agencies include the Calvert Group (Washington, D.C.), Mitchell Investment Management Co. (Cambridge, MA), U.S. Trust Co. (Boston, MA), Franklin Research and Development Corp. (Boston, MA), Dreyfus Corp. (New York, NY), New Alternatives Fund (Great Neck, NY), Shearson/American Express (New York, NY), Pax World Fund (Portsmouth, NH), Working Assets (San Francisco, CA), Pioneer Group (Boston, MA), and Affirmative Investments (Cambridge, MA).
39. *The Star* (S.A.), September 12, 1981.
40. *Yale Graduate Professional*, February 3, 1978.

41. "Embargoes Fail to Check Oil Supply," *Petroleum Economist*, March 1982. South Africa's oil requirements are estimated to be up to 400,000 barrels a day, all of which, except for oil produced from coal by SASOL, South Africa must import. For a general discussion, see D. Myers, *U.S. Business in South Africa* (Bloomington: Indiana University, 1980), pp. 153-88. The importance placed by South Africa on petroleum is revealed by the passage of legislation in 1979 making the publishing of information about sources of petroleum supplies a serious criminal offense. See Martin Bailey, *Oil Sanctions: South Africa's Weak Link: Notes and Documents* (New York: U.N. Centre Against Apartheid, April 1980).

42. See NARMIC/American Friends Service Committee, *Automating Apartheid: U.S. Computer Exports to South Africa and the Arms Embargo* (Philadelphia: American Friends Service Committee, 1982).

43. "Divestment: How much will it hurt?" *Sunday Express* (S.A.), October 28, 1984.

44. *National Student* (Student Press South Africa, 1984), Vol. 4, No. 4.

45. Work in Progress (WIP), "Trade Unions: America Steps In," Yeoville, South Africa, 1982 No. 24. See also D. Thomson and R. Larson, *Where Were You, Brother?* (London: War on Want, 1978).

46. WIP, "Trade Unions: America Steps In," op. cit., p. 1.

47. Ibid.

48. Washington Office on Africa, *Washington Notes on Africa*, Winter 1984.

49. "Reagan's South Africa Policy is a Failure," op-ed page, *New York Times*, September 17, 1984.

50. John Stockwell, *In Search of Enemies—A CIA Story* (New York: Norton, 1978). BOSS (Bureau of State Security) was formerly the name of South Africa's intelligence agency.

52. For discussion of earlier U.S. enforcement policies, see *U.S. Military Involvement in Southern Africa*, Association of Concerned African Scholars (Boston: South End Press, 1978).

53. NARMIC/American Friends Service Committee, "Military Exports to South Africa—A Research Report on the Arms Embargo" (Philadelphia: AFSC, January 1984). This is the source of the discussion here related to military build-up unless otherwise cited. It is based on information obtained under the Freedom of Information Act, interviews with government representatives, and a survey of military-industrial publications and South African patent documents. It includes quarterly and annual reports submitted to Congress by the Department of Defense pursuant to Section 36 of the Arms Export Control Act (various issues).

54. Andrew Cockburn, "An Unsound South African Tie," *New York Times*, op-ed page, December 26, 1984. Cockburn, who is writing a book about intelligence analysis, asks: "Can the United States really afford to bank on the long-term domestic popularity of the Boer intelligence agencies, especially when it is actively supporting them in their struggle for white supremacy?"

55. A.J. Roux, president of the South African Atomic Energy Board, asserted: "We can ascribe our degree of advancement today in large measure to the training and assistance so willingly provided by the United States." *Washington Post*, February 16, 1977.

56. Although a U.S. satellite detected a possible nuclear test in 1979, a U.N. report concluded: "There is no agreement among scientists and observers as to whether the signal detected by the . . . satellite was a nuclear explosion. The South African Government will provide no proof in either direction, and a U.N. group of experts concluded that, although there were some differences from the signals produced by nuclear explosions, the possibility of South Africa having exploded a nuclear device should not be ruled out." (See U.N. Centre Against Apartheid, A/35/402, September 9, 1980.) "Whether or not the 22nd September occurrence was a test, the nuclear technology supplied to South Africa over the last few years has undoubtedly given the South Africans the capability to manufacture nuclear devices." Rev. David Haslam, "The Financing of South Africa's Nuclear Programme," *Notes and Documents* (New York: U.N. Centre Against Apartheid, March 1981). In 1985, Rep. John Conyers, Jr. (D-MI) told a news conference he believed there had been a "scientific coverup" of the 1979 incident by the Carter administration. He proposed a further congressional investigation. ("A-

Test Is Laid to Israel and South Africa," *New York Times*, May 22, 1985.)

57. "Weapons Implications of U.S.-South African Uranium Trade" (Washington, D.C.: Nuclear Control Institute, 1983 and 1984). A U.S. firm shipped an Allis Chalmers Safari I research reactor, and the U.S. government supplied 231 pounds of weapons-grade fuel for it—enough for one atomic bomb—before 1975. (U.S. Congress, Senate Committee on Government Operations, The Export Reorganization Act, 1975, 94th Congress, 1st session, May 24, 1975.) For discussion of the implications for nuclear technology of the computer sales to South Africa, see U.S. Congress, Senate, Committee on Government Operations, The Export Reorganization Act of 1976, 94th Congress, 2nd Session, January 19, 20, 29, and 30 and March 9, 1976, pp. 125-128.

58. See U.S. Congress, House Committee on Foreign Affairs, Subcommittees on Africa and International Economic Policy and Trade, Testimony of Harry Marshall, 97th Congress, 2nd session, December 2, 1982. In 1985, the Nuclear Control Institute released a report stating: "It can be assumed that the South Africans will be able to use their enrichment plants to produce bomb-grade material from their ample supply of natural uranium in the near future, if they already have not done so." John Buell and Daniel Horner, "Issue Brief: Weapons Implications of U.S.-South African Uranium Trade" (Washington, D.C.: Nuclear Control Institute, January 1985).

59. U.S. Department of Interior, *Minerals Yearbook*, Vol. III; *Area Reports: International, 1983* (Washington, D.C.: Government Printing Office, 1985).

60. U.S. Nuclear Regulatory Commission data, cited in *Stopping South African and Namibian Uranium Imports*, Washington Office on Africa fact sheet, January 1983.

61. *Nuclear Fuel*, April 9, 1984. Other U.S. imports of uranium, for example from France, may also originate in Namibia; much uranium mined in Namibia is flown to France for re-shipment; see John Buell, "Issue Brief: Weapons Implications of U.S.-South African Uranium Trade" (Washington, D.C.: Nuclear Control Institute, March 1983).

62. See Chapter 3. See Appendix II for production and export of uranium by South Africa and Namibia, 1983.

63. Joel Charny and John Spragens, Jr., *Obstacles to Recovery in Kampuchea and Vietnam: U.S. Embargo of Humanitarian Aid* (Boston: Oxfam America, 1984).

Chapter Six—The United States and South Africa's Neighbors

1. See Chapters 1 and 5 for discussion of the first strand of the Constructive Engagement Policy.

2. "Bold African Diplomacy," *New York Times*, February 2, 1983.

3. Chester Crocker, "South Africa: Strategy for Change," *Foreign Affairs*, Winter 1980-81.

4. Chester Crocker, "Reagan Administration's Africa Policy: A Progress Report," address before the Fourth Annual Conference on International Affairs, University of Kansas, November 10, 1983.

5. Lawrence Eagleburger, "Southern Africa: America's Responsibility for Peace and Change," speech at National Conference of Editorial Writers, San Francisco, June 23, 1983.

6. George Shultz, "Southern Africa: Toward an American Consensus," address before the National Press Club (Washington, D.C.: April 16, 1985).

7. For earlier U.S. policy initiatives paralleling the Constructive Engagement Policy, see Mohamed A. El-Khawas, ed., *Kissinger Study of Southern Africa: National Security Study Memorandum 39 (Secret)* (Westport, CT: Lawrence Hill, 1976).

8. See, for example, Cheryl Payer, *The Debt Trap and the IMF* (New York: Monthly Review, 1975).

9. International Monetary Fund, *Annual Report*, (Washington, D.C.: IMF, 1984).

10. M. Peter McPherson, "FY 1984 Request for Economic Assistance Programs, Statement before the House Budget Committee Task Force on International Finance and Trade," March 2, *Department of State Bulletin*, May 1983.

11. Lesotho, Malawi, Tanzania, Zambia, and Zimbabwe all called on the International Monetary Fund for assistance; see IMF, *International Financial Statistics*, monthly, country reports. Under pressure from its Western international creditors, Mozambique, too, joined the IMF after it signed the Nkomati Accord.

12. This was typical International Monetary Fund advice. For example, see "Monetarism and the Third World," International Development Studies, Sussex, England *Bulletin*, December 1981, Vol. 13, No. 1.

13. For detailed analysis, see Marcia M. Burdette, *The Political Economy of Zambia* (Lusaka: Univeristy of Zambia, mimeo, 1982).

14. *Moto Magazine* (Harare: April 1983). By 1983, the government of Zimbabwe had almost entirely eliminated expenditures for land acquisition, although it had resettled less than 10 percent of the peasants from the communal areas (the former Tribal Trust Lands). See "Minister of Finance Budget Estimates" (Harare: 1983).

15. For details, see papers from the Workshop on Economic Stabilization Policies, Economics Department, University of Dar es Salaam, 1983. For example, see S.M. Wangwe, "Economic Stabilization Policies in the Industrial Sector"; and H.I. Lipumba, "The Economic Crisis in Tanzania: What is to Be Done?"

16. George Gedda, "IMF Approves Controversial $1.1 Billion Loan to South Africa," *Washington Post*, November 4, 1982; David Coetzee, "Behind Closed Doors at the IMF," *Africa News*, March 1983; "IMF: Calling the Tune," *Africa Confidential*, May 25, 1983.

17. "New IMF Sub-Sahara Policy Highlights Dominant S.A. Role," *The Star* (S.A.), September 9, 1984.

18. Chester Crocker, "Statement, Georgetown University Center on Strategic and International Studies," *Current Policy* (Washington, D.C.: March 3, 1983), No. 462, p. 4. Cited in Elaine Friedland, "The Reagan Administration's Policy Toward the Southern African Development Coordination Conference," a paper prepared for delivery at the 1984 annual meeting of the International Studies Association, typescript, March 27-31, 1984, in Atlanta, GA.

19. Elaine A. Friedland, ibid., p. 13. Friedland's paper includes a content analysis of the "Southern African Section, Daily Report: Middle East and and Africa," 1980 to November 1983. The Foreign Broadcasts Information System (FBIS) publishes translations of materials for use by U.S. Information Agency posts throughout the relevant regions as well as for potential use by the Voice of America. U.S. Government, 1984/5 (Washington, D.C.: Government Printing Office, 1985).

20. *New York Times*, September 4, 1981.

21. *New York Times*, November 30, 1981; December 8, 1981; May 4, 1982. A former South African intelligence agent, Martin Dolinchet, reportedly told Seychelles officials of South African government involvement (*New York Times*, April 22, 1982).

22. *New York Times*, November 18, 1981. See also November 8 and 12, 1981; December 5, 1981.

23. Crocker, "Reagan Administration's Africa Policy: A Progress Report," op. cit.

24. For the Zimbabwe government's understanding of the Kissinger Plan, see "Let's Build Zimbabwe Together: ZIMCORD," Conference Documentation, Zimbabwe Conference on Reconstruction and Development, Salisbury, March 23-27, 1981, p. 1. The proposal was originally reported in the U.S. press as a U.S.-British plan of $1.5-2 billion for compensation to whites for property losses (*New York Times*, September 9, 1976); and Congress was asked to appropriate $100,000 as the first installment of the proposed U.S. $1.5 billion contribution to an International Zimbabwe Development Fund (*New York Times*, May 5, 1977).

25. Information on the Lancaster House Constitution can be found in Jeffrey Davidow, *A Peace in Southern Africa: The Lancaster House Conference on Rhodesia, 1979* (Boulder, CO: Westview Press, 1984); and David Martin and Phyllis Johnson, *The Struggle for Zimbabwe: The Chimurenga War* (Boston: Faber & Faber, 1981).

26. "Report on Conference Proceedings, Zimbabwe Conference on Reconstruction and Development," Salisbury, March 23-27, 1981. The supplement to "ZIMCORD Report on Conference Proceedings" states the donor countries only made a pledge to cover the first of the three years

for which requests were made. Subsequent government budget estimates show that the actual amounts of assistance received fell far short of the amounts anticipated.

| | 1980-81 (Z $000) | 1981-82 (Z $000) | | 1982-83 (Z $000) | |
	Actual	Antici-pated	Actual	Antici-pated	Actual
Development loans	8,146	69,091	14,525	175,200	60,962[a]
Development grants	—	44,601	—	—	—

Note

a. For first three quarters of year—about one-third of amount anticipated. Given the shortfall, the government borrowed heavily.

Source: Central statistical Office, *Monthly Digest of Statistics* (Harare: August 1981, November 1982, April 1983).

27. See Table 1.2 in Chapter 1.
28. Report by Ted Lockwood of the American Friends Service Committee of his interview with Roy Stacey, U.S. AID officer of the U.S. Embassy in Harare (typescript), 1983. See *The Economist*, April 21, 1984; and *Financial Gazette* (Harare), April 29, 1983. The British financed half of the land purchases the Zimbabwean government did make.
29. Lockwood interview with Stacey, ibid.
30. Progress report of research on Zimbabwe's capital goods industry by Dr. Dan Ndlela, Economics Department, University of Zimbabwe, seminar, 1983.
31. See *Moto Magazine* (Harare: April 1983).
32. The Economist Intelligence Unit, *Quarterly Review of Zimbabwe, Malawi* (London: 1984), No. 3, p. 10.
33. Sanford J. Ungar, a senior associate at the Carnegie Endowment for International Peace, argued this cut "will strengthen South Africa's position in the region" ("Foolish Policy on Zimbabwe," *New York Times*, op-ed page, December 28, 1983); Frank Donatelli, assistant administrator for Africa, AID, wrote the *New York Times* (January 16, 1984) that the cause was economic, not "solely" from dissatisfaction with Zimbabwe's voting record. Prime Minister Mugabe's response was that Zimbabwe "could not complain" if the cut was for budgetary reasons, but found it "extremely objectionable" if it was due to U.S. disapproval of Zimbabwe's U.N. votes (*New York Times*, December 24, 1983).
34. See Table 1.2 in Chapter 1.
35. Crocker, "Reagan Administration's Africa Policy: A Progress Report," op. cit.
36. "Linkage Gamble," *Windhoek Advertiser* (Namibia), February 25, 1985.
37. "Radio Reports: OAU Ministerial Council's Resolution on Southern Africa," *Facts and Reports* (Holland), 14th Vol., No. G, March 30, 1984.
38. Crocker, "Reagan Administration's Africa Policy: A Progress Report," op. cit.
39. "Reward for Coddling South Africa," *New York Times* editorial, January 5, 1984.
40. "Luanda Placates Pretoria and Confirms Lusaka Peace Accord," *The Times* (London), March 28, 1984.
41. "U.S. Namibia Mission," *The Star* (S.A.), February 27, 1984.
42. *Windhoek Advertiser*, February 11, 1985.
43. *Boston Globe*, April 18, 1985.
44. In May, Angolan troops killed two South Africans and captured a third attempting to sabotage the Cabinda oil wells, and Pretoria admitted it had mounted military forays into Angola. ("South Africa Admits Spy Mission After Angola Accuses It of Raid," *New York Times*, May 24, 1985).
45. "Namibia Plan Raises Hackles," *New York Times*, April 21, 1985; see also Patrick Laurence, "S. Africa considers new interim rule in Namibia," *Christian Science Monitor*, April 17, 1985.

46. Crocker, "Reagan Administration's Africa Policy: A Progress Report," op. cit.
47. See Chapters 1 and 4.
48. *Solidarity News Service* (Botswana), September 5, 1984.
49. Ibid., March 21, 1984.
50. *Herald* (Harare), March 15, 1984.
51. *Solidarity News Service* (Botswana), March 21, 1984; see also *The Times* (London), March 17, 1984; *International Herald Tribune*, March 17, 1984; *Rand Daily Mail* (S.A.), March 17, 1984.
52. "Revolutionary Mozambique puts its money on capitalism," *The Guardian* (Manchester), May 9, 1984; J. Steele, "Pact with apartheid," *The Guardian* (Manchester), May 22 1984.
53. Joseph Hanlon, "Stealing the Dream," *New Statesman* (Britain), October 19, 1984. This article is based on *Mozambique: The Revolution Under Fire* (London: Zed Press, 1984).
54. *Solidarity News Service* (Botswana), March 21, 1984.
55. Ibid.
56. Ibid.
57. Joseph Hanlon, "Maputo launches raids on ANC," *The Guardian* (Manchester), March 26, 1984.
58. Patrick Laurence, "Swaziland 1982 Pact," *The Guardian* (Manchester), April 2, 1984; J. Hanlon, "Pact puts squeeze on ANC," *The Guardian* (Manchester), April 16, 1984: *Refugees* (U.N. High Commissioner for Refugees: April 1984), p. 172.
59. "Radio Reports," *Facts and Reports*, 14th Vol., No. 1, April 27, 1984, p. 176.
60. "Insurgents fire on train near Maputo," from Johannesburg correspondent, *The Times* (London), April 12, 1984; Joao Santa Rita, "Despite accord, war will escalate—MNR sources claim," *The Star* (S.A.), April 23, 1984; Jonathan Steele, "Maputo demands that South Africa disband the MNR," *The Guardian* (Manchester), May 18, 1984; Jonathan Steele, "Pact with apartheid," *The Guardian* (Manchester), May 22, 1984.
61. Barry Streek, "Machel says SA key to terrorism," *Guardian* (Britain), December 28, 1984.
62. "Relief work being hampered," *Windhoek Advertiser* (Namibia) February 14, 1985; David Rabkin, "Rain, but survival struggle goes on," *Guardian*, (Manchester) February 5, 1985.
63. Rabkin, ibid.
64. Allen Isaacman, "After the Nkomati Accord," *Africa Report* (U.S.), December 1984-January 1985.
65. Ibid.
66. "Cut supplies to Renamo," *Windhoek Observer*, January 1, 1985. Renamo is another name for the MNR.
67. Patrick Laurence, "Rebel sympathizers in S. African army sacked, says Botha," *Guardian* (Manchester), March 18, 1985; see also "Little Gained by Pact," *International Herald Tribune*, March 18, 1985.
68. Joseph Hanlon, "Botswana Groans Under S. Africa Pressure," *The Times* (London), July 27, 1984.
69. Ibid.
70. "South African Commandos Strike in Capital of Botswana," *Washington Post*, June 15, 1985.
71. Press release, U.N. Special Committee Against Apartheid (London: March 21, 1984).
72. Ibid.
73. Sanford Ungar, "Reagan's South Africa Policy is a Failure," op-ed page, *New York Times*, September 17, 1984.

Chapter Seven—Toward An Alternative U.S. Policy

1. Jonathan Steele, "The illusion that armed struggle will solve S. Africa's problems," interview with Dr. Chester A. Crocker by Jonathan Steele and Victoria Brittain, *The Guardian* (Manchester), July 20, 1984.

2. Ibid., printed here as it appeared in the original.

3. Ibid.

4. "ANC rejects talks with South Africa," *The Guardian* (Manchester), July 16, 1984.

5. "Reagan's South Africa Policy is a Failure," op-ed page, *New York Times*, September 17, 1984.

6. Thomas G. Karis, "Black Politics in South Africa," *Foreign Affairs*, Winter 1983/84, pp. 378-406.

7. See Carole Collins, Kevin Danaher, Frank Mont, Melissa Pullins, Jean Sindab and Kenneth Zinn, *American Steel Jobs and South Africa—How U.S. support for South Africa affects your community* (Washington, D.C.: Washington Office on Africa Educational Fund, and United States Steelworkers of America, Civil Rights Department, 1984). In late 1984, the U.S. government was negotiating with South Africa, as well as other countries, to reduce sales to the United States of foreign steel, which still met more than a fourth of domestic U.S. needs. Under the proposed agreement, reducing total U.S. imports to 18 percent of total U.S. steel consumption, South Africa reportedly was to receive a quota larger than that of either Australia or Mexico. (See Clyde H. Farnsworth, "Nations Agree to Steel Curbs," *New York Times*, December 20, 1984.)

Index

THE ROOTS OF CRISIS IN SOUTHERN AFRICA

Shao-Jo Li — de Michelis
4/51

Trung Le — Finding America's
place —
Marc Erdmann — C. Layne
Superpower —